MW00450430

Lean Six Sigma Study Guide 2019-2020

A Complete Review for the ASQ Yellow, Green and Black Belt Exams Including 300 Test Questions and Answers

Copyright 2019 by Six Sigma Test Prep Team - All rights reserved.

This book is geared towards providing precise and reliable information about the topic. This publication is sold with the idea that the publisher is not required to render any accounting, officially or otherwise, or any other qualified services. If further advice is necessary, contacting a legal and/or financial professional is recommended.

From a Declaration of Principles that was accepted and approved equally by a Committee of the American Bar Association and a Committee of Publishers' Associations.

In no way is it legal to reproduce, duplicate, or transmit any part of this document, either by electronic means, or in printed format. Recording this publication is strictly prohibited, and any storage of this document is not allowed unless with written permission from the publisher. All rights reserved.

The information provided herein is stated to be truthful and consistent, in that any liability, in terms of inattention or otherwise, by any usage or abuse of any policies, processes, or directions contained within, is the solitary and utter responsibility of the recipient reader. Under no circumstances will any legal responsibility or blame be held against the publisher for any reparation, damages, or monetary loss due to the information herein, either directly or indirectly.

Respective authors own all copyrights not held by the publisher. This work belongs to Newstone Publishing.

The information herein is offered for informational purposes solely, and is universally presented as such. The information herein is also presented without contract or any type of guarantee assurance.

The trademarks presented are done so without any consent, and this publication of the trademarks is without permission or backing by the trademark owners. All trademarks and brands within this book are thus for clarifying purposes only and are the owned by the owners themselves, and not affiliated otherwise with this document.

Table of Contents

Notice 20

Introduction 21

Chapter 1 – Understanding Six Sigma 23

    A Focus on Statistics 23

    Analyzing Processes 23

    Identifying the Employees' Roles 24

    The Background of Six Sigma 24

    ISO Standard 24

    The Key Parts of the Six Sigma Doctrine 25

    Defects and Opportunities 26

    Lean Value Is Key 26

    The Ultimate Goal (the Sixth Standard Deviation) 27

    The Necessity of Obtaining Six Sigma Certification 28

    How Does This Benefit the Customer? 28

    How Does This Benefit Employees? 29

    The Hidden Factory Consideration 29

Chapter 2 – The Pros and Cons of Six Sigma and How the Cons Are Reversed 31

    Positives 31

    Negatives (and How They Are Offset) 32

Chapter 3 – The Belt Levels of Six Sigma 34

    Champion 34

    White Belt 35

    Yellow Belt 35

    Green Belt 35

Black Belt 36

    Brown Belt 36

Master Black Belt 36

Chapter 4 – The Five Voices 38

Voice of the Business (VOB) 38

Voice of the Customer (VOC) 39

Voice of the Process (VOP) 39

Voice of the Employees (VOE) 40

Voice of Data (VOD) 41

Chapter 5 – The Eight Dimensions of Quality 42

Chapter 6 – The DMAIC Steps 45

Define/Design 45

    Four Keys in the Definition Process 46

    What Is the VOC? 46

    The Storyboard 47

Measure 48

Analyze 48

    What Is a Root Cause? 49

Improve 49

    The Critical Input 50

Control 50

Synergize 50

Replication 51

A Ten-Step Summary 51

Time Frame 52

Chapter 7 – The DMADV (DFSS) Process 53

What Makes This Different from the DMAIC Process? 53

Define 53

Measure 54

Analyze 54

Design 54

Verify 55

What About Existing Products? 56

What If You Accidentally Use DMAIC For a DMADV Task? 56

Chapter 8 – Going Lean (Lean Principles) 57

Defining Value 57

What the Customer Sees Out of the Task 57

Mapping the Value Stream 58

Creating the Flow 60

Establishing a Pull 61

Going After Perfection 61

Consequential Metrics 61

Chapter 9 – The Most Common Types of Waste 63

Chapter 10 – Defects vs. Defectives 68

Chapter 11 – Project Acceptability 69

The WIIFM Point 69

Chapter 12 – The Five Key Deliverables of the Define Stage 71

Chapter 13 – Operating the VOC 73

Internal vs. External Customers 73

Needs and Requirements 73

The AICP Process 74

Certain Methods for Gauging the VOC 74

General Requirements to Keep in Mind 76

The Limits 76

Chapter 14 – The Kano Model 78

The Four Key Parts 79

Three Overall Feelings 80

The Four Quadrants and How to Gather Points 81

Five Questions to Ask 82

An Example 84

A Warning About Time 85

Chapter 15 – The Pareto Principle 86

Chapter 16 – Critical to Quality (CTQ) 87

Needs, Drivers and Requirements 87

The Five Steps 88

Managing Data 90

Process Measurements 91

Producing Targets 91

A General Example 91

The Discussion Is Vital 92

Chapter 17 – Creating a Project Charter 94

Business Case 94

Problem Report 95

Goal Report 96

Scope 97

Longitudinal..97

Lateral 98

Milestones 98

LSL And USL With the RUMBA Limits 98

Specific Roles 99

How Often Should You Revisit the Charter? 100

Chapter 18 – The Stakeholder Analysis 101

Chapter 19 – The Change Acceleration Process (CAP) 103

The Key Steps..103

The ARMI Plan 104

What Influences Change Acceleration? 105

Chapter 20 – The Value Stream Map 107

The "As-Is" Process 107

How Many Parties? 107

The Request Always Starts the Map 108

What Is the Trigger? 108

Analyzing the Flow..108

Cycle-Time Review..109

Value and Non-Value-Added Activities...109

Measuring the Process Efficiency 110

Adding Many Processes...111

Bottlenecks..111

Constraints..112

Lead Time, Processing Time and the Lead-Time Ladder 113

The SMED Process 113

Chapter 21 – Options for Process Mapping 116

    SIPOC..116

    High-Level Process Map...118

    Detailed Map...118

    Swimlane/Deployment Map...120

    Relationship Map 121

Chapter 22 – The 15 Most Important Details for Planning a Six Sigma Task 122

Chapter 23 – Designing a Communication Plan 126

Chapter 24 – The Cost of Quality and the Cost-Benefit Analysis...............................127

    The Five Key Costs of Quality (COPQ) 127

        Indirect Costs...128

    Planning the CBA 129

    Controlling Accuracy 130

    Looking at Your Image 131

Chapter 25 – Choosing the Y Between Effectiveness and Efficiency 132

    Efficiency...132

    Effectiveness 132

    Which Is More Important? 133

    Helpful Tips...133

Chapter 26 – Musts and Wants...135

    Musts...135

    Wants 135

    The Weighted Rating Sheet 136

Chapter 27 – Brainstorming..138

    Mind Mapping...138

Reverse/Anti-Solution Brainstorming 138

Nominal Group Brainstorming 138

Brain-Netting 139

Role-Playing 139

Analogy Technique 140

Channeling 140

Prioritizing the Ideas You Come Across 141

Chapter 28 – Identifying and Managing the X and Y 142

Figuring Out the Qualitative and Quantitative Data 145

Qualitative 145

Quantitative 146

Understanding the Difference Between the Two Choices 147

How Many Variables at Once? 147

Chapter 29 – Variations in the Measurement System 148

What Type of Analysis? 148

Variation Based on Actual Processes Versus a Measurement System 149

Observed Variation 150

The Concept of Conformance 150

Don't Forget Capability 151

Chapter 30 – The Sampling Process 152

Probability Sampling 152

Non-Probability Sampling 154

Avoiding Sampling Bias 156

Acceptance Sampling 157

Essential Questions to Ask in the Sampling Process 157

Chapter 31 – A General Measurement System 160

    The MSA 160

        Five Measurements in the Process 160

        Three Key Terms 161

    Errors in Measurements 162

    Accuracy vs. Precision 163

    Variation 163

    Causes of Variation 163

Chapter 32 – Key Factors for Data Interpretation 165

    Stability 165

    Normality 167

    Sensitivity 168

    How Can the Data Be Distributed? 168

    What to Do If Your Data Is Not Normal 168

    Shape 169

        Exponential 169

        Lognormal 170

        Geometric 170

        Spread 171

    Centering 171

Chapter 33 – Using the Right Measurement Chart (The Basic Tools of Quality) 173

    Charts for Discrete Data 174

        Bar Chart 174

        Pie Chart 174

        Pareto Chart 175

Charts for Continuous Data 176

    Histogram 176

    Box Plot 177

Charts That Work for Both Forms of Data 179

    Run Chart 179

    Control Chart 180

    Variable and Attribute Data for the Control Chart 181

Other Choices for Measurement Needs 181

    Scatterplot 181

    Cause and Effect Diagram 182

    Flowchart 184

    Check Sheet 184

    Spaghetti Diagram 185

Choosing the Proper Measurement Tool 185

Chapter 34 – How Capable Is the Process? 187

Process Sigma 187

Figuring Out the Data Being Calculated (DPMO Measurement) 187

Yield 189

Calculating the Data 190

    The Z Value 190

Cp and Cpk – Specific Points for Capability and How to Measure Them 192

    Cp 192

    Cpk 193

Chapter 35 – Root Cause Analysis 195

Explaining the Event 195

What Was Expected? 195

Reviewing the Event Background 196

Planning a Timeline 198

Have Any Actions Been Taken? 198

The Cause and Effect Link 199

The Five Whys 199

    What If the Final Why Doesn't Have an Answer? 201

Planning Corrective Actions 201

Control Impact Matrix 201

What Are the Incidental Findings? 202

Discussing Solutions 203

Chapter 36 – Cause Mapping 204

Explaining the Issue 204

Process Mapping 205

Chapter 37 – Managing Hand Offs 207

Where to Find Hand offs 207

Identify Signals 208

Review the Middlemen 208

What the Outgoing Sender Must Do 209

What the Recipient Must Do 209

Chapter 38 – Hypothesis Testing 211

How to Test a Hypothesis 211

How a Null Hypothesis Can Work 212

Type I and II Errors 212

P-Value 213

Alpha and Beta Risks 214

Hypothesis Testing Options 214

For Continuous Data from the Input and Output Alike (Chi-Square Test) 215

For Normal Continuous Input Data and Discrete Output Data (Multiple Regression) 216

For Discrete Input Data and Normal Continuous Output Data (ANOVA and HOV Tests) 217

For Discrete Input Data and Non-Normal Continuous Output Data (Mood's Median) 218

For Discrete Input and Output Data 219

Chapter 39 – Producing Solution Parameters 220

Planning a Decision Statement 220

Planning Criteria for the Solution 220

The SCAMPER Process 221

Using the Likert Scale for Your Wants 223

Chapter 40 – Generating the Best Possible Solution 224

Brain-Writing 224

A.   6-3-5 Brain-Writing 224

B.   Constrained Brain-Writing 225

Assumption Busting 226

Chapter 41 – Calculating the RTY 228

Chapter 42 – The Failure Mode Effect Analysis 230

Two Definitions 230

How the FMEA Works 230

How to Tell if Something Is a Not a Serious Problem 233

How to Tell if the Issue Must Be Fixed Now 233

When Should You Carry Out the FMEA? 234

Chapter 43 – Benchmarking 235

Five Keys..235

The Three Forms of Benchmarking..236

A Helpful Series of Steps..237

How Will You Produce Benchmarks?...239

Changing the Benchmarks..240

What About Reviewing the Competition? 240

Chapter 44 – Piloting a Six Sigma Solution 241

When Is It Fine to Pilot? 242

Who's the Target Audience? 243

Steps for Managing Your Pilot...244

Chapter 45 – The Validation of the Measurement System (R&R) 248

Calculating Gage R&R 248

What to Do When Fixing the Issue 251

Chapter 46 – New Process Mapping 253

Working with the Opportunities 253

Producing New Targets 253

Special Workflow Plans...254

Chapter 47 – Statistical Process Control...257

How Will You Implement SPC? 258

Chapter 48 – Choosing the Right Kind of Control Chart 259

Charts for Variable Data..259

    I-MR Chart...259

    Xbar and R-Chart..260

    Xbar and S-Chart..260

Charts for Use When Reviewing Defective Units..261

NP Chart 261

P Chart 261

C Chart 262

U Chart 262

Chapter 49 – Deming's Four Rules for Tampering In SPC 263

Chapter 50 – The Central Limit Theorem 266

Chapter 51 – The Control Chart and Control Limits 267

Control Limits 267

What Does It Mean to Be in Control? 269

Out of Control Issues 269

Common Types of Trends in Maps to Notice 271

Chapter 52 – Specification Limits 273

Using One Limit 273

Chapter 53 – Leading and Lagging Indicators (KPIs) 275

Leading Indicators 275

Lagging Indicators 276

Chapter 54 – Managing All Risks 278

Analyze the Operational and Reporting Goals 278

Talk with Current Members 279

The Poka Yoke Process 279

Three Types 279

The Process 280

Chapter 55 – Getting a Control Plan Ready 282

What To Get In Your Control Plan 283

Chapter 56 – The Gemba Walk 284

Chapter 57 – Kanban 286

The Six Rules of Kanban 286

Four Added Principles 287

The Steps for Kanban 288

Additional Chart Formats 290

What About the Gantt Chart? 290

Chapter 58 – Signing Off of the Six Sigma Task 292

Chapter 59 – Planning a Six Sigma Presentation 294

Chapter 60 – Managing Conflicts In the Task 296

Chapter 61 – Agile Project Management 298

The Basic Concepts of Agile 298

The Keys of the Agile Manifesto 299

The Four Key Values 299

The 12 Key Principles 300

The Positives of Agile 300

Any Issues? 301

Chapter 62 – Running an Agile Project 302

Planning a Road Map 302

Changing the Road Map Around 303

Planning Your Agile Requirements 304

Ideas for Creating and Changing the Requirements 305

The Single-Page Dashboard 306

Producing the Backlog 307

Trust Is Critical 308

Chapter 63 – The Use of Epics, Stories and Themes in the Agile Process 309

Creating an Epic 310

The Use of Stories 311

Chapter 64 – Using Story Points in Agile Work 312

Chapter 65 – How to Incorporate Agile into a Six Sigma Routine 314

Process Increments 314

Concentrate on the Planning and Not the Design 315

Skills of the People 315

Accept Change 315

Chapter 66 – The Scrum Process 316

The General Uses of Scrum 316

Three Parts of the Scrum Theory 317

An Additional Word on Transparency 318

Chapter 67 – The Three Roles of the Scrum 320

Chapter 68 – The Project Backlog for Scrum 323

The Key Features of the Backlog 323

Checking the Backlog Throughout the Work 324

Changing the Backlog During the Process 324

Planning a Backlog for the Sprint 325

What Are Increments? 325

Chapter 69 – The Events of a Scrum 326

Sprint 326

Planning the Sprint 327

Canceling a Sprint 328

What Is the Daily Scrum? 328

Questions For the Daily Scrum 329

Can Others Attend the Daily Scrum?...330

Planning a Board...330

Chapter 70 – What Does It Mean to Be Done in the Scrum? 332

Chapter 71 – Planning a Review for the Scrum Process 334

Planning a Retrospective...334

Chapter 72 – Helpful Tips for Six Sigma Efforts 335

Chapter 73 – Handling the Exam 336

Yellow Belt...336

Green Belt..337

Black Belt...337

What Your Certificate Includes 337

What About Recertification? 337

White/Yellow Belt Certification Questions..339

Answers to White/Yellow Belt Certification Questions 361

Green Belt Certification Questions 369

Answers to Green Belt Certification Questions...390

Black Belt Certification Questions 398

Answers to Black Belt Certification Questions..422

Conclusion..430

Notice

The following guide includes information on the Six Sigma process and relevant subjects that are related to it. The guide also features a full test that may be completed for certification. Be advised that the questions in this guide are not guaranteed to be a part of the actual certification exam. Also, the exam will vary based on the type of certification that you are aiming to attain. This guide is appropriate for all people looking to obtain Six Sigma certification, although further training and experience will be required for those looking to attain the highest levels of certification.

Each of the processes you put in place will vary in intensity based on how effective the solutions may be. The effectiveness of Six Sigma is based heavily on your adherence to the standards that Six Sigma encourages. Furthermore, the resources and funding required to follow what you learn in this guide will vary based on your specific plans for keeping the Six Sigma routine going forward.

There are no guarantees that every step in the Six Sigma process or any other related field will be required for your particular task. You can use many of the points in this guide, but you must remain aware of the demands involved with your work. Part of this includes focusing on certain routines based on the overall process. Be aware of the plans involved for your Six Sigma routine and follow the considerations listed in this guide.

Introduction

Having a business can be a thrilling endeavor. You will enjoy taking control of many functions and processes while working alongside many people. Your ability to help your community and its customers will also be to your advantage. But at the same time, it may be difficult for you to keep your business active. The processes and functions within your business may hit several snags that keep the entity from operating as it should.

The importance of keeping your workplace organized and ready for action is critical to its success. You must ensure that all people in your workplace can handle the best possible processes for operation. This is where the Six Sigma techniques can come in handy. It is through Six Sigma that it will become easier for businesses to grow and thrive. This guide will help you understand what you can do when using the Six Sigma standard to your advantage.

Six Sigma entails reviewing not only your business' infrastructure but also the people involved and the values that your customers have. Six Sigma takes a full approach to everything that is happening in your business. You can use the points introduced in this guide to help you recognize how to keep your business running right and how to improve upon its functionality. More importantly, you will discover that your business will be more profitable and efficient, not to mention being easier for people to trust. You can even use Six Sigma to make the people in your workplace feel confident about what they are doing.

You will learn in this guide about how the Six Sigma system works and what you can expect out of it. The guide features details on how to use the Six Sigma layout and ensure that all products that are manufactured and prepared for sale the right way. By using the Six Sigma standards, you will ensure that the manufacturing processes in your workplace are consistent and that the risk of defects will be minimal. The businesses processes that are used in the system are also designed to be fluid and consistent. Knowing what you will get out of the Six Sigma system is critical to your success in the workplace.

This guide includes details on not only the Six Sigma system but also on the Scrum framework. The Scrum setup helps people on a team to figure out answers to various problems in the workplace. The goal is to produce products that offer the highest possible value. The process works particularly with taking projects and breaking them down into smaller segments. But the greatest part of using the Scrum framework is to ensure that the right people are consulted for getting the task up and running without delay.

Agile project management is another aspect that will be covered in this guide. APM is a vital point for Six Sigma that often uses the Scrum setup for your advantage. The practice is about more than just completing projects with small sections in mind. The practice is also about helping a business to respond to change while focusing on the needs that users have. This includes knowing how to handle the uncertainty that comes with a task. Knowing how to handle changes and any outside concerns that may develop will help with correcting the many issues that might develop in the workplace. Testing and integration points and functionality considerations are all vital points to notice.

You will also find a full test at the end of this guide. The test is comprehensive and includes hundreds of questions to help you with studying for your Six Sigma certification. You can use this guide for various belt certifications, including for the Black Belt certification. The points in the guide should prepare you well to understand what goes into the exam. Passing the exam ensures you can show your ability to handle Six Sigma functions properly.

By using the Six Sigma process, you will improve upon how your business operates. It's most likely your business will grow without problems. You must look at how well the effort involved can work, so it helps to see what makes the Six Sigma routine that you put in so effective and useful as you see fit. This guide will provide you with details on everything you need to do to make the most out of your work.

Knowing what to do for organizing the functions and processes within your business is a necessity for your success. You have to know what to expect out of the Six Sigma program if you want your business' manufacturing process to work out right. The efforts involved should be planned right based on various points relating to getting your projects organized correctly. Besides, your business will surely need the competitive advantage that only the Six Sigma program can provide it with.

Chapter 1 – Understanding Six Sigma

Though the art of Six Sigma is complicated to many, businesses must use the Six Sigma principles to improve upon manufacturing processes. The Six Sigma process spans production efforts at the start all the way through to the handling of servicing. The data-oriented nature of Six Sigma helps businesses to identify what they can do to move their functions forward and to produce the best error-free manufacturing processes.

A Focus on Statistics

Whereas average businesses use guesswork to attempt to resolve manufacturing and procedural issues, Six Sigma operates based on a full statistical analysis of how a business operates rather than on an analysis of what could potentially happen. The statistical review helps with identifying the problems that have developed in the workplace. The program also assesses how a business operates based on how it both measures and resolves problems. Studying how problems have evolved and what can be done to statistically reduce them is critical to the Six Sigma process and to keep a business growing.

Using statistics helps a business operate as predictably as possible. You can use various types of statistics in the process. Descriptive statistics may be used to identify data with charts, numbers and other bits of data that are easily noticeable. Inferential statistics may help with identifying the relationships between certain items. The reviews may support different concepts analyzing what makes the work distinct and unique. More importantly, the statistics focus heavily on what makes specific work useful.

Analyzing Processes

Six Sigma is designed to look at the many processes that a business utilizes, including how well those processes run. You can use a Six Sigma routine to look at how each step is run and assess whether there are certain gaps or problems getting in the way of work.

You can use a Six Sigma analysis to figure out how well your business is being run and whether any changes should be made. Sometimes only one part of the process needs fine tuning. Other times a process may need to be overhauled completely. Scrapping a process altogether based on what Six Sigma recommends might be a challenge, but in some cases, it is the only solution.

Six Sigma helps you to reduce workplace waste including unnecessary processes. Part of this includes carefully studying routines in order to determine whether they are both efficient and productive. Minimizing the waste of time and employee efforts will go a long way toward strengthening a business.

Identifying the Employees' Roles

Using your employees to their best potential is a critical aspect of Six Sigma. Employees are just as important to the success of a business as the manufacturing process. You can use Six Sigma to figure out what your employees should be doing based on the resources, processes and other key factors that play a role in your business. Six Sigma ensures that you can plan out your processes and routines so all the people in the workplace are clear on their designated tasks. This can enhance productivity. For example, a call center, after its processes are analyzed and employees' routines are revised, might produce a Six Sigma task that entails employees handling more calls at a time.

The Background of Six Sigma

When it comes to quality control processes, Six Sigma is relatively new. It was first introduced in the 1980s by Motorola for use as a process improvement standard. General Electric adopted the Six Sigma standards in the 1990s, with Ford, Honeywell and many other companies eventually jumping on the bandwagon. Over the years, the Six Sigma standard became commonplace throughout the manufacturing industry, then spread into other industries such as finance and customer service, among others.

The name is a reference to the Greek letter Sigma. The letter, σ, is used in mathematics to refer to the standard deviation. As discussed later in this chapter, Six Sigma states that the manufacturing processes should be within six standard deviations. When the Six Sigma standards are met, a business will meet all its opportunities for staying productive and operating at an efficient level. A business that fails to meet the Six Sigma standards will not be as productive; the system is designed to create a near-perfect standard for manufacturing that is still easy to follow.

ISO Standard

Six Sigma is now officially recognized by the International Organization for Standardization (ISO) (ISO certification 13053-1:2011) as a method that manages process improvement functions. The standard focuses specifically on process improvement in order to improve upon a business' functions. The Define, Measure, Analyze, Improve and Control process (DMAIC), which will be discussed later in this guide, is a vital aspect of what makes Six Sigma so useful and efficient.

Businesses may have certain standards for how the Six Sigma process is used. Some standards may vary from what ISO recommends. All practices must be geared towards producing a leaner and more efficient environment where regular business functions can be easily supported. You can use as many changes to the Six Sigma process as you want, provided that each of the changes involved is planned based on your needs for keeping the business operational.

The Key Parts of the Six Sigma Doctrine

The Six Sigma doctrine uses several critical points dedicated to ensuring the system works to its fullest potential:

1. The results produced in the Six Sigma routine should be consistent.

The consistency of Six Sigma comes from how variation is reduced. While not all variation can be eliminated, what with manufacturing practices entailing many assets that can change over time, Six Sigma does at least reduce the variation in question. The process also ensures a sense of stability. When it knows what to expect, a business can operate without worry. Standards of operation should become consistent after a while.

2. There are set, measurable definitions to the manufacturing processes in the workplace.

The definitions should entail specific routines or activities that can work for every practice that develops in the manufacturing process. In addition to each of these established definitions, the actions in the process should be measured and reviewed. There must be a sense of control in each action, not to mention the ability to improve upon those actions. Actions should be easy to measure.

3. The full organization will be responsible for producing the best results.

The results must be sustained by every person in the workplace. These include not only the people who study Six Sigma but also employees and managers. That said, the highest levels of management are responsible for most of the work. Those persons will need to identify how well orders are prepared and what can be done to make those orders eventually actionable by employees.

4. There must be a sense of control for the inputs and outputs alike.

A tenet of Six Sigma is that those who can control the inputs can also control the outputs. When the processes are clearly defined, it becomes easier for a business to operate. A clear analysis of each process in the workplace should be made available in order to review the efficiency of the various functions. This allows you to not only control the inputs but also to analyze what comes out of the processes while adjusting your efforts appropriately.

5. All evaluations must be continuous.

Every point in the work environment has to be analyzed. Regular evaluations are needed to identify how well the Six Sigma approach is operating. All changes must be made as soon as possible. The evaluation process should be the same all the way through but must be adapted according to what Six Sigma determines is and is not working.

6. By eliminating variations, you will save money and reduce any deficits in the workplace.

The lack of variations in the Six Sigma process ensures that there are no errors or waste in the business process. Waste includes extra time expended on resolving problems. By maximizing the use of resources, including time, a business is more likely to stay under budget and to achieve its goals efficiently.

Defects and Opportunities

An important term in the Six Sigma process is the **defect**. This is a reference to any kind of process output that does not work to the specifications that the customer or the business wants to utilize. For instance, a company might make thermal cotton bedsheets. Each bedsheet set uses a certain number of threads to produce a comfortable surface. When a sheet set is made with fewer threads than what the company deems acceptable, the product is not adhering to business standards and customers will feel that the product is not what they were told it would be. Therefore, that product is a defect.

A defect is not always about a general product issue, but rather about the process in general. A business has to follow the correct processes for generating items or handling functions without any errors. A business that has too many defects may be interpreted as being disorganized, improperly managed or simply poor quality. Customers may shun a business that has too many defects. They might find the business difficult to trust. Employees may also feel conflicted in not knowing how to resolve some of the problems they might come across in the workplace.

The **opportunity** is another aspect of manufacturing to note. The opportunity is a measure of when certain actions take place in the work environment. A hand off to another party or another action that directly influences responsibility in the workplace may be interpreted as an opportunity. A successful opportunity will result in a product being correctly made, or a general practice running as intended.

The opportunities and defects both combine into the DPMO. The DPMO is a measure of defects per million opportunities. It analyzes the defects in a workplace with the intention of resolving those defects before they can become worse. For opportunities, the number of faulty processes must be reduced, along with any defects in each process.

Lean Value Is Key

One interesting aspect of Six Sigma entails how a business works towards producing a **lean value**. For this reason, Six Sigma is also referred to as "Lean" in some cases. The lean value in the workplace refers to a minimal amount of processing in business routines. That is, everything that does not add some value to the business is reduced.

Every step in the process must be based on concepts and values that are useful to the business in question. Keeping moving parts in check assists in producing a more efficient and cleaner work environment. The more unnecessary processes, the more waste, inefficiency and likelihood of developing errors.

The Ultimate Goal (the Sixth Standard Deviation)

The ultimate goal for a business is to reach the Six Sigma level. **Sigma** is a reference to the standard deviation that occurs within a larger group set. It is a measure of how many standard deviations a result is from the main specification limit and of the variation in a data set that is collected surrounding a process. The measure is designed with the knowledge that natural variation is a common, unavoidable part of the manufacturing process. But with Six Sigma, the business is supposed to keep from losing control of its ability to keep the manufacturing processes consistent and regular.

The goal is to create a series of limits that are easy for a business to operate within. This, in turn, produces a setup where the manufacturing process fits within the data being utilized. As a result, the number of defects that may develop will be minimized.

For instance, a company that makes soft drinks and packages them in cans needs to ensure that each can includes 12 fluid ounces of a drink. The product may be planned as having between 11.98 and 12.02 fluid ounces per can. The variance is part of the natural variations that are bound to occur in a manufacturing process. That is, there is no genuine way to ensure that every single product made will be truly identical. The process mean in this situation is 12 fluid ounces, right in the middle.

The standard deviation should be as minimal as possible. A deviation should be around 0.005. 11.98 should be six standard deviations from 12. A business that obtains Six Sigma will ensure that its products are made within six standard deviations, thus ensuring that each can is prepared right. The general measure for Six Sigma is that only 3.4 defects will occur within every million products produced. That is, only three or four cans out of a million, in this example, will have the incorrect amount of soft drink.

There are also lower Sigma levels that can be obtained. For example, a business may obtain three Sigmas to get to about 66,800 defects per million. Eventually, the business can move to four Sigmas or 6,210 defects per million, and then five Sigmas for 230 defects per million. But the continuing process of attaining the Six Sigma ranking is the ultimate goal for a business.

Sticking with the Six Sigma standard is especially critical when certain industries are considered. For instance, a pharmacy might reach three Sigmas and still produce about 200,000 incorrect prescriptions every year. This can be dangerous as people might not get the prescriptions they require. But a business that gets to six Sigmas will produce only about 50 to 70 wrong prescriptions in a year. Another example entails a three Sigma electric company having power outages for about three to four hours a month, while a six Sigma electric company will have only one hour without electricity every two to three years.

Not all businesses have to meet the 3.4 defect standard. This standard may be too lofty or difficult for businesses to attain due to some of the natural variations that may develop in the manufacturing or operational process. But the goal is to create a layout that ensures a business continues to improve upon its functionality. Aiming for a 99 percent efficiency rating makes it easier for a business to grow. More importantly, as its processes involved become more predictable, a business will become more trustworthy and easier to support.

The Necessity of Obtaining Six Sigma Certification

It is vital for you to get the Six Sigma certification. The most important benefit of obtaining your certification is to reduce the number of errors within your business. By identifying opportunities within the workplace, it will become easier for you to determine the solutions necessary for fixing your business. Your business will also save money on its operations when the problems within its operations are fixed.

The Six Sigma certification can be applied to an assortment of industries. In the sciences, Six Sigma is used to identify how chemical tests and actions work and what can be done to ensure certain results. In banking, Six Sigma helps to review how banking functions are planned and what can be done to correct any errors or concerns that may develop. The marketing industry may use Six Sigma to identify possible opportunities and/or potential for waste. Having more control over one's work is a universal concern, thus making Six Sigma ideal for businesses of all kinds to use.

More importantly, Six Sigma can help your business to maintain compliance. Various inspection boards and organizations use Six Sigma standards for identifying functions and actions in the workplace. Part of this includes looking at how well machines work and how employees are capable of managing tasks, among other factors. Inspection boards may use Six Sigma standards to ensure that there are no problems with business practices.

How Does This Benefit the Customer?

The customer is always the top priority for a business. The customer expects a business to produce high quality products while also remaining competitive, reliable, timely and offering the best possible service.

The Six Sigma approach ensures that products are made to the best standards possible. When consistent standards are maintained, the customer will know that a business cares about quality and will then be likely to support that business. You must always do what you can to please the customer. After all, that old adage is correct—the customer is always right.

How Does This Benefit Employees?

The employees in your workplace will benefit from the Six Sigma process as well. Employees will be able to create results for your business by designing processes that are easy and efficient to follow. You can expect your employees to work better together as everyone will be on the same page. When employees work together with the Six Sigma process, it becomes easier for the business to grow and thrive in the long run. The best part about the Six Sigma routine is that the process works well for everyone in the workplace.

The Hidden Factory Consideration

The best analogy to describe the Six Sigma process is that of clearing out the "hidden factory" that is within your business. But what does the hidden factory entail, and how is it so important to the Six Sigma effort?

The hidden factory refers to the things that take place within your standard operating procedure (SOP). While you might think the task at hand is moving forward as desired, that effort might actually be slumping or struggling to move forward. Part of this might come from the sudden issues or waste concerns that are slipping into your Six Sigma task. These issues might make it harder for your business to stay functional or capable of providing you with the best possible results for the work you are putting in. Those issues have to be identified so they can be corrected.

The hidden factory suggests that there are things in your workplace that are going on that are anything but normal. Those problems have to be resolved as soon as possible so you can keep defects or issues from arising. Furthermore, there is always the chance that the things happening in the hidden factory will spill over into the rest of the workplace, so addressing any problems immediately is paramount to a business' success.

Think about a simple question when looking at the hidden factory: what if the customers knew about what was going on in your hidden factory? Do you think they would want to buy into your products or services? People might not want to spend lots of money on products or services produced in a way where defects are more likely to occur than not.

A great goal for Six Sigma is to reduce the influence of the hidden factory, allowing your work to be more visible and useful to everyone. The process will produce a better result thanks to every part of the task being revealed and studied for efficiency.

One way to manage a hidden factory is to make it into a visual factory by offering pictures, diagrams, manuals and other things that illustrate your new Six Sigma process to all your employees. The things you can do when planning the visual factory can be diverse and varied. You have to look at what people can understand. Some courses or discussions with your employees may be required. You need to review what people want to get out of a task and how the work in question is run. Only by being aware of every aspect of every process can you implement solutions as necessary.

Chapter 2 – The Pros and Cons of Six Sigma and How the Cons Are Reversed

This guide will help you understand what makes Six Sigma a sensible approach for your business to utilize. But, as you will notice, there are some negatives associated with Six Sigma. The great news is that there are far more positives that come out of Six Sigma as you go along, which will neutralize any negative issues.

Positives

1. Your business may save money.

Six Sigma helps you to identify problems of inefficiency in your workplace. As a result, your business will save money by streamlining carefully defined strategies and processes. Your employees will learn better ways to go about their daily tasks, keeping the business running at peak efficiency. The resulting additional profits may help with enhancing other functions in your business or with providing your employees with more benefits, thus making Six Sigma all the more valuable for everyone concerned.

2. Six Sigma is a data-oriented approach.

You do not have to worry about guesswork any longer. Everything you do with Six Sigma is based on data collected over time. This keeps the process of finding information through Six Sigma from being too hard to follow. You can measure ongoing processes in the workplace to figure out how they work and what you can expect out of them. Analyzing this data makes it easier for your business to stay efficient and current. This can be critical for your success.

3. Six Sigma is a continuous process.

While many efforts you put into your business to keep it active and operational may be beneficial, your business may forget about certain functions or processes after a while. But with Six Sigma, it becomes easier for your business to grow and thrive. You can use Six Sigma to review information relating to your business' processes while recognizing what can be done if the processes ever falter. The continuous effort of Six Sigma ensures that the process is maintained and monitored properly.

4. Information in the process should be easy to convey to your employees.

During the Six Sigma process, what is expected of employees is clarified. With clear expectations now outlined, employees will work harder and more efficiently. As you perfect your Six Sigma routine, the processes and strategies you use will become easier to follow. Having a sense of control is vital for everyone's success. Individual lines and efforts in the workplace should become easier to operate.

5. Everyone plays a role in Six Sigma.

The best business processes are the ones where everyone has a say in the action. Everyone in the workplace will want to be active and contributing to the process. Six Sigma provides consistent routines that all people can work with. Everyone can be educated to recognize what can be done to move forward with Six Sigma. People will not feel left out in the Six Sigma process, thus making the effort all the more enjoyable for everyone concerned.

Negatives (and How They Are Offset)

The problems that may arise with Six Sigma are often temporary. As your business becomes used to the Six Sigma routines it enters into, it becomes easier for the business to grow and to use the Six Sigma efforts for their needs. However, you should still be aware of the initial growing pains that you will come across so you are prepared for what to expect. Knowing what the Six Sigma process entails is vital to its success.

1. More resources and funds may be used.

Although Six Sigma can help with improving upon how a business operates, it can also be a tough endeavor to enter into. You may need to invest in more resources like newer machines or additional training functions, among other things. This will require spending money which could total thousands or even millions of dollars over time, depending on your business' specific needs. The good news is that, although the initial Six Sigma investment may be prohibitive to some, you may also save money in the future by avoiding problems. Check your Six Sigma plans to figure out what, specifically, will be involved in the process you are entering into.

2. You might have to increase the values of the products or services you are offering.

The costs associated with implementing Six Sigma might make it to where your business will have to increase the price of the final product in order to offset costs. Thus, customers might not be as likely to buy what you are offering. But as you grow your business through the Six Sigma process, that added value may be worthwhile. You will show an attention to quality and a desire to produce the best product for customers while getting it on the market sooner. Customers are more likely to shop with businesses that they can trust even if it means paying a little extra for something.

.

3. You have to keep monitoring the Six Sigma process no matter how far you get into it.

The Six Sigma process can last for as long as it has to, ranging from months to years. Part of the process requires continual monitoring. The routines that you put in might take a while to establish. However, the Six Sigma routine can be easier to follow once properly implemented. You may use the Six Sigma efforts you put in to analyze what is happening in the work environment and to fix problems that suddenly show up.

4. Six Sigma requires the participation of everyone in the workplace.

As exciting as Six Sigma can be, it must be supported by everyone since all of the people in your workplace will be required to operate under Six Sigma guidelines. These include the guidelines for handling processes and routines. But the good news is that it won't take long for everyone in the workplace to recognize what can be done to make the Six Sigma process easier to follow. Educating everyone in the workplace about what it takes to make Six Sigma run right, and why it will be good for business, is vital for helping your company grow.

5. The process for gathering information can be time-consuming.

The information you get out of the Six Sigma process will be critical for your business. But it may also take a while—and quite a lot of effort—for you to obtain said information. What makes this negative a positive is that the data you gather will be both accurate and precise based on what you want. Thus, you should have a much easier time analyzing the data and using it appropriately.

The thing about Six Sigma is that the process focuses on both precision and accuracy. You will use Six Sigma to give your business an extra bit of control when it comes to managing its data and content. This can make a world of difference when trying to make the most out of your work environment. You must see how well Six Sigma works while not being too worried about the negatives. Those so-called negatives will do more to help you with your Six Sigma work when all is said and done.

Chapter 3 – The Belt Levels of Six Sigma

Similar to various martial arts forms, Six Sigma uses a series of colored belts to recognize the proficiency levels of Sigma Six practitioners. The belt will vary based on the level of certification you have obtained and certifies you to work within certain functions. The belt levels listed in this chapter are organized from the lowest level of certification to the highest and most powerful.

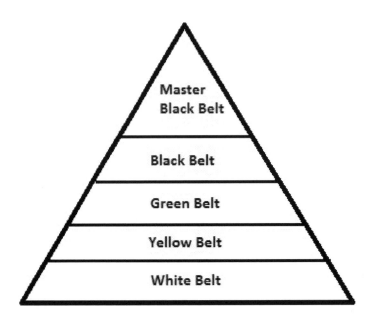

Champion

Although the term "champion" sounds like a huge deal, this is actually the lowest level of Six Sigma certifications. A person with Champion status understands the basic concepts and values of the Six Sigma process and what it takes to make the process easy to follow and use. However, a Champion does not yet have the quantitative skills necessary for success. A Champion may be a part of a larger committee and should have the influence to move the task forward so the organization can grow. A Champion will work well alongside Black Belts and Master Black Belts.

A Champion will be responsible for identifying a project during the work process. The objectives for the project will be developed and organized with the support of management partners. You can select a Black Belt for any project when looking for a leader, or you can use a Green Belt for a smaller or less complicated project. The timetable of a project, the focus for the task and the resource management plans can also be organized. The role of a Champion is vital to the success of the Six Sigma process even if the person involved is not necessarily responsible for all the functions in the process.

In most cases, a Champion may be an executive in the workplace. That person may have an idea of what needs to be done and can tell others who have received Six Sigma training to take care of the project. A Champion might also be someone who has participated in a Six Sigma task in the past and has some kind of belt certification but is responsible for other functions outside of the routine. Think of a Champion as the general boss who engineers the process and tells others about what has to be done with the effort at large. Better yet, a Champion may be interpreted as a sponsor of sorts

White Belt

A White Belt will focus on problem-solving efforts but will not participate much in the design of the Six Sigma task. A White Belt can study further and take a test to receive a Yellow Belt, followed by a Green Belt. A Six Sigma task can include as many White Belt participants as necessary so long as they are not given too much control over a particular task.

Yellow Belt

A Yellow Belt is a person who has completed the Green Belt certification but has yet to complete a Six Sigma task. A person who finishes a Six Sigma task immediately becomes a Green Belt. A Yellow Belt can progress well if that person understands how to handle the tasks associated with managing a process right.

Yellow Belt participants can participate in projects and receive training for handling any foreign concepts in a Six Sigma task. All process issues are reported to Green and Black belts. A Yellow Belt is not responsible for training White Belts. After completing a Six Sigma routine, a Yellow Belt will become a Green Belt and will have extra control over future procedures and tasks.

Green Belt

A Green Belt will take on more Six Sigma tasks thanks to their prior experience with other projects while in the Yellow Belt status. Extra research is a part of a Green Belt's duties. This includes work with extra analytical tools and further help through the DMAIC process or identifying how to move forward with a lean task. A Green Belt will still report to a Black Belt.

A Green Belt is a person who works on smaller projects that are easy to follow such as producing a project charter and determining what members of the team will participate in the program. A Green Belt also communicates with other people in the Six Sigma project; the communication is consistent throughout the entire project to ensure a sense of control.

A Green Belt schedules project meetings. Data collected during the project will be analyzed throughout the duration of the program. Other team members may also be trained by the Green Belt to handle various tools and functions relating to how Six Sigma operates. A Green Belt must work well with all team members to keep the project running smoothly at all stages.

Black Belt

A Black Belt is a person who has more expertise in the Six Sigma process. The person has more technical skills, understands statistics and other complicated processes and is capable of organizing meetings. A Black Belt should understand the psychology of the people who are on a team, thus producing a more controlled setup and arrangement for managing the content being used in the Six Sigma routine. Any reviews from a Champion or executive committee will be supported by a Black Belt.

A Black Belt should be especially easy for a person to work with. He or she needs to manage an extensive amount of work and effort in the process, ensuring tasks are handled smoothly and efficiently. A Black Belt cannot afford to feel intimidated by anyone and must have a strong customer focus. A Black Belt understands that it is the customer's needs that will determine how an overall work process is managed.

A Black Belt will also handle many tasks in the Six Sigma process. He or she should be supported by a Master Black Belt. That Black Belt may also report to his or her manager for any further instructions. All Green Belts in a project can also be monitored and mentored by a Black Belt, although this is for cases where projects are limited in how they are organized. The power that a Black Belt holds is vital for managing the tasks at hand.

Brown Belt

A Brown Belt is similar to a Yellow Belt. In particular, a Brown Belt is given to a person who has completed Black Belt certification but has yet to participate in a project or complete a Six Sigma task. When he or she completes a task for the first time, that person will receive a Black Belt.

Master Black Belt

A Master Black Belt is the highest level of certification that a person can obtain. This is the main leader of any Six Sigma task. A Master Black Belt will have led at least ten teams through basic Six Sigma tasks and should have worked for at least two years on

Six Sigma tasks of all types. The person should be an expert in Six Sigma practices and therefore will be able to handle any issues that might develop.

A Master Black Belt will talk with all senior executives and managers about the Six Sigma process. New projects may be organized with the goal of identifying what can be done to move a task forward. All actions in the Six Sigma process will be monitored and analyzed to see that the processes move forward correctly. A Master Black Belt may talk with the sales and HR departments alongside any call centers or IT groups that the company hires. Any important statistical considerations that have to be resolved should also be handled by a Master Black Belt.

A Master Black Belt can work with every lean and DMAIC concept that may be introduced. He or she can teach other people about Six Sigma theory with an emphasis on analyzing the tools and methods. The mentorship skills that a Master Black Belt offers are vital to the success of a task while also confirming that a group can handle all the necessary Six Sigma tasks.

Remember that, no matter where on the totem pole you are, your role in the Six Sigma routine is important. You must work towards certification in your work and with getting more experience in Six Sigma tasks if you wish to get to the higher belts. Those who have the highest belts will have more control over assigned tasks. But remember that a Champion will tell you what the task is for, even if that Champion does not have much control over the actual Six Sigma routine. You will find it is not hard to carry out a task efficiently if you look carefully at your efforts and manage your content the right way.

Chapter 4 – The Five Voices

As you work on the Six Sigma process, you will come across five voices. You can use each of the five voices to figure out how the process is working while using them to gauge your business' operational functions. Understanding how your business works is critical to its success.

The five voices are used when designing the Six Sigma routine. Seeing how well the five voices change throughout the DMAIC process helps you to see what is working or whether you need an extra bit of help with planning a project. You need to know what will make the task run well based on the voices involved.

Voice of the Business (VOB)

The first voice to look at is the Voice of the Business or VOB. The VOB is a measure of the needs that a business has. The VOB does not have to be directly discussed, but it must include enough information on what a business requires. The VOB may also be related to shareholders. Shareholders have as much of a value to a business as the people who operate that business.

The VOB involves reviewing current leadership issues and struggles within the workplace. You will use the VOB to analyze how a business is growing and what can be done to keep it on the right track. VOB can also be used to review what you want to do in terms of customer service, retaining employees and shareholders or reducing the cycle time within the business. As you review the VOB, you may also consider general advancements in technology. You can reduce the costs involved and find ways to make the content you are handling more flexible, or even use the VOB to figure out what you can do when trying to grow your business in overseas markets.

Your analysis of your business should be as thorough as possible. You can talk with managers, shareholders, affiliates and anyone else about current processes or regular events that occur in the workplace. Talk about what is working and what customers are most interested in. More importantly, discuss the problems within the workplace and what has to be done to resolve those issues before they become worse.

You must ensure the VOB is handled as confidentially as possible. Some people in the business might not be willing to share information with you unless their identities are kept private, particularly if the information they want to share is negative. Even if that is the case, you should listen to them carefully and respectfully. They might introduce you to flaws or issues within the workplace that you may have overlooked.

Voice of the Customer (VOC)

As important as the needs of the business are, the customer always comes first. Without customers, a business will fail. Therefore, the Voice of the Customer or VOC is the next important measure to look at. The consideration here is that a "satisfied customer" is a thing of the past. Customers no longer want to feel just satisfied with what they are getting out of a business; they want to be delighted.

Customers want great prices on high-quality products. They want those products to be made available in many forms. More importantly, they want those products right now. The Six Sigma process reviews what customers want based on the VOC. The goal of Six Sigma is to figure out a way to give a customer what he or she wants even if a business doesn't have that specific content at the precise moment it is requested.

For instance, the automobile industry used to only produce black cars in its early days. People were not satisfied with that; they wanted to have different-colored cars so they could have more unique vehicles and/or at least be able to tell cars apart from each other. Thus, companies began making cars in different colors.

The VOC is relatively easy to gauge. You can talk with various customers about what they are looking for. Surveys and focus groups are often held to identify what customers want. The reviews can be as extensive as necessary, so long as they are done carefully and with your target audience in mind. You can use these points to gain a clearer understanding of what to expect out of customers that you wish to contact.

You can talk with as many customers as you want when you're trying to find answers to your questions. That said, make sure you have a plan for getting the most out of the work you are putting in.

Voice of the Process (VOP)

As you look for information on what people within the business and its customers want, you need to also look at the process being planned out and review how well that routine is moving. Any errors within the process must be identified. The opportunities surrounding said processes should also be explored in detail. The Voice of the Process is an essential part of your business operations that cannot be ignored.

The Voice of the Process or VOP is an analysis of what is happening in the workplace and how your business' processes are working. You can use the VOP to identify opportunities, but the most important part is to assess what the process is telling you in general.

The VOP should tell you what the processes in the workplace are capable of achieving. The analysis should be based on how well the process is running versus any possible opportunities that come about and what you can do to make the most out of those occasions. The most important part here is to see that the data you are handling is managed right.

You can use a control chart to identify how the VOP is running and review how certain events in the process produce results based on what you are getting out of the practice. The chart can identify how well the process is running and help you determine what you should be doing to resolve issues. You will learn more about the control chart in a later chapter.

The best rule of thumb surrounding the VOP is that you should be looking to obtain a state of Gemba. This is a Japanese term for a real workplace where you go and see what you want to achieve. This is different from a workplace where you wait and listen to see what is happening. Gemba is the state a business operates in when established standards are consistently attained. Failing to reach that state may result in significant struggles within the process your business is trying to perfect.

Remember that, if you have complex business processes, the VOP will be a little more complicated to assess. The effort might take a while, but it will help you establish the best possible control for your business.

Voice of the Employees (VOE)

As important as it is for your business to be in control and your customers to be satisfied, none of this is possible without the support of your employees. It is through your employees that your business will (or will not) continue to progress and be profitable. But in some cases, your employees might not have the training that they need. They may struggle to complete their jobs because they don't have the necessary resources or education. This is where the Voice of the Employees or VOE comes into play.

Employees might not have the skills they need, let alone the additional employees necessary to take on some of the most complicated tasks. The VOE will help you to identify what those employees need. You can talk with employees in the workplace and ask them about what they want. Then follow up by discussing how the things they want can be attained, whether that involves hiring a few new people, establishing some new processes, purchasing additional resources or anything other solution that is specifically helpful to the situations you and your employees are assessing.

Let's look at a baseball team to get an idea of what the VOE is about. Team members might be confident in their abilities to hit and run the ball. But the starting pitchers might be concerned about the lack of proficient relief pitchers. The starting pitchers know they cannot go an entire nine-inning game every single time they get out on the mound. They need reliable backup pitchers. The VOE suggests that those new relief pitchers are necessary to ensure the team succeeds and the starting pitchers aren't at risk of injury.

That example relating to a baseball team is just one way the VOE can be utilized. Any business or entity, whether it entails a manufacturing plant or a sports team, can use the VOE to figure out what the people directly associated with the organization want to get out of the process. The best part of reviewing the VOE is that doing so gives a business the opportunity to figure out what it can do for success and to move forward with various plans to keep an establishment active and running smoothly.

Like with the VOB, the VOE must also be gathered confidentially. Any changes within the business will directly influence the feelings that your workers have toward its operations. Knowing what to get out of the VOE means allowing people to speak their minds. You never know what you will get out of the VOE if you don't let people speak freely about the problems they have.

Voice of Data (VOD)

The fifth voice is the Voice of Data or VOD. The problem with data in the workplace is that it abruptly can change without warning. What worked well in the past might not work so much later on. But with the VOD, you can better determine what you want to get out of your business. You can use the VOD to your advantage to figure out what should be done to resolve problems in your workplace.

The VOD can be reviewed as often as needed when gathering data on your business. You can do a general data analysis every week or month if you have to. You can also keep a closer eye on that data depending on the changes taking place within certain periods of time. Knowing what to expect out of your processes is a necessity for moving forward and making your business stronger. More importantly, the VOD may help you with understanding how technology may improve your business practices.

You can use all five of these voices in the Six Sigma process as necessary. The Six Sigma process is a full routine that focuses on every aspect of your workplace and how it operates. The voices will help you to get a comprehensive idea of what should be done for the general success of your business to ensure it continues to grow and thrive over the years.

Chapter 5 – The Eight Dimensions of Quality

Every Six Sigma project, no matter what your objective may be, needs to work within appropriate **dimensions of quality**. There are eight particular dimensions of quality that you may utilize when planning your task. Some dimensions might be more relevant in your field of work than others. Let's look at the specifics surrounding these dimensions of quality and what you can expect out of each.

For this chapter, we will use a sports car as a measure of quality. A Six Sigma task will produce end products that efficiently support all eight dimensions of quality. The car you want to produce should be planned with all dimensions so the customer will be satisfied. However, the standards that have to be met will vary based on the particular dimensions of quality within which you wish to operate.

1. Performance

Performance is a measure of how well a product or service does what it is designed to do. When, using the example of the sports car, certain parts have defects, their impaired performance will produce unsatisfied customers. For a vehicle, the engine must be built to specific technical standards to ensure it can produce enough acceleration within a precise time frame. Other parts, like the suspension or control, may be monitored to ensure that they are working together as intended.

2. Features

A product or service needs all the features that it has been advertised as having. All features must be planned with precision and accuracy while ensuring they are suitable for their required purposes. A sports car might need to be manufactured with leather seats that are thick or strong enough to handle most people's weight. Meanwhile, the car needs an audio system that produces enough power for entertainment use. Six Sigma routines will ensure that each car feature is planned out and engineered correctly.

3. Reliability

A product or service has to work consistently and efficiently. For Six Sigma, the product or service should be produced at the same rate with every item being manufactured so it is accurate and safe. The reliability rating may be very high if the Six Sigma plan is prepared without lots of waste or with a simple set of instructions for all to follow. For the process to be reliable, a sports car manufacturer will need to produce the same number of vehicles each day. In addition, those vehicles must pass other tests for dimensions of quality to ensure the vehicle can be made available for sale without problems.

4. Conformance

All items being handled or offered must be linked to a certain specification or standard. Conformance rules can include anything from specific performance goals to the ability for something to meet specific product descriptions. A conformance standard might entail something like using the right materials to obtain a specific result from a product or service. For example, a car manufacturer might use the same type of leather every time, along with using the same consistent cuts to the fabric, to produce a high quality, consistent result.

5. Durability

A product or service has to last for a while. As such, the sports car in this example should be produced with materials that will not tear, rust or fade over time. You can plan a Six Sigma routine that focuses on using the correct materials to ensure the routine is run to your specific liking.

6. Service

Service is a critical part of the total cost of ownership. A business should ensure it has the proper tools on hand to assist a customer with a product or service. The service may be important for ensuring that the cost of operation is reduced. This is a useful point for businesses in Six Sigma as those entities can review the ways how their items are offered. A sports car manufacturer may look at how well a call center works to see that any questions people have about their cars are being answered swiftly and accurately. This includes keeping people from waiting too long on the phone while also preventing any possible cases where someone is forwarded from one line to the next.

7. Aesthetics

The general appearance of something can make a difference to customers. Sports cars have distinct appearances that make them stand out from every other car on the road. Six Sigma plans should be organized based on what you feel is suitable for your plans. This includes an analysis of how well a material is produced and what specific measurements might be suitable for obtaining the aesthetic effect you want to achieve.

8. Perception/Experience

Perception is often tough to measure, but it is a part of quality that is critical to any Six Sigma task. Perception refers to what people notice when it comes to products and services they consider buying. People have to feel confident in what they are finding and they need to believe they can benefit from whatever is being offered in terms of a product or service. For a car manufacturer, a product that offers a top-quality experience like a fancy sports car can make that company look more appealing.

Perception is also known as experience. A Six Sigma routine has to be planned out to where each end product or service provides people with the best experience. Whether it entails a fast customer service call or the thrill of driving down a road in luxury, the end product or service should be worth a customer's time and money. A company that is perceived as offering a better all-around product might be easier for people to trust.

Chapter 6 – The DMAIC Steps

The way you handle your Six Sigma approach is vital to the success of your task. In fact, this chapter might be the most important one you read in this book as it focuses on the general guidelines that you will follow throughout the Six Sigma process. These include steps designed to cover everything you wish to utilize in your work routine.

One of the most important principles surrounding Six Sigma involves the DMAIC steps. These are critical steps that improve upon how well a business can develop its various functions. You must use these steps to plan Six Sigma routines. Failure to follow the DMAIC steps will keep you from understanding how a process works, not to mention what your business needs for success.

The DMAIC order should be systematically followed to give you a plan for how people will serve your business and how different parts of the business will grow and progress. Every step *must* be followed in a specific order, as outlined in this guide. Getting everything done with realistic parameters and within a logical time frame is paramount for your business' success. The good news is that DMAIC is not a hard process to follow.

Define/Design

The DMAIC process is designed to resolve problems after they are identified. To start, you need to define what you wish to do when handling the DMAIC process. You must define a tangible issue that needs to be resolved. This will be the basis for the Six Sigma process.

This process of clearly defining an issue, followed by determining what needs to be done to resolve it, helps you to identify what *specifically* you can do to improve upon your business efforts. There are three things in particular that have to be done:

1. Identify the initial problem.

2. Identify the customers who will be influenced by it

3. Review the VOC to identify customer needs

You will need to use a value stream map to identify workplace processes and to review how information is flowing within the work environment. The practice lets you see how people interact with each other and allows you to assess whether there are certain flaws in the overall business' processes. The value stream map will be discussed in a later chapter in this guide.

Four Keys in the Definition Process

As you define your Six Sigma task, it's important to determine how clearly that definition is established. If it's not clearly defined, employees will not be able to fulfil the task's requirements. The four keys to a clear definition are:

1. Objective

The objective is based on the problem. Tangible issues you might have identified early on should be re-examined based on the solutions you are considering. For example, if there is a tangible problem that has been identified with a particular manufacturing process, your objective must be written so as to address that problem. You can be as specific with your objective as you want. This includes establishing specific procedures to use or a time frame during which the problem must be resolved.

2. Benefits

Benefits entail anything relating to the success of fulfilling your objective, including improved manufacturing standards or enhanced processes. As you are enumerating the benefits, be specific about they will help with improving upon the Six Sigma process.

3. Project Team

The project team elaborates upon who is responsible for running the Six Sigma task. This includes the Black Belt, Master Black Belt and other people who hold designating responsibilities throughout the process. You can have as many people on the project team as you would like, but each person's role should be clearly defined, and the team has to be organized appropriately.

4. Schedule

Although you don't have to create a specific work schedule, it can be helpful. The schedule can include specific dates for when each of the DMAIC steps should be attained. The time frame can be as long or short as necessary for your objective. You can also use a range of dates if you want to create a more flexible work schedule. Be sure, if you use very specific dates, that they are realistic.

What Is the VOC?

The VOC, the Voice of the Customers, was mentioned in brief a little earlier, but it is a concept that deserves a little further explanation. It is a measure of the expectations and demands that the customer has. The typical customer will have unique expectations and interests, not to mention concerns. All these can be organized based on order of importance.

You can use customers to guide you through the Six Sigma effort while designing a plan that fits their specific needs.

The VOC can be gathered in many ways:

1. Focus Group

A focus group is a group of people (there is no fixed number of participants) who discuss a business' perceived purpose, what they want out of it or what they are interested in. You can also hold several of these focus groups if that's helpful to your objective. You should review the demographics of these groups so they suit your business needs. Make sure that all people have a chance to participate in the discussion and that no one participant is doing all the talking.

2. Basic Interviews

Individual interviews are often helpful. You can change the questions as needed to suit the person and situation. Just remember to consider your budget and how much time you have for individual interviews. And don't forget that the interview subjects will probably want something in return for their time.

3. General Studies of Your Market

Large-scale studies of your market can be utilized to help you identify the VOC. These include reviews of your business finances and how certain actions or events might have triggered changes in your workplace or how people supported your business. A basic review of your market can help you with identifying how well your business is established and what can be done to improve or maintain it as needed. The more specific details you can gather during your review, the better.

After you gather the VOC, you can utilize many processes to help you get more out of your work. First, figure out the needs that people have based on the interviews or focus group you have conducted. After that, organize those needs into a hierarchy that focuses on what people want most versus other less critical wants/needs. Prioritize the list based on urgency.

Any parties in your workplace that focus on product development must be present during this process. The developmental team should create a group sampling of customers to interview. After this is done and the data is analyzed, the business can then move forward with resolving issues as necessary.

The Storyboard

A storyboard may also be used in the design process. A storyboard will help you with recognizing task specifics. It may include a business case that illustrates the things you want to do with your work and how you will carry out your tasks and efforts in general. You can include the problem and then the goal statement, followed by a scope for the task. Milestones can also be incorporated in the planning process.

You can also look at the resource plan to see what roles you should be utilizing. Every team member, particularly any White and Yellow Belts, should have specific, predetermined roles. You can use the definition part of the DMAIC process to identify how well those roles are planned out, thus producing a thorough and detailed approach to the work routine.

Measure

The second part of the DMAIC process involves measuring your project's progress. At the start of the project, you must establish baselines for how your business is going to improve. Part of this includes collecting data regarding how your business is moving forward and making necessary changes. The baselines should be measured at the start and then measured once again, later in the process, to determine whether any improvements can be seen.

The measurements can entail any parameters and may be gauged based on the improvements that you feel need to be analyzed. The most important part of this entails ensuring that necessary data is appropriately gathered and assessed. You may also measure the process capability of whatever you are working on to get a clear idea of how processes in the workplace are established and what needs to be done to improve them, if anything. Every measurement must be as accurate as possible.

You can produce a cause and effect analysis in the measurement process. The causes of problems are identified with the intention of fixing problems and adjusting plans to achieve desired effects. The measurement process is designed for analyzing the concerns or controls that have to be factored into the Six Sigma process.

The measurement process must also include a review of the Y-axis variables that you will utilize. This refers to the base guideline that you are going to work with throughout the process. A general analysis of the measurement system and how well it might work can be planned out in your work as well. Any baselines that you wish to incorporate in your work can also be included, although you have full control over whether or not certain standards or concepts might be utilized. The measurements you come up with will dictate how well your task operates and where you might go with the work you put in.

Analyze

Analysis is the third aspect of the DMAIC effort. Analysis involves reviewing the content that was measured at the start to see if there are errors that need to be corrected plus what should be done to resolve those problems before they can become worse. Your goal is to figure out what you can do to eliminate problems that are keeping your business from developing or from meeting your established requirements or standards. This root-cause analysis can be planned and utilized in any way you see fit.

At this juncture, you might come across several root causes relating to a problem. You must factor out the most significant concerns and come across ways to fix those issues before they can become too significant. The efforts you put into the analysis process will vary based on the subject matter or concern. The work may include the creation of process maps to identify where, exactly, the root causes for problems are developing and what can be done to resolve them.

While the Y-variable is all about what you are measuring something along, the X-variable is about time frame, quantity or anything else you want to analyze. The potential causes of something can be explored in detailed at this juncture, provided you have a plan on hand for managing your content. A relationship may also be found between the X and Y points.

What Is a Root Cause?

Root cause refers to the issue that initiates the concern in the workplace. In some cases, the earliest problem will come about during a routine practice or an already established process. In other situations, the root cause may be the entire process itself. In that case, the problem may have become too significant to handle. Identifying the real root cause may require an analysis of a very large sample size relating to your business, including information regarding your business' operations.

Improve

After you determine the problem, you must improve upon how your business operates. As difficult as the improvement process can be, it is often the best part of the DMAIC effort. You will get a clear understanding of what you can do and will then see, based on your efforts, how your business changes for the better.

The improvement process is all about creativity. The best solutions will be unique and also simple and easy to follow. Your employees should feel comfortable with what you are doing as you get the new routine or process up and running. Your ideas can also be deployed in any way you see fit so long as you avoid anything that is too unrealistic or difficult to convey.

The possible solutions you want to use can be analyzed to see what their probable results might be. A pilot solution that you test out later may also be planned. The pilot can be thorough and include any new targets you want to establish. The detailed pilot should be clearly planned out and should be simple to carry out.

The Critical Input

The most important part of the improvement stage is the critical input. Critical input is the process that entails the items that are handled at a time. You can use anything in the workplace as the critical input, although you need to confirm that whatever you are planning will be organized accordingly. The input can be managed for as long as necessary. Keeping the critical input under control for a little longer is a necessity for seeing your business consistently improve.

The improvement stage requires you to both verify the critical input and to optimize that input. The optimization process involves changes to the input while keeping notes or reports on how you are modifying that input. Your work can entail as many steps as you wish so long as it remains realistic and efficient.

Control

The fifth part of the DMAIC process is the control stage. If the four stages before this have been systematically followed, the control stage should be easy to implement. You may produce a formula that identifies what is happening in the workplace and what you have to do to fix problems that might develop.

A control chart may be incorporated at this point. The control chart is a full analysis of how your business works plus a general measurement of what is happening in the workplace. You can use the control chart to confirm what your business is doing and to see if the business is maintaining the Six Sigma standards or is, at least, very close to getting there. You can use your chart to see if the business is consistently improving.

Any plans for developing new ideas or transitioning certain parts of the workplace to new standards may also be listed in the control process including things like how the process develops, how a business can transition from one point to the next and a schedule for how actions might develop in any situation. The benefit-delivery process and confirmation process can also be reviewed.

After a while, you can sign off on the Six Sigma task, provided that the results of the task are consistent. At this juncture, the risk of something changing for the negative over time should be minimal.

Synergize

There is a sixth step associated with the DMAIC process that can also be explored. This is the synergize step. The process involves sharing the benefits of the Six Sigma process as a whole, helping everyone in the workplace to understand how the Six Sigma routines are working and ensuring that procedures in the workplace move forward as desired. You can use the sixth step to analyze how well employees' roles are established and how people in the workplace are making individual progress. You may also use the synergize step to identify any irregularities occurring within the DMAIC process.

You can always use the synergize process after signing off on a Six Sigma task as well. The process works for cases where you're trying to review how well a task is running. You can get a better idea of how well the Six Sigma task is working and determine whether you need to resolve certain problems that have arisen.

Replication

The replication process involves taking what you are doing in the DMAIC process and applying it to other avenues of action in the workplace outside of the one that you are trying to improve upon. You can use the replication process to analyze what people are doing in the workplace and to recognize any challenges that might come along in different departments. Knowing how to make the most out of your replication effort can be vital for the success of your work and to helping many people in your workplace understand what should be done to succeed.

A Ten-Step Summary

The best way to explain the DMAIC process is to use ten steps to explain what is happening and what may be done to solve problems. Each step focuses on certain actions that develop in the workplace and establishes what can be done to allow the business to grow. This includes resolving the problems that occurred in the workplace that led to the need for Six Sigma efforts. The ten steps here may be used throughout the Six Sigma routine:

1. Define the problem.

2. Map out the process that will fix the issue. (This is provided the problem can be mapped out.)

3. Gather the necessary data for handling the issue.

4. Perform a cause and effect analysis.

5. With the data that was gathered, verify the root cause

6. Determine the necessary solutions for the task. You can also talk about preventative measures for resolving the problem.

7. Prepare a pilot test for the implementation process.

8. Complete the implementation. This includes establishing how all steps in the practice are organized.

9. Complete the monitoring process.

10. Document any lessons that were learned in the process.

Having more control over your work and seeing how a plan is clearly laid out, step by step, is vital to your success in making the DMAIC process work. You will be impressed with the final results.

Time Frame

If you have time constraints, you might be concerned about how long a Six Sigma task will take, especially if you are trying to compete with other businesses. The good news is that you don't have to rush your way through a Six Sigma process. You can work with the process with as few or as many details as you want while spending a little more time confirming that the work in question is being managed right.

The average amount of time spent on a Six Sigma routine can vary by organization. Some people will spend at least three to four months on their tasks. Others might spend as long as a year. A task will vary in length based on how intricate a process is and any other standards that you need to manage throughout the work process. You can talk with others in the Six Sigma routine about how long you should keep the process in place. Be advised that you might have to talk with your Champion for details.

The Six Sigma process is different from the Scrum process, a related part of Six Sigma that will be discussed in a later section of this guide. The Scrum has a set time frame and requires individual processes to be carried about approximately within a month. This is best for cases where you already know the individual processes and efforts you will be planning out.

Chapter 7 – The DMADV (DFSS) Process

While the traditional DMAIC process can be utilized to help you with managing your business' existing functions, there is another process that can be used if you wish to introduce something new. This is known as the DMADV or DFSS process. The process is also called the Design for Six Sigma process and uses five steps designed to help improve upon how a new product or service is created. You can also use this when establishing a new process for anything in the workplace. The effort involved is designed with many actions in mind, but this focuses on understanding how certain actions might work.

What Makes This Different from the DMAIC Process?

The basic difference between the DMAIC and DMADV processes involves the creation of something of value. The DMAIC process focuses mainly on improving existing content. The DMADV process is about creating something new. The two processes both focus on managing and supporting customer needs and determining how well a business operates. However, the DMAIC concentrates more on stringent requirements for improving upon a business' functionality, while DMADV is about keeping a project organized.

The DMADV process focuses on what immediately happens when developing something new. The DMAIC process involves a sense of control over how content may be utilized and how things can be developed. Knowing how to make this content work to your liking is vital for your success. You can choose to use the process you wish, although the DMADV routine is best for cases where the subject matter is easy to plan.

The good news is that the steps involved with the DMADV process are similar to what you would get out of a DMAIC effort. With this in mind, it's time to look at the steps involved in DMADV work.

Define

The first part of the DMADV process involves defining the design goals that you want to use. You will create new goals that are consistent with certain demands that your business and your customers have. The process can also include research and interviews with the public to determine specific needs. The key is to keep the definition process separate from anything else you wish to work with so whatever you want to do is planned out right.

The definition process is designed to expand upon whatever you have already introduced within your workplace. The definitions have to be specific and unique based on what you wish to highlight. The plan works based on what your business is doing *now* versus what you expect to get out of it later on.

For instance, you might be running an auto body shop and want to offer a unique service like the ability to install specialized high-power audio systems. You could define a process that entails ordering the parts needed for those systems, training people to install them and finally, actually installing the system. The goal is to define efforts such that installing the new systems is easy and doesn't waste anyone's time.

Measure

The second step involves the measurement process. You will measure Critical to Quality (CTQ) content. You can use this to figure out what items or concepts are most important for your business. You can also look at the capacity of your business. The risks associated with what you are doing should also be analyzed in order to plan for how to lessen those risks.

There is also the option to measure the opinions of customers, employees, managerial staff and so forth. A measure of those values may help with figuring out certain concerns that people have, their particular needs and what they feel you can improve upon. Look for connections in the data you gather from these discussions and measure it appropriately. Those connections lead to the next step.

Going back to the auto body example, the installation process should be measured based on the resources and time that will be required to complete the work to the highest standard. You can also measure the approximate time frame required for consistently installing systems correctly and efficiently.

Analyze

The analysis process is nearly identical to the one in the DMAIC routine. The analysis involves studying the cause and effect of anything you are doing, any root causes of problems you have identified and an understanding of possible solutions to be implemented. You can analyze the data to develop alternatives that are appropriate to your needs. The most important part of the analysis process is figuring out whether the new ideas being introduced are worthwhile and/or whether any problems might develop.

The analysis stage is where you make some of the final decisions regarding your work routine, based on things like the life-cycle cost of a project, or what you can do once you have enough resources on hand. The analysis gives you a closer look at what might make your work stand out or be efficient.

Design

The design process will help you to produce a new efficient routine or effort based on what you identified in the first few steps of the DMADV. You must look at how well the efforts involved will work in any situation that arises. More importantly, the work you put in must be organized so that results are measurable and consistent over time.

Any specific needs you defined earlier can be designed at this stage provided that the data you are using is easy to follow and you have a clear plan for proceeding. The car installation process may include a review of specific directions for installing the stereo system. You know what you will use and how it's going to be measured. You just need to know how you're going to plan the process based on what you feel is appropriate for the task.

You have the option to use as many alternative designs as you wish at this stage. You can plan different routines based on your definitions and what you feel is appropriate based on your measurements and analysis. You might have alternative solutions for installing the car stereo system, for instance. You will then need to communicate that information to everyone else so all people are aware of the particulars of the plans.

Verify

The fifth and final DMADV step is the verification process. You will confirm the design and set up a test run to determine whether the product or service works right. The testing can take as long as necessary. The goal is to keep the procedure or effort you put in as consistent as possible while avoiding problems that could cause the business trouble and be wasteful in terms of time and resources. The verification process should be monitored and data should be carefully gathered to obtain a complete analysis.

Let's go back to the car stereo sample one last time. You might have a plan for expanding upon the portfolio of services you want to offer by including car stereos in the offering. But the project should be planned out well and tested before presenting it to customers. You might have different employees test the routine to see if everything is working and that there is no waste being produced in the process.

You might have to run several test pilots to see how your DMADV work is or is not successful. You can confirm any project expectations at this juncture. You may also discover problems. Any issues that are identified will then have to be analyzed and corrected. You might need to restart the DMADV process or at least go back a few steps if you come across certain problems.

Use the DMADV process if you are planning on producing something that is unique and new. The DMADV process is similar in some ways to the DMAIC process, but the DMADV is specifically all about helping you to easily and efficiently create new products and services.

What About Existing Products?

The DMADV process can be utilized if you've got something to work with already. This can work in cases where you have existing products that need to be maintained and planned out properly. You might have an existing product or service that has gone through the Six Sigma process but has yet to reach a specification you want to attain, let although the Six Sigma standard. You can use the DMADV routine to define the issue with that existing item and then find a new solution that can expand upon a process (or adapt) that is already in place. DMADV is best for when you're trying to make minor changes; the full DMAIC process is best if you've got a much larger task to work with and aren't certain where you will go with the work at hand.

What If You Accidentally Use DMAIC For a DMADV Task?

A significant difference between DMAIC and DMADV processes is that DMADV is brief and does not entail as much of a thorough output or plan as a DMAIC task. You might still end up using the DMAIC process for something that could have easily been done via the DMADV route. But that does not mean that you did something wrong. Rather, you are planning your work with an extra bit of detail. You might be working with more elements than expected, but you are at least working with many of the same principles that you would use within the DMAIC process. You can always restart the project if needed, although that might not be necessary if you are seeing improvements. If anything, you might benefit more from using the DMADV process to make slight changes to an existing DMAIC routine.

Regardless of where you go with your DMADV task, you have to look at how you're going to make this work and ensure that you have a clear-cut plan in mind. The DMADV work you put in can be efficient and useful provided that the work in question is managed to your liking. But the DMADV effort is primarily for completely new ideas above all else. You might be surprised at where you will go when using this choice for handling your Six Sigma routines.

Chapter 8 – Going Lean (Lean Principles)

One of the options you have in the Six Sigma process entails going lean. Lean Six Sigma can be utilized with the DMAIC process, especially as you look to reduce waste and other common problems. But in some cases, you may consider a fully dedicated Six Sigma routine that focuses exclusively on eliminating waste. In order to make the process of going lean work, you have to look at the five lean principles.

Defining Value

The value of the work in the Six Sigma process has to be planned out carefully. The value concerns the needs that a customer has regarding a certain project. This might include rules for manufacturing a product or service, how it will be delivered and how much a customer is expected to spend. It's critical to illustrate the value of a product or service to clients.

Lean work involves removing waste. This applies to value in that every product element has to be relevant to a customer. Although you can incorporate some extras into the process, you should avoid anything that might otherwise be deemed unnecessary.

For instance, you might plan a work task for Six Sigma that entails producing a new refrigerator for customers. An appliance factory might need to produce a new refrigerator model based on customer demand. You might plan a manufacturing effort based only on the materials that customers have expressed they believe are valuable in a refrigerator. Thus, you might focus on manufacturing a refrigerator model that includes flexible shelves that can be removed and/or shifted around. The value of the project should be defined based on what the customer might feel is suitable for the task.

The interesting thing about waste is that it can be anything in the workplace. This includes cases where you might be utilizing too many steps in the process. You might also be purchasing excessive resources for said overly elaborate process. The key to going lean is to plan a process out so unnecessary tasks and resources are eliminated.

What the Customer Sees Out of the Task

The customer will identify your routine and notice three things that relate to the amount of value that is added to the work.

1. Value-Added Work

Value-added work refers to things that have to be done. This includes things that fix a process or make an end result work. The content in the valued-added process can entail anything. For a shipping plant, the value-added work might entail identifying where pieces of mail or packages are to be sent. Certain numbers might be reviewed on packages so they can then be shipped out to the right places. The value here ensures that the process moves quickly and with as little delay as possible.

2. Non-Value-Added Work

Non-value-added work does not add anything to the product in question. The shipping factory in our example might do non-valued-added work like trying to find certain shipping numbers or reviewing the quality of the boxes being produced or utilized. The efforts could take a while and might even last longer than what you're getting out of the rest of the value-added content.

3. Non-Valued-Added Work That Is Necessary

There comes a time when non-value-added work is necessary for the success of a task. This non-valued-added work can entail anything in the effort including clarifying the numbers on the boxes for shipping or rectifying any packing errors that might lead to product damage if left untreated. This form of non-value-added work should be kept to a minimum, but it will still be more useful than anything that might entail your workers waiting around and hardly doing anything.

Be advised that the second and third parts of the process are invariably going to produce waste. That waste makes it harder for a task to run successfully. Knowing how to keep that waste in check is vital for any efficient operation.

Mapping the Value Stream

The value stream is the measure of what you will use versus the ways materials will be handled. It entails the use of raw materials based on what customers feel will be suitable and useful. You can get the value stream for a refrigerator to work with only a few resources such as lightweight metals for the unit's construction or cooling agents for keeping the model chilled. You can also always plan to use other materials like glass surfaces for shelves. The resources in the value stream should only be based on things that are deemed necessary for the work.

Your resources should be planned based on how they will be designed and utilized. The procurement and HR processes may be handled alongside the processes that entail delivery of the final product and customer service. Manufacturing is only a small portion of the total effort to produce a product.

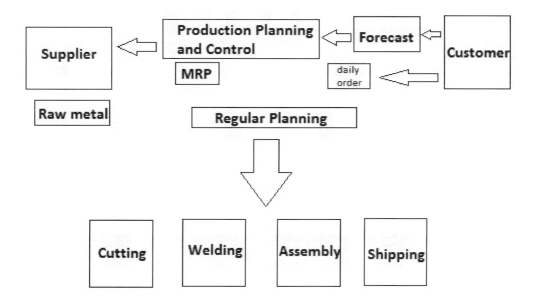

Your map can include many features that illustrate the many ways your Six Sigma routine is working. You can post things in your work based on factors like how long you need to wait to get a specific problem taken care of, or the time it consistently takes to manage certain functions. You do not have to worry about a set template for the map, as the above example shows. You can put as many details or standards into your map as you see fit. You can also look at the lead time relating to how long it will take for you to manage a step based on factors that you might not be able to fully control. This includes cases where you might need to wait for a delivery of a particular material without which the process cannot proceed. You can always use such lead time to prepare for whatever might come next in your routine.

The best part of managing the value stream is that you can keep it working with as many tasks or actions as you see fit. The value stream refrigerator example might include how the resources for the model are acquired and then organized. This includes planning the construction process based on what you feel is appropriate and helpful. You must remove any steps that might not be appropriate or useful for the task.

For the refrigerator, you might find, in the building process, that there is no need to use a certain number of materials. You might not have to work with as much aluminum or carbon fiber for the refrigerator's body as you had originally estimated. You can produce a map of the value stream to identify how well the task is run. Additional details on the value stream map will be included later to help you identify the ways that certain functions might change over time. The goal is to allow the process to run lean while ensuring the task is easy to follow.

The following image gives an example of how the value stream may be organized. The stream flows out from one central point to a series of steps and processes. The routines involved can be thorough and detailed, but they have to be organized to the point where they are easy to follow without anyone in the process being confused or frustrated. You can use this example of a hamburger restaurant to figure out what makes the routine unique. The process is a simple sample of what you might expect out of a procedure.

As the map shows, there are many steps that take place in the process of producing a final product for the customer. This includes many contingencies surrounding how the final product is created. You can use this as an example to see how a business functions with a value in mind. A company can use the concept here to figure out what should be done while also identifying what things are necessary and where waste can be lessened or eliminated.

If there is one positive thing that can be said about the work process you put in, it is that you don't have to worry about having to reveal to your customers whatever it is you have to offer. But even then, you must always look at your map and ask a simple question— what steps do you feel your customer should not have to bear with? These include steps that are considered to be unnecessary and therefore might cause the person who is using the service to not appreciate what is being offered.

Creating the Flow

A good flow is helpful for the Six Sigma effort. A lean process involves creating an easy-to-manage flow. A good flow lets you clearly see how a process works. The burger example you just saw is illustrative of a clearly defined flow.

You can always review any problems within the flow that are keeping the process from moving forward appropriately. These flow issues might entail concerns like being unable to handle several materials or steps, or maybe errors that are making the manufacturing or delivery process harder to follow than necessary. The Six Sigma process should work with enough of a lean flow to produce a healthy sense of support.

The most important part of creating a flow is to end the silo mentality that often comes with some processes. The silo mentality entails many groups in one larger organization not sharing information with one another. Departments with a silo mentality have different ideas of what should be done in a workplace. By not sharing important information, the groups are isolated from one another, thus possibly creating a limit on what can be done in the workplace.

The good news about the lean Six Sigma effort is that it helps with reducing the confusion or frustration that comes with groups not communicating with one another.

You can use a lean process to work with as many departments as possible, provided that the task is clearly outlined and that the departments are linked up with each other.

Establishing a Pull

The pull is a useful part of the lean process to note. It specifically refers to how a customer can pull a product or service from you as needed. The pull involves getting material to the market as soon as possible. The problem with some manufacturing processes is that items might be stuck in a warehouse for a while, thus causing a team to spend more money than necessary. Also, anything built in advance, or things that are not pulled out well enough might be hard to maintain or promote. If the pull is poor, you may have to charge less for some inventory items that you are holding for far too long.

Going After Perfection

The most important thing you can do for your work is make the improvement process a part of your regular work culture. You can plan the Six Sigma effort based on what you feel is more important than anything else. You can work with many tasks to obtain perfection, but it helps to notice how well certain routines may work.

To obtain perfection, you need to be consistently aware of your employees' abilities. Each employee should be consulted based on what you want to do with a task and how you're going to streamline the work. Proper education and information, especially when getting away from the silo mentality, is vital to helping you manage lean work appropriately.

The lean process maximizes customer value and helps you get the most out of your routine with fewer resources and processes. Keeping resources down reduces the amount of money you spend on the task and is also vital for an orderly process.

Consequential Metrics

An important aspect of Six Sigma entails how you work with particular metrics. These metrics may be used to figure out what is going to occur in the task and how it will evolve. In particular, you will have a primary metric and a consequential metric. These will directly influence how well your work is laid out and what you can expect to get out of the process.

The primary metric is the measure of the thing that you want to attain. The metric is a measure of a task's key goal. The process entails a full review of how well a task can be resolved by using simple standards and routines. You can use as many details in your primary metric as necessary, although the most common metrics entail a desire to reduce the costs associated with a task or to manage difficult functions that occur in any case. You must be clear with your metric.

The consequential metric directly influences the results of a Six Sigma task. It occurs as a direct result of what you are doing with the primary metric. For instance, the consequential metric might entail something such as the amount of waste being reduced as a result of costs going down. The cycle time may also be reduced since a process now involves fewer steps. Anything that directly benefits the company and enhances a process will work if planned out appropriately.

Chapter 9 – The Most Common Types of Waste

A big part of the Six Sigma process entails reducing waste in the workplace. Waste is a problem that keeps a business from providing value to the customer. Eliminating waste ensures that the customer gets the most out of a business and therefore, the business will likely thrive.

When waste develops, processes in the workplace become disorganized and disorderly, thus increasing the likelihood of defects. For instance, a hockey team might have a process for practice. But if power play or penalty kill practices are inconsistent, this could hurt the process as the team will not be on the same page when trying to work together.

When waste is removed, processes become easier to handle. For the hockey team, the Six Sigma process can help with organizing how the team's practice routine is structured. In this case, the penalty kill and power play practice will be set up at a consistent time during the practice session. Thus, the entire team will get a clear idea of how they can handle these two special situations in a hockey game. This allows the team to practice better. As a result, the team can score more power play goals, prevent an opponent from scoring short-handed goals and score goals while short-handed. This can lead to more success, which the fans or consumers will be happy about.

So, how does Six Sigma work for a business with this in mind? Getting rid of the waste in the work process ensures a task is easier to manage. The process works with fewer steps and therefore costs less and wastes less time. You can increase your profit margin as a result. Better yet, you may keep customers from having to bear the excess costs associated with your employees doing extra, unnecessary work.

Waste is divided up into eight parts, each detailing different actions or functions that immediately impact the way a business runs. These segments can be identified individually. They may also be combined. A business with several of these waste problems can be hard to manage.

1. Defects

While defects are a basic problem that can occur in any business process, defects can also be extremely specific. Defects are products or services that are not working to their proper specifications. For instance, a vacuum cleaner might have a defect where the motor is not generating a consistent amount of suction. The defect may be found in more than one vacuum cleaner on the market and that defect will upset customers and keep the business from growing.

Resources are necessary to correct the defect. For the vacuum cleaner company, new products might need to be ordered for use in the manufacturing process. These include items that help to replace old parts that kept the vacuum cleaners from producing a consistent level of suction. Some changes in manufacturing procedures may also be examined. The Six Sigma process requires a business to not only replace individual components but also to understand various points that should be followed.

2. Overproduction

Overproduction is a process where a company produces more of an item than necessary. This includes a case where a business has too much inventory to work with before it can be sold. A business may not know what to do with all the excess. Even worse, more resources may be expended than what the business might be able to afford. The cost associated with overproduction can be very high.

Let's go back to the vacuum cleaner example. The factory might have produced more vacuum cleaners than it really needed. This could cause problems where the business cannot move its products. Eventually, the business might have to sell some of those products at reduced prices just to get them out of the way. The profits that the business could have earned will have been dramatically reduced due to the overproduction process.

The overproduction process will also cause your business to expend more time producing items than necessary. That added work might become cost-prohibitive after a while. It is true that you might be producing extra value by having more items ready to sell. But even then, there are zero guarantees that the things you are doing will work to your liking. You must analyze how well the task is working and have a plan in mind for manufacturing your product without producing more than what you require.

3. Waiting

In some cases, a business will wait far too long for a process to move forward. Instead of employees being productive, they are idle and are unable to do anything. Even worse, people might not understand what they should do in terms of procedures and actions in the workplace. They won't have a consistent routine to follow.

Let's go back to the hockey team from earlier in the chapter. During a practice, hockey players might not be certain what they should be doing next. Some players might end up waiting a while, unable to do anything to practice their skills and/or team communication efforts. Some players might also go on to other things; while some people are practicing passing, others are practicing how to physically contact players without producing penalties. Because the players are not on the same page in the practice routine, the team will become disorganized and unsuccessful.

Waiting can be unappealing because it means the people in the work environment aren't doing anything. This is worse if those people aren't trained to do anything aside from the tasks they routinely perform. Those people will be idle and will do nothing while on the clock. This is a waste of both your time and of your money. Keeping a Six Sigma plan handy is strongly recommended to avoid such scenarios.

4. Non-Utilized Talent

A business or group may use talent incorrectly. Some employees might not be fully invested in the routine. The employees might not be given tasks that suit their skills or efforts. Other employees may not understand how to complete those tasks. The lack of information or education could hurt how the business operates.

A retail store might have many employees who specialize in certain actions. For example, a store might have some people who work in the customer service department, while others focus on visual displays. The store might not use its customer service employees appropriately; it might ask those employees to do other tasks or routines. This is in spite of those employees possibly not knowing what they should be doing. Because of this, the customer service department may not be supported by employees who *do* understand how to handle tasks in a particular department.

You can always try to control this form of waste by looking at how you can train those people to work with many kinds of tasks in mind. You can ask your workers to handle certain tasks based on what you feel they can work with, so long as you are realistic and sensible about their capabilities. You can be flexible with the training process, but even then, you have to think about what's right for the business. Also, you should plan the training by looking at the number of roles that may be handled at one time and who is able to work with each of those roles based on what you are comfortable with entrusting the people in the workplace.

5. Transportation

The transportation waste issue entails products or items being moved around too much. Things that are not necessary for a process may be transported to different places. This transportation waste will keep a business from having the materials it needs. The waste may also cause the business to spend more money on its expenses for handling materials. A business' carbon footprint may also become greater than necessary.

A retail store that needs to collect assets for its operations might end up taking in items that it does not need for its operations. The company will then have to ship those items back out somewhere else, thus wasting money and time, not to mention causing added pollution due to the unnecessary transport. Meanwhile, that same retailer may also pay lots of money for trying to rush some resources that it needs at the last minute. These issues can keep a business from success.

Transportation problems can also be an issue within the workplace. You might have to move items from one part of a store or warehouse to another. This may cause an unnecessary amount of effort. You must keep transportation waste down in your business by ensuring anything that doesn't have to be shipped can be removed.

6. Inventory

Whereas overproduction involves producing more items than necessary, inventory entails items that are not being processed. The inventory waste issue involves a business struggling to appropriately use its assets. A factory that makes vacuum cleaners might have too many motors. The company is not doing anything with those motors, which is a waste.

The concern with having idle inventory is that it is easy for people to forget about what is happening with one's resources. The idle materials may be ignored to where a business will order new items when it could have utilized what it already had. The lack of control over idle materials may cause the business to waste money, not to mention space for handling other forms of inventory. Businesses are at a huge risk of hurting their bottom lines when they are unable to manage their inventory totals the right way.

7. Motion

Motion is a waste involving people making far too many physical movements in the workplace. They go from one spot to the next and might spend lots of time getting places when they could get their objectives completed without walking around so much. Cutting down on motion is vital for business efficiency. Also, the employees will be less tired and more productive if their motions are limited.

Let's say that a retail store has different stockrooms for various products. One stockroom is for clothing while a second is for hardlines. A person might have to go between the two stockrooms when collecting items that have to be brought out to the salesfloor. The employee is wasting time/motions going from one end of the store to another. This causes that employee to become worn out while also having to put in far too much effort to a meaningless task. Finding a way to combines those stockrooms so that the person requires less motion is critical to allowing the business to stay active.

8. Excess Processing

The last of the eight parts of waste involves excess processing. This includes cases where a business or group engages in activities that are not necessary for a business' productivity. The business will use far too many steps to produce something. This could involve the use of more inventory items, more labor or anything else that could be detrimental. The excess processing causes the business to waste both money and time

Going back to the store example, that store might have lots of work moving inventory out. But the store may also use steps like moving certain pieces of equipment out of the way or shifting items from one stockroom to the next. The need to use more computers to scan items than necessary may also be a problem. The store will waste lots of time trying to process its goods.

If you have not figured it out yet, the eight types of waste can all be laid out to create a simple acronym: DOWNTIME. When your business experiences any of these waste issues, it will not be working at peak efficiency. The business will enter a state of downtime due to time being wasted, things being idle and overall processes being more complicated than necessary. These eight wastes are all problems that have to be resolved. This guide will help you to figure out how to do that.

Chapter 10 – Defects vs. Defectives

You may come across something interesting when working on a Six Sigma routine. While you are trying to figure out what defects are in the system, you may also come across something that is defective. The two terms might sound similar to one another, but there is an important difference between a defect and a defective.

A defect is something that does not work based on a particular manufacturing or work process. The defect might be gathered with data that is distinct and has substantial changes from what might be expected in the production process. A defect causes a product to be imperfect, but. the item in question can still be functional and useful.

On the other hand, a defective product or service cannot be used. The problems might be too hard to manage or overcome. The defective may be counted through testing processes or other extensive reviews to figure out what problems might have arisen within the work in question.

Here's an example of how a defect can be different from a defective. A restaurant might produce burgers and fries, but the process of producing the foods might be improper. A burger might not have enough lettuce or mustard on it. Meanwhile, the fries might not be evenly seasoned. These are defects in that they are still things that can be fixed without having to scrap a process altogether. The burger and fries can be consumed, although the experience of doing so might not be as ideal as a customer hopes.

A defective entails something that cannot be used at all. In the same burger joint, a burger might not be cooked to a proper temperature, thus possibly causing a person who consumes it to become ill. Meanwhile, the fries might be burned to where they're inedible. This poorly made combination is a defective in that people will not want to consume such food. They will have to throw the meal out because it is both unpalatable and risky to consume.

The key is that the defect can be used, but the defective cannot. Your Six Sigma task is all about ensuring that you produce things that people can easily use.

Chapter 11 – Project Acceptability

As important as it is for all people in the Six Sigma process to agree upon whatever is being planned, you have to look at how well the overall task is operating. You have to get all people in the workplace to agree upon a task's parameters and overall importance. The project acceptability rate is a measure that identifies how effective a task is and whether the people involved with the work are following the correct instructions for making the task run smoothly.

The project acceptability is based off the following equation:

1. The goal is to obtain 100 percent effectiveness.

2. The quality of the solution should entail 20 percent of the task.

3. The acceptability should involve the other 80 percent.

Project acceptability focuses on seeing what can be done to get everyone one board. This part of the design effort involves seeing that more people are prepared to complete the Six Sigma work and that enough effort goes into knowing what can be done to move forward. The best way to describe the project acceptability process is that it focuses on changes in order to move forward and ensures all people are onboard with the project and understand its value.

The WIIFM Point

The What's In It For Me? (WIIFM) is critical to project acceptability. Every person in the project has to understand what makes a task important. When everyone recognizes what they can get out of a task, people will want to move forward efficiently with the job. Conversely, a person who has no buy-in and feels there's no value to the work will be far less motivated. Therefore, it will be hard for that person to go all in on the project and to work on the quality aspect.

A shared need can be incorporated into a project to counter any WIIFM issues. Shared need is an idea that is provided to everyone in the workplace that might be interested in a task. When people are told what makes a task so useful, it becomes easier for them to want to move forward and participate in a certain effort. Those people will also feel as though they are worth something and that they are cared for. As a result, everyone will feel confident with what is being planned out.

It also helps to explain the changes in the workplace by talking about any parameters that are shifting in the routine. You can mention things about visible and tangible changes as well as any impacts that the Six Sigma work is having on the customers and the standing of the business in general. Being open about the changes and how they are planned out is vital for getting everyone on the same page.

It is even more important to think about any processes that might cause an increase in the cost associated with the task. The WIIFM consideration might be hard for people to swallow if the process entails extra expenses. In that case, you will need to clearly explain what makes a more expensive process worthwhile.

So now that you understand the ins and outs of the Six Sigma effort, you can get started on a Six Sigma task of your own. Next, you will learn how the Six Sigma concepts in this guide work based on each of the five main points in the DMAIC process. You will be impressed with how well the DMAIC routine works when getting your Six Sigma efforts up and running.

Chapter 12 – The Five Key Deliverables of the Define Stage

We're about to look at the define process in the Six Sigma routine. This is around the point where you notice that there's a problem in your business. You'll have to determine what the issue is, how you are going to resolve the concern and then determine what you will measure your success or progress based upon. You can use all of these factors to find a solution for your work that fits the desires or goals you have for success and moving forward with your work.

To make the most out of the define stage, you need to look at five deliverables that are critical to your success.

1. Process Map

You will need to produce a process map for the Six Sigma effort. The map shows people what the project is about and what you will do when changing plans in your functions. A flowchart, fishbone diagram or any other kind of map may help you plan out the process. Other possibilities include the SIPOC, High Level Process Map, Swimlane and Relationship Maps.

2. Project Scope

Look at the general scope of the project as you plan it out. The scope of the project should be planned out based on the boundaries of a task. You have to look at the boundaries based on factors like the things that come into the workplace and how realistic certain actions might be within your work. You can look at project goals, tasks, timelines and other things of value here. You must establish a sensible, realistic scope. Don't forget to look at the leaders in the project to identify which people will be responsible for handling specific content.

3. Identifying the Stakeholders

The stakeholders are critical to your Six Sigma task as they are the people who will benefit the most from what you are doing. The stakeholders should be analyzed based on what they are investing in and how they can serve you. These are the people who will be reported to when getting the Six Sigma task running. In other cases, the stakeholders might be customers. Either way, getting clear input from the stakeholders is important for your success.

4. Define the Stakeholder Requirements

You should be clear on the expectations that the stakeholders have. The Six Sigma work should be to meet their demands while remaining logical and easy to use. The process should also include objectives that can be met over time. You can use any kind of requirement or objective in this situation.

Stakeholder requirements can entail anything. These might include things like a company's revenues increasing or its market share going up. The rate of profitability could also be a factor. You must also look at the image of the business and any processes used for getting a task ready. You can use your stakeholder plan to review what is happening in the workplace or what needs to be corrected.

5. Create the Plans

The plans for the Six Sigma work should be incorporated in the design. You can establish plans based on how you're going to communicate things with others, how the scope will be kept under control and how the cost/benefit parameter is considered. Your plans for the Six Sigma should be thorough enough to where all people will have a clear idea of what will happen in the process.

Chapter 13 – Operating the VOC

Everyone should have a say in what can be done with the Six Sigma work. But it takes an extensive effort to help you create a task that benefits everyone. The best way to start is to look at what the customer is going to think. A general analysis of the customer lets you figure out what problems might arise versus what should be done to keep those customers happy.

The voices that come with Six Sigma are critical, but the Voice of the Customer or VOC may be the most important part of it all. Without the customer, your business will be worth nothing. Customers are vital for not only buying and using your products or services but also for referring your work to other people. Customer satisfaction is vital for success. Therefore, you must look at how the VOC can be planned out.

Part of managing the VOC entails not only knowing the customers you are trying to contact but being familiar with how you will gather data from them. Part of this includes reviewing what people need versus what people simply want. Knowing what you are getting out of your customers assists you with understanding what you should be doing to improve upon your processes, not to mention having an easier time growing your business.

Internal vs. External Customers

The VOC will be planned out based on two types of customers: internal and external. The internal customer is a person who is within the organization. The person might be a manager, executive, employee or anyone who is directly associated with the business. Internal customers are the first people to see what is produced.

The external customer is a person who is outside of the organization in question. That person is someone who will use a business' products or services and who will, therefore, have some interest in the organization. But that person is not going to directly control the process. Rather, that person's preferences and information are to be factored into the VOC process. External customers can not only include basic customers who buy or use your products, but also any shareholders you might have working in the process.

Needs and Requirements

Although the terms **need** and **requirement** are both similar to one another, they are surprisingly different. Need is a term that involves the expectation that someone has from a product or service. A person might have various needs that could make or break a sale. A hotel guest might demand that a hotel have a shuttle service that goes to a local airport or a complimentary breakfast or conference room. A hotel that does not have such features might not be all that useful to the client.

Needs are not to be confused with wants. A need is something that a person absolutely must have. A want is something that the person prefers to have, but it is not necessarily a requirement. Those who do not get their wants might not be all that happy, but someone who does not get his or her needs will be far less pleasant.

A requirement is different as it entails something that fulfilled those needs. A customer will define a requirement as a must. Returning to the hotel example, a person might need to utilize a complimentary breakfast feature. A requirement might entail the person having coffee in the morning. While the rest of the breakfast might be pleasant, to that person, the coffee is more important than anything else being offered. When the requirement is met, the customer will feel pleased with his or her experience.

The AICP Process

One distinct part of managing the VOC involves using the four-step AICP process to figure out what people want to get out of something:

1. Voice of the Associate – feedback from employees

2. Voice of the Investor – feedback from shareholders and management

3. Voice of the Customer – what the clients are saying

4. Voice of the Process – what happens when measuring the CTP to CTQ

Each voice will provide you with a statement. You would review that statement and use this to figure out the need that the particular voice produces. For instance, a customer might say, "I want a whirlpool at the pool in the hotel." This simply states that the person has a need for the whirlpool. The requirement is that the person wants a little luxury.

Certain Methods for Gauging the VOC

You have many choices to consider for measuring the VOC. These are all distinct for offering certain ways information can be gathered. Each of these five options for gauging the VOC can help you with figuring out what people might be most interested in. Here is a look at each of these choices for figuring out what the VOC might be:

1. Survey

You can start by producing a survey where customers are asked various things about whatever it is you are offering. You can ask as many questions as desired while also being as thorough as you wish. There is also the option to ask people about things based on a grade scale, although you can ask for one of two or three specific answers if you wish. Be advised that while you can get a good response out of a survey and get specific results, you might experience a low response rate. Furthermore, some people might not always be truthful in a survey in spite of a promise of confidentiality.

2. Interviews

You can hold one-on-one interviews with various people to talk with them about the things that they want out of your business and what products or processes they may prefer. You may ask as many questions as you want out of an interview subject. You may also have parameters for the types of people you want to speak to including individuals within specific demographics that fit whatever you are interested in.

In an interview, you can discuss any issue that relates to your business. The interview may be extensive or short, depending on your need to talk with many or few people. The process for chatting with a lot of people can be a hassle depending on how many have to be consulted and what you want to get out of each interview.

3. Focus Group

Maybe you want to talk with many people at a time about whatever it is you are offering. A focus group can be held in a conference room and provides you with the opportunity to simultaneously talk with many people about what they want and what they might be most interested in. You can get information on things that are vital to the quality of whatever you are offering. At the same time, the focus group might be difficult to generalize. Also, there is the risk of one or two people dominating that group. Having multiple groups with a diverse array of people based on your business' possible demographics always helps.

4. General Suggestions

Have you ever seen one of those comment boxes at a workplace? You can use such a box to let customers, employees and other parties tell you about what they want. The suggestions that these people provide you with can help you with improving your projects as you figure out the things that individuals are most interested in. That said, the comments in a suggestion box might not be fully comprehensive. Also, you have to look at how each action being suggested does or does not link to another, forming a larger picture.

Comment cards can help with finding the VOC, although it is best to avoid using these as your primary choice for data. The problem with the comment cards is that not all people in your workplace are going to fill them out. If anything, people who had extremely positive or negative experiences with your business are more likely to fill out those cards than anyone else. They might feel more empowered to voice their angry or positive feelings if they are highly unhappy with something that was offered.

5. Observations

The observations you make during the work process refer to the things you notice when completing tasks. These observations can entail anything from what people are doing in the workplace to ideas or concepts people recommend. Observations can vary based on what you notice, but you will need to do plenty of monitoring to really assess how a workplace is operating. Also, you might need to use covert methods so people aren't likely to notice that they are being monitored for the purposes of reviewing their activities.

General Requirements to Keep in Mind

Every customer has certain requirements. One way to find out what customers need is to look at the specific requirement points that you might wish to operate. A customer might have a certain voice which results in a requirement that needs to be met. Here are a few samples:

1. "I want to get something that I ordered" = Accuracy, getting the right product to the specific customer

2. "I want to get something when I ask for it" = Timeliness, getting something to the customer within a certain time frame

3. "I want someone to be friendly to me when I'm doing business" = Courtesy, or a general sense of respect or care for the customer

4. "I don't want to pay lots of money for this product or service" = Price, including ensuring that the price is equal to or less than what another party is offering

Your Six Sigma process may work with different plans based on the different things you want to offer to your customers. The plans may be as detailed as they have to be, but you should provide clear answers to each of the people you are working for. Those people will respect you if you offer a simple solution to their questions or problems. Don't forget that the many methods you're using for finding the VOC can help you with identifying particular requirements. All you need to do is carefully review a process in question and be clear in your objectives.

The Limits

The limits that may be found in the VOC process are the Lower and Upper Specification Limits, or LSL and USL. The specification limits are generated from the requirements that customers have. These limits refer to the minimum and maximum acceptable standards that people want to get out of a process. These refer to the best results that can be produced versus things that might not be required but which are still recommended for use. You can use the VOC to figure out the needs that people have for products and services to determine what people might be most interested in.

For instance, a company that builds doors for houses might analyze what people want to get out of their doors. People might be surveyed about a door that will be about 3.5 inches thick. The LSL and USL may be calculated to figure out what people want. The LSL might be 3.485 inches and the USL 3.515 inches. Attaining Six Sigma will involve ensuring that the doors all fit within those limits without going outside of them.

The limits that you produce on a bell curve chart may be different from what your process might suggest. The process may have different numbers based on what is appropriate for the manufacturing process. You will have to figure out the similarities between the two bell curves so you can obtain a more precise measure for what the Six Sigma process entails and your established goals. The measure may prove to be more accurate or useful than what you might come across elsewhere.

Chapter 14 – The Kano Model

As you look at what you can do to get your business to grow with Six Sigma, you have to think about the VOC and finds ways to satisfy each customer's needs. Part of this should involve using the Kano model. Designed in the 1980s by prominent professor Noriaki Kano, the Kano model focused on what should be done to make it easier for a business to grow its operations by pleasing the customer. You can use this model to organize the customers preferences into different categories.

You can use the Kano model after you go through the VOC phase of the process. This is also a part of the Define process in the DMAIC routine. Use the model to determine how something you are offering relates to with what a customer wants or what the public might be interested in. The most important part of this is that the model concentrates on what people want the most versus what they might be merely pleased with.

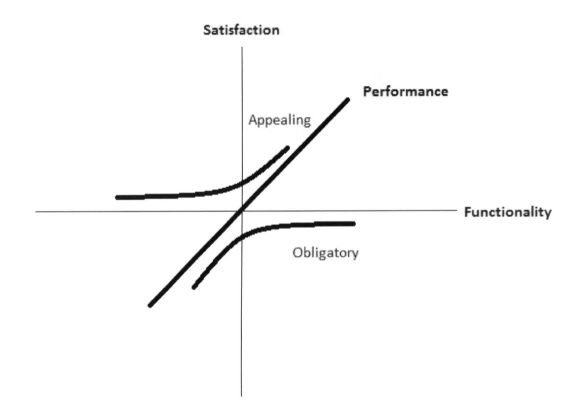

The illustration above should give you an idea of what to expect out of the Kano model. The model is designed to give you an idea of what might work when you're trying to make your efforts more appealing to audiences of all kinds. You can produce a layout showing how people are satisfied with your work versus how well something needs to function. People want high-performing items that are functional and satisfy their needs.

The Four Key Parts

The Kano model measures the things that are offered with four key parts in mind. These four parts vary based on how conditions are met, whether a customer is satisfied or if that person rejects something:

1. Dissatisfying materials

Dissatisfying materials refer to any features or qualities in a model that might not be enjoyable to those people using your product or service. These include features that are annoying and unattractive and which are therefore avoided by customers. These include things like products or services that have too many unnecessary or confusing features.

Dissatisfying items are things that do not fulfill the condition that someone has for a product or service. Outright rejection is a problem. A person looking to buy a boat motor might reject that motor because it does not come with certain key connections for a battery, for instance. Because those connections are not included, the customer will outright reject that product and not bother with your business. Knowing what people might be unhappy with will help you to recognize what should be done to fix a problem.

2. Mandatory needs (must-haves)

The mandatory requirements of people in the Kano model are the general basics of something. A person might feel that a product or service must have certain features. For instance, a car manufacturer might be asked to produce vehicles with air conditioning systems. Some people might have a need for a dual-zone climate control system that is more intricate than what might come with basic AC units. When the mandatory needs are met, the customer will feel as though his or her needs have been fulfilled. However, it is the quality of the feature that might make or break the process; knowing what people need will help a business to fine-tune its resources or processes.

The Kano model states that mandatory needs require a business to meet all the standards that someone has. This condition must be fulfilled while the customer is also satisfied. Anything less than this is a sign that the specific things that someone absolutely requires are not being offered. But for this to work, the mandatory needs have to be logical and easy to follow without the business struggling. The best way to view a mandatory item is as a must-have that cannot be ignored.

3. Customer needs

Customer needs are not things that absolutely have to be included like mandatory needs. Rather, basic customer needs involve certain expectations that don't always have to be met, but it helps to get as close to those needs as possible. For example, a customer might ask that a car come with an air conditioner, but that person does not necessarily need a dual-zone AC unit, for instance. An example like that shows how the customer needs that someone has might be factored into a manufacturing process.

On the Kano model, customer needs are measured based on whether conditions are fulfilled. The customer might choose to reject the product if those needs are not met. That person might also be fully satisfied if a company's need fulfillment appears to be above average.

4. Delighters

Delighters are the unexpected useful and/or unique features that customers might not expect to come across but which pique their interest and are different from what your competition has to offer. For instance, a car company can make a model that offers an air conditioner with an easy-to-remove-and-clean filter and ionizer to keep the inside of the car cabin cleaner. This is a delighter as it goes well beyond the needs that most people have for an air conditioner in a vehicle. It requires an extended bit of thought to figure out what delighters are necessary, but producing the right delighters makes it easier to satisfy people.

After a while, a delighter will become a necessity. This happens as the industry evolves and people start to expect certain things of value. While the air conditioner was once valuable many years ago, it has gotten to the point where people expect such a system in every car. What was a delighter is now something that has to be offered or people will be dissatisfied.

There may also be times when people are indifferent to some products or services. Indifference is not necessarily bad provided that the items are ones that perform well and meet particular standards. An air conditioner in a car might be something that people are not too concerned about, but it's good enough if the AC unit is working appropriately. Not all customers will demand the world of you. Of course, adding a special feature like a dual-zone control system or a special filtering material always helps, but that is useful only if you have the time and budget needed for planning that feature.

Three Overall Feelings

As you noticed in the chart at the start of the chapter, there are three feelings that customers might have: the Attractive, Performance and Must-Be points. These are three concepts that will change what the customer might want to get out of the effort or what someone might think about the work in question. Your goal is to produce something that a customer will appreciate and support. With this in mind, let's look at the three feelings that customers have towards what you are offering and how they might work to your liking.

1. Attractive

The attractive feeling is that something will be executed well and be highly satisfying. The customer will not only see that something is effective, but also that there are more things than he or she might have expected to get out of a product or service. You might have to spend an extra bit of time determining how to satisfy customers in such a manner. Thus, the added effort you put into satisfying the customer should be carefully determined.

2. Performance

The attractiveness of a product might not be all that concerning to some people. They simply want things that can perform to their best potential. Maybe a luxury car that does not have all the unique features of others might not be as attractive, but it may also have an engine that works harder than what you might find elsewhere. The car may also be very reliable and do what the driver wants every time. Performance is important. People like it when something runs well.

3. Basic

The basic point is all about the must-haves that people often take for granted. Whereas a luxury car might be attractive and a sports car might focus on performance, a company car is the basic choice. This car does not have lots of power in its engine, but it is be good enough to fulfill its transportation purpose. The simple design of the basic process can be enough to keep people moving forward.

The Four Quadrants and How to Gather Points

The Kano model requires you to use four quadrants. These quadrants are laid out with an x-axis and a y-axis being used on the same chart. The x-axis refers to the product or process. The y-axis involves the customer's feelings. You can use the Kano model to use the VOC to measure what people think about what you are offering.

The x-axis will range from the condition being unfulfilled on the left to the condition being fulfilled on the right. When the condition is reached, the customer will feel happy about what is offered. You will find that what you are doing is right when the people who buy your products or services agree with you about what is being offered. Meanwhile, the y-axis goes from the customer rejecting something on the bottom to the customer being fully satisfied when the plot point reaches the top of the chart.

You can gather information on many people in the VOC process and use that to identify where people appear on the Kano model chart. Assess how well they feel based on whether the product offers what they want and whether customers are willing to accept what you are offering. Knowing how customers feel is vital to organizing the data and reading right. You can also use this to find certain trends and ideas. This includes cases where people favor certain things or feel that what you are offering is not overly unique or intriguing.

Every chart featuring the four quadrants should be saved and dated to list what people are thinking about your products or services at a specific time. You can gather new reviews from customers in the future if you wish. You may find that some things that are delighters at the start might end up being mandatory things for people to have after a while. For instance, a car in the 1950s might have had things like a roof or seatbelts as mandatory features. But in the 2010s, the mandatory needs may instead entail things like a large stereo system. The technology for producing cars has changed so much over time that the things people want have evolved (and continue to do so).

Five Questions to Ask

As you work with the Kano model, you have to look at several things relating to what people are providing you with when asking for feedback in the VOC process. You have to ask the customers about what they might like the most and how they feel about certain ideas or points you want to incorporate into something. These things relate to the chart that you have produced, but the information that comes through has to be clear and accurate enough to where you can produce a better plan for what your customers want. Here are the five questions you have to ask as you plan your Kano model and analyze what you get out of it:

1. What are the things that people are expecting and might be taking for granted?

Over time, people will want certain things in the products or services they see. They take them for granted in that these are everyday items. A refrigerator might have an ice maker or water dispenser, for instance. People expect all refrigerators to have these items, what with them being so commonplace in most models. But the feeling of satisfaction will vary based on how well something is produced. When a must-have item is handled right, the customer will not express any feelings. But when that must-have is not produced well enough or is nonexistent, the customer will have a negative impression of the item.

2. What one-dimensional qualities do people have?

Customers are often one-dimensional in what they want. They demand that certain products or services be made to their liking. A person shopping for a refrigerator might have a one-dimensional need for a model that comes with shelves that can be positioned in many spots and are easy to add, remove and clean. Based on those needs, a person might comparison shop for such appliances. When the one-dimensional need is met, the customer will be satisfied. Your Kano model study should analyze what people are looking at and what drives them to respond to a product based on what they most want to get out of it.

3. What makes things attractive?

The greatest challenge with attractive items is that people are not always going to directly address what they like most about something. A person might like that a refrigerator unit has a control on the door that allows the user to see what the temperature inside is, not to mention a control for adjusting that setting. Not all people are willing to directly mention that they like this feature. You have to dig deep into how people are responding when being asked about the things that they like the most out of what you are offering. The attractive items are often the things that delight the customer without that customer thinking twice about those features before they are first introduced.

4. What things are people indifferent about?

When gauging customer needs, you might learn that they are often indifferent about many things. A customer might not be all that concerned about how heavy a refrigerator is, for instance. Sometimes indifferent attributes might be interesting, but not all people are going to focus on them. You can therefore put these considerations to the side in the Six Sigma process and focus on other key processes.

5. What attitudes are people expressing significant differences in?

There are often times when certain people have an interest in specific attributes, but those same features are then turnoffs to other people. For the refrigerator, a models that is overly complicated and includes lots of technical controls for temperatures, defrosting and self-cleaning functions might be a turnoff to people who just want a basic refrigerator. But for others, some people might love a refrigerator that offers all those intriguing controls and features. You have to look at the differences between people in the VOC process while analyzing what people are most interested in. You should see how those people are responding to the things you are offering and ensure that what you have to give to them is interesting enough but not excessive.

You can use the Kano model to analyze everything that your customers are feeling about what you are offering. You can use these points in the model to figure out what might be important for your needs while also remaining realistic. You can also use this for comparing and reviewing everything that comes along with the VOC. The process has to be detailed enough to be suitable and easy to use while generating a smart idea for what to expect for the Six Sigma process.

An Example

The Kano model might be a challenge to work with, but the following example makes its use clear. Let's look at how a hotel may be organized.

You might notice consistent processes/services at a hotel such as an extensive continental breakfast in the morning, television sets with cable access in every room and coin-operated laundry machines. But what could be done to make that hotel even better? You can use the Kano model to determine that.

The Kano model requires an extensive amount of analysis. The VOC can be obtained by reviewing questionnaires or doing interviews with both people who have stayed at the hotel just once and those who have been frequent guests. You can talk with people at the hotel about anything of value, but it is critical to notice how certain trends come about. You can always add incentives to people who talk with you, but that is always optional.

You might notice a few things in the model for the hotel. Let's start by going to the bottom-left of the model to see the things that people rejected as unsatisfactory. You may notice things like the people at the front desk not being careful or friendly enough. There might be a perceived belief that the hotel employees do not recognize the needs of the customers.

Go to the bottom-right and you may notice things where the things a person is being offered are not strictly to standard, but some conditions are at least being fulfilled. These include cases where employees might be punctual or polite. People might state that the cleaning service offers consistent service while also being friendly and respectful. Meanwhile, customers might also state that while the television sets in the hotel rooms are not necessarily of the best quality, they appreciate that the sets have an extended assortment of cable television channels to choose from.

Next, go to the top-left part of the chart to review the cases where people are satisfied with what is being offered, but feel as though their needs are not being met all the way. The check-in and check-out process might be listed here. A person might be satisfied with the process because that person is quickly getting in and out of the hotel. But while the simplicity of the process might be important to note, a person might also state that the contract or terms for renting out a room could stand to be a little easier to understand.

The top-right part is the place where you want all the good things to be. This is where people are delighted by everything they see as they enjoy the experience and the features offered, not to mention people might be pleasantly surprised at what they are getting. The top-right section can include anything, but the section works best when the things involved are unique. These may include things like an easy-to-use AC unit in each room, a whirlpool in the pool area, a self-serve waffle maker at the breakfast station and a high-definition television set in each room. Anything that is distinct and offers an interesting way for people to enjoy their stay at a hotel is always worth checking out.

You can use the details you get on a Kano model to see what is happening within your business and what people might be interested in the most. The Kano model should be detailed enough to be analyzed without being too complex or hard to follow. But you must always ensure that the data being listed is appropriate and that the content in question is easy to follow. Knowing how well the content is organized in the Kano model should help you to make the most of your business.

A Warning About Time

There is one last aspect of the Kano model to note. This relates to time. Time can influence how satisfied a person is about something. Specifically, satisfaction may go down as time passes. A person may feel as though whatever is being offered is not as appealing as what he or she found in the past. The product or service in question might also become stale.

Think about what might happen when driving a car. Maybe you have become less interested in your vehicle over time. The things that delighted you or fascinated you are not as unique as they used to be. You might want to get a new car just to get a vehicle that you find somewhat interesting again.

Individual features that were once exciting might not be as unique as they used to be. A dual-zone climate control system might be initially appealing, but eventually that feature will become outdated. Something new, like a climate control setup that handles multiple rows in a car or every single seat, might then come along. Something a little more technologically advanced might become the norm. Another example is that, while the driver's airbag was a popular feature for years, people no longer expect just one airbag in their cars. They want airbags all around; more must therefore be added in order for people to be satisfied with a car model.

You should look at such things in your Six Sigma plans. The risk of time changing the attitudes and feelings of people is something that cannot be ignored. There will always be the potential for people to think differently about what you are doing and what you have to offer. Those people might not feel confident in your offerings after a while, especially as they notice that there are newer and potentially more interesting things for them to try out. But when you remain innovative while still offering a good sense of value, it becomes easier for people to stick with you and respect what you are offering them.

Chapter 15 – The Pareto Principle

The Pareto principle is a Six Sigma concept that focuses heavily on understanding what you are putting into your work within the process. The Pareto principle is also called the 80/20 rule. This states that about 20 percent of all causes produce about 80 percent of the effects that might come about in a task. This can be used in business by saying that about 80 percent of a company's sales may come from 20 percent of customers.

The important thing about the Pareto principle is that it shows how important a task may be and illustrates what you can expect to get out of your work. The Pareto principle demonstrates that you must work with a few changes to improve upon how your efforts are received. Think of the principle as something that helps you to explore the things in your work. You can also use it to consider some of the root issues that are triggering problems you wish to fix within the Six Sigma process.

For instance, a call center might look at some of the complaints it is receiving. A vast majority of the problems might be occurring due to people being put on hold for too long. Meanwhile, the call center might see that too much time is being spent explaining automated options to customers who just want some help. In other cases, people who have specific needs for the call center might be more likely to bear with certain problems. You can use the Pareto principle to identify how often certain problems are occurring while also resolving concerns that may develop in the work environment.

A good idea to consider for analyzing the Pareto principle in your workplace is to produce a chart that illustrates the problems or defects in the workplace. You can do this by gathering the variables and problems in the work environment. After you get that data, you can arrange everything in a descending value. Look at how these items compare with each other; the chart above is an example of this. See if the Pareto principle is in play with about 20 percent of the concerns or causes triggering 80 percent of the problems in the setup. The results may assist you with figuring out the problems that are arising in your efforts.

Chapter 16 – Critical to Quality (CTQ)

As you design your Six Sigma process, you have to pay attention to the Critical to Quality or CTQ measure. The CTQ refers to the quality standards that your business must attain if you wish to meet the needs that a customer has. When you review the standards in question, you can get closer to producing measurable characteristics or ideas that can be utilized in the workplace. These standards can be as important to your business as anything a customer might think is valuable.

The CTQ is different from the Critical to Customer or CTC standard. The CTC is about what the customer feels is important and is vital to the success of the company. The CTQ produces the points that meet the CTC requirements that a person has. Knowing what the customer needs is vital for your CTQ hopes. You can always use different VOC points to help you appropriately plan your CTQ efforts.

Knowing what the CTQ are for your business is vital. You must plan the CTQ to reduce variability in the workplace while figuring out what people most want out of something. This includes a look at the functions that people are interested in. Using the best CTQ plans ensures that the value of a project will grow and that the customer will be more appreciative of a product or supportive of whatever is being provided. Knowing what the CTQ is can also result in helping you keep up with your competitors while also reducing any barriers to entry in other markets or fields that you wish to work with.

Needs, Drivers and Requirements

As you start your work for the CTQ, notice the three points that make any task worthwhile. These are the needs, drivers and requirements that have to be followed in your work. This chart should help you get an idea of what will work within the CTQ standard:

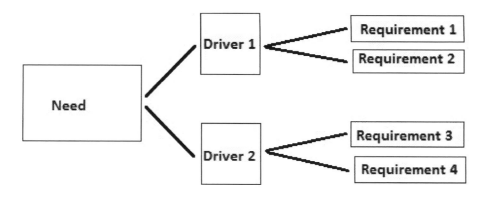

In this CTQ tree, you are looking at the need that someone has. This will follow from the drivers that trigger said need. These drivers will influence the feelings that people have about the initial need and what can be done to get those demands met to the standards of whoever needs help the most. The drivers can work in any way, but they should always be easy to follow. Also, some requirements will be produced based out of those drivers. These requirements entail many things that might change in the task and how the work might move along.

You can work with as many needs as necessary, although each need should have unique drivers and requirements. Be prepared to study how well your efforts are organized and ensure that you have an idea of what to expect out of your subject matter. This is to produce a better plan or idea for what will work in the CTQ effort.

Here's an example of how the CTQ tree can work to your liking. At the start, you might look at how a business needs to build on its customer service rating. This can be done by analyzing how well the business is producing various materials and making its work accessible to all. You might review some of the drivers that directly dictate what you will get out of the process. This can include many things like the waiting time being produced in the process. The quality of the staff might also be considered. You can produce a few performance requirements at this stage based on those drivers that you have come up with. The five steps you will read about here should give you an idea of what to expect out of the work in general.

The Five Steps

Five steps are used in the process of gather the VOC and planning the CTQ. These are critical for producing the CTQ tree in question:

1. Figure out the characteristics of a product or service.

All customers have certain desires for what they want to get out of their products or services. You can talk with those customers about the things they are interested in the most. Terms surrounding the specific features of a product or service are the focus here. You may talk with a customer about the timing for certain functions, the sizing of products or how certain items are to be used. Review what people most ask for.

2. Measures and operational actions should be noted.

The operational definitions are how products or services can be defined. You can use many definitions to identify what people want to get out of what you are offering. Let's say that a dry cleaner is trying to grow its business; you could consider talking with customers about the time it takes to dry items or specific cleaning cycles available for individual fabrics. Your goal is to look at the concerns people have surrounding operating definitions and what they feel can help to get a business to grow and be more successful.

3. Target values must be defined.

A target value is a specific goal. You can produce one of many target values for your business. These include goals like producing a certain objective without any possible variations or at least as little variation as possible. The dry cleaner in the above example might have a target value of completing a cleaning task within 24 hours after the clothes are delivered.

The target values should be planned within the performance requirements on your map. You can use these to measure the specifics of what you want to get out of your efforts. For the waiting time requirement listed earlier, you can analyze a target value of at least 90 percent of the customers being satisfied with the waiting time. A target where customers do not have to wait longer than x time can also be planned out at this juncture. You can use any kind of performance standard you wish, although it is best for the work to be easy to follow and plan out.

4. Look at the tolerance limits.

Every customer has a tolerance limit. This refers to how much of a variance a person is willing to accept. For a dry cleaner, the 24-hour time frame for completing a task might be hard to attain. This could be due to concerns like operating hours, materials on hand and how many items are being cared for at a time. You can ask customers about their tolerances to see how long they are willing to wait. Customers might be fine with getting their items about 26 to 30 hours after the order is placed and the clothes are received. The important point here is to figure out what is acceptable to the customer without going overboard and setting unrealistic expectations for yourself.

5. Produce a defect rate.

The defect rate is based on the number of times a service or product fails to meet the tolerance limits. For Six Sigma, a business will want to have no more than 3.4 defects for every million opportunities, although the specific goal may vary based on each organization. It is critical to be aware of the defect rate in question to see that there are no problems involved. Keeping as close to the acceptable defect rate as possible is a necessity for making the Six Sigma process work.

The defect rate should be realistic. That allows customers to notice how committed you are to certain ideas and shows them you want to make the most out of your work. Even better, you might show your customers that you care about the requirements and needs that they have when using the things you have to offer.

After you gather all that date, you can start working with the performance requirements that you want to use on the CTQ map. You can ensure that the staff at a customer service team is pleasant and greets customers within 60 seconds of entering a store, for instance. A defect rate should be planned based on how well the people involved can work with the tasks being handled. The goal is to produce a sense of satisfaction for everyone to where the process is consistent and helpful every time someone needs the right service.

Managing Data

Not knowing how well the CTQ process works can result in sizeable delays or a general inability to get a process to work appropriately. All information gathered must be accurate for the best results.

You can use many pieces of data when figuring out what the CTQ process will involve. You can work with content from sources such as how available certain services are or how complete that content is. The definition of anything you wish to introduce and the format of the data should also be explored to give you a better understanding of how content works. Anything that is timely or relevant is also helpful. The demographics associated with the data may also be explored, but that is optional.

Continuous data should also be gathered in the CTQ process. This is data that can be found at many points in a process. The continuous data should be easy to follow and gauge. You can break down that information into many segments so you can get specific details on certain points that are coming along in your work. You can also use discrete data if you want to focus on very certain events or parameters, but continuous data will give you more support for information on what to get out of the CTQ effort.

After you figure out the data you will use, you have to plan a series of measurements for your content. The measurements can be as extensive as you want them to be. But you must produce limits for what you will analyze and set parameters for how that content is to be explored and reviewed. Having an idea of what you want to get out of the subject matter is vital for the success of the task. The best thing to do here is to avoid any parameters or measurements that may be used after the process is developed; these include measurements like any complaints people send your way or how the customers are satisfied with what you are offering.

You must also produce the best possible metrics at this juncture. You can simplify the project and also reduce any confusion over what you are doing, not to mention reduce the possibility of errors in your work. You might want to use many metrics for different entities or customers, what with each group having specific standards. Each metric can also be independent from one another to produce a more accurate readout.

Process Measurements

Process measurements are a necessity in the CTQ effort. Any CTQ that a customer has should be subjected to certain processes that a business is capable of supporting. The need to manage any product or process right will require many steps, but the metrics used will vary by each business. You can use a plan for process measurements to figure out what should be used in any situation you encounter. The measurements should factor into what you choose to utilize in the CTQ process so the data involved is easy to work with.

Producing Targets

As you review what your customers want, you can produce rules for what the business needs right now. There are no extremely specific processes to follow when you're trying to prepare a target you can agree with and support. But the target you plan can entail many variables. To start, you will look at both the considerations that the customers have and the drivers that influence what those people are going to expect out of your business. The customer and the business' capability of producing such results should be incorporated into any decisions being made.

A business' capacity to produce results is important to consider. That capacity may entail how well a business meets certain standards or the variations that might be utilized at any moment. The drivers that influence a business, including the VOC and customer behavior, not to mention the competitive benchmarks involved in the workplace, should be explored just as well.

A General Example

To fully understand the CTQ process, it helps to look at an example. Let's say that you are operating a pizza parlor and need to simplify the delivery process. You are trying to figure out a pattern for how the delivery process will work while ensuring customers are satisfied with everything you are offering. Part of this includes not only seeing that the pizzas are prepared to the specific needs customers have, but also that the pizzas are delivered within a logical time frame.

You may find that the CTQs people demand include quality standards like ensuring the orders for pizzas are accurate and are sent out in as timely a fashion as possible. You can use these standards to produce a CTQ plan that is appropriate for your business and which meets the needs that people have. Specific guidelines for what you want to do should be monitored as well; these include rules for getting pizzas out within a certain period of time.

Your CTQ tree can review every driver. The company might have drivers based on how long it takes for a pizza to be delivered or how much effort goes into making the pizzas.

General customer satisfaction can also be reviewed based on how well the team is working and whether the customers feel their pizzas are of the best quality. The work that goes into the CTQ map should identify the things that have to be done to make the task worthwhile and efficient.

You can produce a metric based on how accurate or expedient your pizza delivery plans are. You can also use measurements where the pizzas are designed to be produced to extremely specific needs that people have, including standards for what toppings are used. A target rate for success should also be explored.

You can then produce tolerance limits for what people might expect to get out of your work. These tolerance limits should entail things that people are likely to accept. You may review the VOC to figure out what people want in a pizzeria based on how much time they are willing to wait for something. You may set a tolerance limit stating that a pizza will be ready and delivered in up to 40 minutes. While the 30-minute standard may be promoted well, a 40-minute limit may also be established. The window can be produced in response to how busy a business get based on number of orders or how long it takes to get a pizza sent out within a reasonable amount of time.

The final definition should be planned out in the CTQ routine. Your goal is to plan a setup where you not only produce the best possible pizzas but also get them out to people within 40 minutes if possible, but preferably within 30 minutes if you can. The definition should then be utilized as the base for the Six Sigma routine. You can plan the Six Sigma efforts based on what you feel is sensible for your work. You have the option to change the final definition depending on what you come across when planning your Six Sigma routine, but the goal is to try and keep to the same standard.

The Discussion Is Vital

While the measurements of what you can expect can vary, the discussion surrounding the CTQ routine is the most important aspect. You have to talk with others in the workplace about what you wish to do and how your business will move forward by establishing a good plan. The discussion will help you to save time as you work with others in the business to determine what is suitable and useful for your business' particular needs.

Everyone should feel comfortable with the objectives being planned. The task must be clearly organized and ready to run based on the standards that you feel are appropriate enough for work. The discussion can be as thorough as it needs to be, but it should focus on realistic ideas. Feel free to share your thoughts on the standards you want to follow.

Whatever happens, you will find that a CTQ process does not have to be hard to follow when planned out right. The steps involved with getting the CTQ plans ready should be followed when designing your Six Sigma plans. You can use the design to create a better experience for your clients. The process may also help with identifying some of the things in the review process that might influence what you are going to do with your work so you can get more out of the content or subject matter you control. This is especially important for when you're trying to figure out what a customer might want out of your business and how to deliver to those expectations.

Chapter 17 – Creating a Project Charter

As you start the Six Sigma design process, you have to know what you're going to get out of the work you put in. You have to see what the objectives of a Six Sigma plan are alongside a rationale for allowing the effort to work. Those who try to begin the Six Sigma process without thinking about what should be done will struggle to keep the charter moving along right.

A project charter may be established in the Six Sigma process. The charter introduces the Six Sigma task and analyzes what people will do with the routine. The goals and extent of the task should be incorporated in the process. The milestones that may be attained in the effort should also be mentioned in the planning process. Don't forget to look at how team roles are established as you plan your project charter.

The charter is similar to what you might see when a business is first established. A charter is often used to explain an organization's goals. But a charter doesn't have to be limited to when a business first starts up. An organization can produce a charter at any time. A project charter is one such example; the charter here helps with managing a task that will last for months or possibly years.

Think of the project charter as a mission statement that a business puts out. That mission statement might be extensive or detailed depending on what the business wants to do. The statement should be sensible and easy for the business to stick with. Your project charter is like a mission statement for your Six Sigma routine. The charter might seem brief, but it is about showing that you have a plan for getting more out of your work.

Business Case

The first part of the project charter is the business case. The business case is a layout of the objectives that come with the Six Sigma task. The business case explains the basic reasons for why the Six Sigma effort is being planned out. The task should be explained based on what people might expect to get out of the routine or what people might be interested in the most. The following questions should be asked as you look at the business case:

1. Why is this project so important?

2. What resources are to be utilized in the Six Sigma routine? Those resources should be necessary for the effort and relevant to what you wish to plan.

3. Why is this so vital to the business in general? Is there a potential for the business to grow or experience some other special reward for the effort?

4. Is this going to be useful to the customers? What benefits will the Six Sigma effort provide to the customers? You can extend this question to concentrate on any shareholders or investors involved with the business as well.

5. What makes right now the best time for the Six Sigma effort?

6. What consequences will occur if we don't complete the task right now?

7. How is the task going to fit in with the targets and goals of the business?

The business case should then be answered with a simple, clear statement. You can incorporate all of those questions above into the statement. For instance, you might run a bakery and need help with delivering fresh goods to customers. You could have a goal to find an effective process that makes it easier for cakes and large-scale baked goods orders to be sent out to people within a reasonable time period. Your business case could read as follows:

"As we reduce the time frame needed for producing large-scale baked goods orders, we will satisfy the needs that customers have. The customers will appreciate our precise and expedient nature, and the business entity will have an increased potential for getting more customers and revenue. Positive changes via a simple approach to work may also enhance the experiences of customers while also reducing the expenses associated with dead time or excessive material usage."

The business case only has to be a few sentences in length. By planning the statement right, it becomes easier for the business to figure out what should be done in the Six Sigma process. You can also use this statement to give the people in the workplace an idea of what should be done in the workplace. Everything becomes a little easier to run thanks to the business case. But you have to look at the other factors that enter into the Six Sigma process.

Problem Report

Next, you need to focus on the issues you have while figuring out goals for what you can do to resolve those concerns. To start, you have to look at the problem report or statement that first introduced the issue. Explain in your problem statement what the issue in question is and where that concern is arising from. Explain how often the worry arises and whether it is recent. You can also talk about how long the problem has been present and/or the extent of the problem.

Going back to the bakery, you can talk about the problem based on when something occurred, what the issue is, the intensity of the worry and what consequences have arisen. An example problem statement may read like this:

"During the last two months, the bakery has been struggling to get its wedding cake orders out to people as quickly as possible, with some orders not making it in time for the reception. The risk equates to about 30 percent of the revenue that the bakery can earn. By not getting the cakes out to the weddings on time, the business will lose sales and future clients, not to mention revenue. Any efforts to try and produce wedding cakes within a certain time period may also be ineffective as the cakes might not be produced as well as possible or with enough detail."

The problem may be the most important thing to discuss in your work. You have to explain your problem to others in your workplace to confirm any issues or worries your business has encountered. The report has to be as specific as possible. The information should be detailed enough to let people see what measures should be planned. The goal here is to confirm what the problem is and to find a way to resolve the problem in question as soon as possible.

Goal Report

After you look at the problem, you can produce a goal report. Your goal statement should not list a cause that might have produced the concerns, nor should it include any solutions. You can fill in those points as you move along with the Six Sigma effort. But the goal should have a deadline for when you need to get answers. A focus should also be set up with the goal being something that you can legitimately take action on.

The SMART process can be used when producing your goal report. The SMART process entails five steps:

1. Specific – You need a certain goal that can be defined and which is not vague.

2. Measurable – The results should be easy to identify and measure.

3. Attainable – Realism is vital for the goal report. The goal should be something that can be attained.

4. Relevant – The goal has to be relevant to the business.

5. Time-bound – The time for when the goal should be reached must be listed.

The bakery's goal statement may be:

"The goal is to reduce the number of late deliveries on wedding cakes by at least 30 percent within the next four to six months. This is to increase the possible number of positive referrals we may get in the future."

That goal is suitable in that it specifies what the bakery has to do and includes a measure for what has to be completed to get a task to move forward. The goal is not overly lofty;

it just requires reducing late deliveries by around a third within a few months. Most importantly, the goal is relevant to the business. You can use any kind of time frame you wish, provided that the timing is reasonable.

Scope

Every Six Sigma project requires a certain scope that can be followed. The scope is a measure of when the task starts and ends. You can use the scope to get a realistic look at what can be done within your business and how your organization can grow based on the Six Sigma task you are operating. The scope creates a better focus and lets you know what should be done versus what might need to be corrected as the task moves forward.

The scope helps team members maintain a sense of interest in the task at hand. This interest is vital for allowing all people to feel positive about the work. When the scope is defined, the project becomes easier to carry out. Also, the team will focus on real things that have to be accomplished. By keeping things specific, the team will be active. But to make the scope work, you have to look at the two forms of scoping that may be used in your Six Sigma effort.

Don't forget that the scope can work for as long or short a time period as necessary.

Longitudinal

Look at the longitudinal scoping at the start. This part of the scope focuses on the length of whatever process you are working with. The practice works from when an order is taken to when the distributor gets the item out to the customer. The longitudinal scope focuses on how well the effort is run through the entire practice while remaining easy to follow. The start and end points may be fixed. The definitions help with understanding a specific process that is to be followed.

The longitudinal scope for our bakery example is as follows: The business will review the process from when the order for a wedding cake is sent out to when the cake itself is delivered to the reception on the big day. Your scope can include an analysis of everything in the business from when the store takes in an order to the scheduling for the order. The process of gathering ingredients and the manpower needed for designing and producing the cake may be analyzed. All parameters are measured based on how much time is needed versus how much effort is required. You can do anything you wish when defining the scope, but all the events must be relevant to the time frame that you find to be suitable.

The process maps you produce will help you with identifying the general process you wish to manage. This includes a visual layout of the many tasks that will be completed in the work environment. You can use this to review the longitudinal process to see how well the entire effort you put in works. This might take as long as needed, although your goal should be to keep the steps efficient and easy to follow.

Lateral

The lateral scope relates to how well the process extends from one spot to another. The scope looks at the events that take place within the task. The bakery example here would include a review of the people who might be suitable for work when preparing a cake. All orders from certain vendors or the communication between people within a party should be explored at this point. You can review the efforts that vendors put in to recognize what you are doing when handling the order.

Milestones

As your task moves along, you have to look at the milestones that you are putting in. Milestones can be produced to create a plan for how well a work routine is to be run. You can also use these milestones to progressively produce some rules for what someone might experience in the work routine. You can use as many milestones as necessary. Creating milestones produces a plan for what you wish to do when planning your Six Sigma routine. You can use these milestones to gauge how well your task is running.

A milestone will be placed midway through the Six Sigma effort. Going back to the bakery example, the bakery might set milestones on how well wedding cakes are delivered. The first milestone may be a five percent reduction in late deliveries before the end of the second month. The second milestone could be a 15 percent reduction before the fourth month ends. This all leads to the final goal of having a 30 percent decline at the end. The progressive layout of the milestones ensures that you have a timeline for getting all the tasks in the workplace accomplished in a timely fashion.

You can share information on your Six Sigma milestones with other people in the workplace. Talk about the milestones based on what you expect to plan out while keeping them sensible. Establishing a clear plan for moving forward is crucial to your Six Sigma success.

LSL And USL With the RUMBA Limits

You will have to incorporate some specification limits within your work to enhance how a task runs. These limits entail the LSL and USL, the lower and upper specification limits. Anything that goes above or below these levels can be interpreted as a defect. You'll want to arrive at the middle point between the LSL and USL. But to make the LSL and USL work, you have to plan the limits with the RUMBA standard in mind. RUMBA is a measure for what can be used when setting the limits within a project charter. These five points refer to the following features:

1. Reasonable

The specifications used should be based on what you have determined to be the customers' needs. Those needs have to be as reasonable as possible to produce a better result in the testing process. You can use this to see how people demand products or services and what people expect to get out of them. You can use as much research in the process as necessary to get a clear idea of what people might be asking for.

2. Understandable

Everything has to be clearly explained so everyone will know what has to be done. The specifics should be stated and defined to where no one is going to misinterpret what you are saying. You can offer a plan for managing content to where the people involved will recognize what should be done while the plan remains easy to follow.

3. Measurable

You have to know how to measure the limits that you use. These limits should be measured based on your business' output. The performance of anything you are planning in Six Sigma should be measured with as much of a definition as possible. The criteria needed for managing a task should be analyzed well. Failing to produce a measurable standard will make it harder for you and your customers to agree upon things, what with the parties having different ideas on what counts as a successful task or something that does not meet expectations.

4. Believable

People should buy into the specifications that you are offering. Employees should feel that the limits are attainable and can be managed. The shareholders should feel that the business is going to be in good standing after a while. When everyone agrees that the objectives are sensible, it becomes easier for the task to move forward.

5. Attainable

The objective should be attainable. There has to be a realistic opportunity for the business to attain its results within the two limits that have been imposed. The business should work within the same range introduced in the task. Keeping a particular specification going is vital for the success of the business. This especially involves seeing that the risks involved with a task are not any harder than they have to be.

Specific Roles

Several roles have to be planned in the project charter. The roles should be divided up between people based on the belts they have been certified for. A Master Black Belt may be tasked to complete very specific routines or tasks. Those who have lower-level belts will also have strong duties and responsibilities that are vital to the success of the overall task. It is up to everyone to ensure that the roles being filled are correctly assigned.

How Often Should You Revisit the Charter?

The project charter should be analyzed as many times as is necessary during the Six Sigma routine. You can review the results of a task while comparing them with the charter. The general goal of the charter review should be to see that what you are doing is simple and that you have a plan in mind for making the most out of your work.

Chapter 18 – The Stakeholder Analysis

The stakeholders within your Six Sigma task are among the most important people you will come across as you design your work. You have to go lean to ensure those stakeholders are happy with the business. Therefore, there should be a sense of understanding about what they are asking for in the Six Sigma effort.

A stakeholder analysis can identify how well the people involved with the business support things of value. A chart may be utilized in the analysis process to help determine what such people are thinking and to assess what needs to be done to ensure their continued support.

The process for handling the stakeholder analysis is as follows:

1. Determine the people who are going to support the task.

The stakeholders can be executives, business partners, owners, high-end shareholders or any other individuals that have a massive amount of control over the effort. You can also choose to include managers or other leaders that you are regularly in touch with. Though most stakeholders will not directly participate in the Six Sigma work, they will focus on what can be done to maintain a task and make that work move forward successfully.

2. Review how much of an impact someone will have.

A stakeholder may include someone who is providing funding for a task and who may expect some kind of return for his or her investment.

You can produce a rating from 1 to 5 illustrating the approximate rating that the person has. You can also include a desired rating for each person. Explain why you are rating someone a certain way. Talk about the things a stakeholder might do and what that someone might feel is appropriate to a task. Your goal should be to help that person have the best possible impact, whether it entails the stakeholder having more control over the task or not having any kind of control whatsoever. The latter is best suited for cases where you feel the stakeholder might not have a full idea of what is happening and/or isn't someone people in the workplace can fully trust with the job.

3. Determine the level of support that someone has for the Six Sigma task.

The greatest concern here is that, while some parties might be fully supportive of a Six Sigma task, others might resist. They might feel that the Six Sigma work is unnecessary, possibly because they're not fully aware of the benefits involved. The chart might list those who are supportive enough to where they are willing to provide full funding and support for a task.

4. Look at why a person is or isn't supporting a task.

There are many reasons why the Six Sigma task might not be supported by some stakeholders. People who have helped design a process that is currently in place might not see the need for a change. Meanwhile, some individuals might opt for creating a task simply because they think it will make more money. Review the reasons that people have for supporting the Six Sigma process, but also look at the people who don't support it.

5. Determine the actions that should be taken to address certain prominent stakeholders.

Talk with stakeholders about what they feel is appropriate for a task or what they would like to see done differently. Review what actions you can take to get people to side with you, even if this requires an extensive amount of persuasion.

You can work with as many details in the stakeholder analysis as you desire. But the goal of the task is to see that you have an idea of what to expect out of the process. The analysis process helps you figure out what people are thinking. Ensure that you have an idea of what to expect out of each person.

Don't forget that stakeholders may come from both inside and outside the work environment. "Inside" stakeholders may include executives and managers. "Outside stakeholders" might be shareholders or individuals you regularly do business with. It is always worthwhile to take the time to analyze such people's thoughts on your operation.

Chapter 19 – The Change Acceleration Process (CAP)

The next part of the definition phase of Six Sigma is to review the Change Acceleration Process or CAP. At this point, you are looking to transition the product or service in question from its current state to an improved state. However, to make this work, you have to ensure that the CAP includes the right people.

The Key Steps

There are many steps to be followed as you work with the Change Acceleration Process.

1. Share a need with people.

All people in the Six Sigma group must develop a shared need that everyone in the workplace agrees upon and participates in. This need can be anything relating to improving upon a business. Most importantly, the shared need must be stronger than any resistance people have towards change.

Consider a seafood restaurant. The restaurant might need to ensure it gets its entrees out to people as quickly and accurately as possible. There might be a possibility of cooking entrees faster, thus ensuring customers don't have to wait a long time for their meals. This fits the needs of everyone in the workplace including chefs, waiters, busboys, etc.

2. Establish a vision.

The need must be transformed into a clear, easy-to-understand vision that everyone in the business buys into. The seafood restaurant may determine that customers need to be served within a specific period of time. This includes following certain routines to prepare food after an order is placed.

3. A buy-in should take place.

While the people within the Six Sigma group might agree with certain ideas, it's vital for stakeholders to also buy-in. One way to achieve this is to involve them in your plans for the vision and explain what will make it work and why it's important.

The seafood restaurant in our example might talk with a parent company or owner about what needs to be done to achieve the established vision. This includes an emphasis on any plans introduced in preliminary meetings. The stakeholder, the owner in this case, can talk with the people in the Six Sigma about the process and share feedback. After this, the Six Sigma process for improving upon the business should begin.

4. The change must be planned for long-term needs. The effort must last as long as possible.

The Six Sigma process has to be planned out to where a routine is as easy to follow as possible and is a consistent, sustainable long-term effort. This is not always easy to achieve, but it can work if appropriately handled, with enough alternatives to keep the business functional.

5. Keep reviewing the progress as the task moves along.

Progress on the task should be consistently monitored. You can review the benchmarks or milestones that you have established to see how well the Six Sigma effort is working. You might have to change some things around depending on any problems that arise. The indicators that you use should be well established to where you can guarantee that people are accountable.

Going back to the seafood restaurant, the team must continue to monitor how processes are impacting the shared vision of delivering food within a certain time frame. A detailed analysis of progress (or lack of progress) should be regularly carried out.

These five steps are designed mainly to monitor what is happening with a situation. But these steps may also help you with planning a routine so your task is easier to carry out. You might spend some extra time setting things up, but the positive impact on your business will make the extra effort worth it in the end.

The ARMI Plan

The ARMI setup is the next part of the CAP effort. The ARMI layout is used to determine the people who will be working on a task. Everyone in the Six Sigma team, from Champions to trainers, will be organized based on the many steps in the DMAIC process. Each person can be defined within each step of the DMAIC setup within the parameters of four different roles:

1. Approval – A person approves of the decisions that the organization is making.

2. Resource – An employee or partner's skills or knowledge will be required for a certain step. That knowledge is considered a resource. The leader who uses Approval will request help from that person/the use of that resource (knowledge) to keep the task moving forward.

3. Member – A team member works based on whatever was introduced earlier in the charter. He or she will provide feedback to whoever offers Approval.

4. Interested – Interested parties will not have too much of a role at this point, but they will keep people informed about everything that occurs throughout a process including the direction that the business is going and any findings during a task.

You can use as many people in the ARMI setup as you wish. All people must still be defined accordingly. Be aware that the Approval stage will often entail a fewer number of people, while the Interested stage will have the most people. In short, those who have the most power will be the least in evidence. Talk with each member to see what tasks they are all comfortable with and discuss how they are going to help you with your task efforts. Ensure they know what is expected of them.

The ARMI review can include a look at whether or not the people in question are supportive of whatever you are planning. You can ask people about anything relating to what can make your work more useful or discuss their individual concerns.

What Influences Change Acceleration?

Although the CAP work can be useful, it is especially important for a business to analyze a few factors for figuring out how well a task is working and what further changes might have to be implemented. Such changes should be regularly measured to ensure things are moving in the right direction.

1. What metrics are used?

The metrics in a process can influence its acceleration. A seafood restaurant might use metrics like the timing needed for producing an order for a customer or how many orders can be planned at the same time. Sharing a task's specific metrics is vital to ensuring that people are comfortable with what is expected.

2. How is the data made available?

The data produced within the project should be posted with regular updates based on the certain parameters that the business wishes to utilize. The restaurant in this chapter's example might post information on how many customers were served within a time period each day. That extra data should show people in the workplace how the specific task is helping the business grow and thrive.

3. How are resources made available?

The resources needed for completing a task can entail extra materials, schedule changes or added personnel. Whether it entails extra people coming on shift to handle high-pressure situations or people switching to a work schedule that is more comfortable for them, such decisions should be carefully planned out. All people should be consulted over how resources will be allocated. There's always the option to allow people to ask for extra help if necessary, but only if a concern is truly significant.

4. How close are the people to the Champions involved with the Six Sigma routine?

There needs to be access to those who have power in the Six Sigma process. When a leader is accessible, others are more likely to feel confident about whatever is being planned out. Everyone in the workplace will understand the parameters of the Six Sigma work and what new routines are being established. But this only works when the Champions associated with the task are readily available for answering any questions that people have about the task.

5. How difficult is the task?

The CAP might be tough to manage if the task is very hard. That's why it is so important to maintain a realistic approach to the Six Sigma effort and set reasonable parameters and goals.

You might have to reorganize your task based on its difficulty. This includes changing the goals based on what you feel works best. You can be as flexible with this aspect of the task as you wish, so long as you consistently remember that the task needs to remain feasible to complete within your established parameters.

6. What benefits will be derived from the task?

The benefits should be explained to everyone involved so they feel invested in the effort. No one wants to participate in something if the benefits involved are not clear. People need to have a stake in a project and that can only happen if they are clear on why the project is being put into place and what its specific benefits will be at the end.

The CAP is a key aspect of managing the Six Sigma effort that cannot be ignored. The CAP effort makes it easier to organize data. It allows for better communication between people and helps ensure that everyone is prepared to handle any problems or unexpected concerns that might arise.

Chapter 20 – The Value Stream Map

As you plan a reasonable process for your business to operate within, you will have to look at how well the data you are utilizing is organized. Part of this comes from the use of a value stream map. We briefly discussed the application of value stream maps earlier. In this chapter, we'll further articulate the importance of this map that illustrates how a business operates based on its processes, allowing you to identify areas for improvement. This is a critical aspect of Six Sigma's definition phase.

As you produce your map, you will identify the waste that has developed within your business and will assess what has caused that waste. Specifically, the map starts with a look at the "as-is" functionality in the workplace, particularly what you are doing right now. The "to be" state refers to a new process form and flow that you can utilize.

The goal of the value stream map is to find a way to get the order process to go from the customer to the business and then back to the customer again. In such a case, the customer requests the service and the business completes a series of steps or triggers to then give the customer what he or she wants. After the steps are finished, the customer's request or need should be fully satisfied. The process needs to be streamlined so as to minimize waste that includes unnecessary steps. This includes ensuring that the process does not run into any dead ends.

The "As-Is" Process

The "as-is", which is the current process, begins the value stream map. You will observe the ongoing flow of information and functionality in the workplace. Part of this includes interviewing people and assessing how machines, materials and employees are working. The as-is process may end up being very different from any manuals, handbooks or other employment guidelines that you might be familiar with. There is a potential for irregularities and other problems in the workplace to keep the as-is process from running as well as it normally should.

How Many Parties?

The number of parties involved in the value stream map will vary. The parties will often entail the customer and the supplier, although the shipping group and production control team may also be factors. The parties should be organized at the start to determine the main players in the process.

Consider a sporting goods store that needs to order hiking shoes. An order is sent to a supplier or a production control team. The supplier will need to send an order to a production control group. The same supplier must also review the orders that the store or other client has to work with. A shipping team will be incorporated into the process to figure out how the materials are to be sent between all parties.

The parties in the value stream map should be analyzed based on how they play their parts in the process. You may find that there are too many people involved. There might also be problems with organization. This includes the customer sending an order to the supplier before that supplier is able to get the production control team to establish a plan for handling the order.

The Request Always Starts the Map

A request is necessary for a business to start a process. For example, a beauty shop might need to order hair gel. The beauty shop puts in a request to get more hair gel from the company that manufactures or ships the product the shop uses. The process entails the company eventually getting the gel out to the beauty shop, thus allowing that shop to serve its customers who require certain hair treatments.

What Is the Trigger?

Several steps will follow in the value stream map after a request is sent out. These steps are known as triggers. That is, each step triggers another step in the process. The process can include as many triggers as needed so long as no triggers cause problems.

The trigger on the value stream map can be the issue causing the irregularity to develop in the workplace, whether large or small. For instance, a retail chain might have a large shipping area that moves merchandise to many locations around the country. The chain should have a plan for shipping to different parts of the country based on demand, necessity and budget. But in some cases, the shipping plan might become difficult to manage.

A computer might be responsible for managing the schedules for where items are to be shipped. That computer might stop working properly. Or it might use incorrect algorithms for figuring out what should be mailed out. In other cases, the products might be shipped to the wrong locations or even not at all. The problems with the computer are the trigger since they are the cause of the main problem.

This does not mean that the trigger is always bad. A normal process entails a trigger that operates as planned. When the computer in the above example uses an updated and carefully managed algorithm for moving shipments to certain parts of the country, that trigger is working properly. Each trigger should be explored based on how it is working and assessed to see whether it is consistent with your overall plan. Any triggers that are not working correctly should be fixed as soon as possible.

Analyzing the Flow

Each trigger in the value stream map entails a process. The natural flow of that process is based off the triggers moving in a sequential order. A predetermined process for those triggers must be incorporated into the mix. Each step must then move forward as intended.

A good way to identify the flow is to use the verb and noun layout for identifying steps. "The computer receives the order" may be followed with "The order is sent to the shipping center." The steps show that there is a subject or entity involved and that some action is being produced to support the business' purposes. This can work with as many steps as needed.

Cycle-Time Review

Cycle time is the amount of time it takes to go through each step within the business flow. The time may be divided up between value-added and non-value-added time. As discussed in an earlier chapter, value-added time refers to the work that a business actually puts into the process. Non-value-added-time is when nothing is happening. Every process that comes along might impact your work. You can time these processes as necessary to determine the length of the cycles and whether or not they're proceeding as planned.

The goal is to keep the non-value-added time to a minimum or to eliminate it altogether. For instance, a team that processes medical insurance charges might take an excessive amount of time processing bills. Because of the poor time management, customers may not get their claims appropriately managed. A Six Sigma routine can help the processing team to go lean by cutting down on non-value-added activities.

Value and Non-Value-Added Activities

Value-added activities are the actual forms of work that customers are ready to pay for. The activities that make the product what it is and which will transform a product or service from one form to the next will be analyzed as value-added activities. These activities can only be utilized when the actions are completed right the first time around. Therefore, planning is vital for the success of a project.

For instance, a business may manufacture a part for a larger appliance. The manufacturing process is a value-added activity because it involves making a key part of a product. But to make this work, the parts have to be built correctly. Any failures to do so will result in waste, which is directly related to non-value-added time.

Non-value-added time is the other part of the as-is process. It refers to anything in the work environment that reduces productivity. In some cases, parts might be idle because they are waiting to be sent out. Customers aren't paying for the storage processes for managing inventory; they're only paying for items that have been manufactured.

Product transportation should be interpreted as non-value-added time. The queueing process, where items are being set up so the next step can start, might also be non-value-added time. The value-added time will not start until the next step itself begins. Your goal is to keep non-value-added times from being a burden to the manufacturing process.

As you look at your value stream map, you have to look at how the map is organized based on whether the actions involved are worth something. You should review each action on the map to determine whether it is something that people will want to spend money on. An appropriate transformation from a series of raw materials or parts into something new and desirable to customers should have taken place during the process—without any errors or defects. Anything that meets all of these criteria will be interpreted as being value-added time. Anything that doesn't meet said criteria is non-value-added time.

Measuring the Process Efficiency

To complete the process efficiency measurement, you take the total number of cycle-time hours by combining the value-added time and the non-value-added time together between each step. The value-added time should be divided by the cycle time. This gives you a percentage for how efficient the process is. A process that is more effective will have a higher percentage total, what with the task requiring less time spent on functions that your client is not going to pay for.

For instance, you might have a process for building an engine for a luxury car. The value-added time involves processes such as receiving an order, taking in materials and getting the engine manufactured and then shipped out. The total amount of value-added time you might have spent could be six hours. But the overall cycle time may be 60 hours. The 54 hours of non-value-added time might have involved things like the engine being shipped by truck over the course of a full day or the engine sitting in a storage space, waiting to be shipped.

In this example, you would divide 6 by 60 to get 0.1. This means that the process efficiency is 10 percent. You are spending 10 percent of the time from when the order is received, until the product is shipped, manufacturing the engine and ensuring the material is processed and made ready for use. You might need to reduce the non-value-added time by using a faster shipping process or finding a way to streamline the manufacturing and shipping process.

A good way to think of this is to look at a sample chart of something that might work based on how efficient a cycle might be. A company could create a plan for producing work with regards to identifying specific tasks that can be done. The goal would be to keep the non-value-added tasks in check while also focusing on any value-added work that comes in.

Consider another example, the team is looking at the value-added efforts and the non-value work. The process of identifying shipments, checking the labels, scanning them, entering identifying numbers and then moving the product along should be efficient. There will naturally be plenty of non-value-added tasks.

Let's suppose there is a total of 860 seconds being spent on the task and 182 seconds are value-added. By taking 182 seconds and dividing it by 860, we get 0.221. This means that only 22.1 percent of the time being used for handling the task is value-added work. The team has to plan a new routine or process that lessens the non-value-added tasks.

You can establish any goal you'd like. For instance, you might decide that 30 to 40 percent of all the work will be value-added, although that will require you to make some substantial cuts. The example listed here might be accentuated with new processes that entail changing the routine around for finding identification numbers. A new plan might also entail setting aside any damaged items first, thus expediting the overall process. Whatever the case might be, the work should be organized for ease and efficiency.

Adding Many Processes

You have the option to incorporate as many processes into your as-is and value stream map analysis as needed. While you will use a few main processes at the start, later you will dig deeper into a subprocess that is loosely based off the main one. After that, you will establish another subprocess for each of those smaller processes if applicable. You can make this part of the value stream map as detailed as you wish. But you must also ensure that the subprocess in question is kept under control and that you have a graphical interface ready for linking each of those smaller efforts with each other. Reviewing how processes are interconnected allows you to find errors and problem areas.

Sometimes there can be two smaller subprocesses that will link to one final result. The scope of the task will have expanded enough to allow for a calculation to be handled many different ways. The added scope might take an extra bit of time to resolve, especially considering how detailed some of the smaller processes might be. While it is fine to design these processes, it is best to avoid adding too many of them at a time.

Bottlenecks

There are two particular issues that you might discover on your value stream map. The first issue is the bottleneck. This is a problem that entails a department or functionality whose necessary capacity is less than what the demand being placed on it might be. The bottleneck gets its name for how the needed capacity or the width of the bottle is too slim for all the items that have to come out of the bottle. This occurs when a business has too little space to move out the many items it might have.

An example of a bottleneck is an appliance manufacturer that has a limited amount of space for manufacturing and shipping its appliances. The appliances might not be moving out of a warehouse as well as they should be. This becomes hard on the manufacturer as the company will not have the ability to produce new items like it might have planned. The company will struggle with trying to move out its products, thus resulting in excess supplies and delays in the production process. This may also entail pressure from customers who want something but aren't able to get it due to how slow the process is. Employees may also become dissatisfied with their inefficient work routine.

Constraints

The other significant issue to look at is the constraint. This problem, which can also be identified in your value stream map, is a factor that keeps a business from working to its best possible potential. When a constraint develops, the company is not using its resources, whether people or raw materials, the right way. Therefore, the business will not be as efficient as it could be. Customers may not be served, and the business may not turn the best possible profit.

Constraints include issues like when a business does not have the funds available to handle a task. The business might not have the necessary resources. A manufacturer of vacuum cleaners might not have the money needed to acquire the unique motors or suction devices it needs for producing its cleaners, for instance. In other cases, the business might not get the resources it requires even if it has the money.

The schedule and time for a project is another constraint. The business may not have the time to complete certain tasks. Businesses often try to cut corners to manage their schedules, and in many cases, the customer will notice defects in products as a result of the rush job.

The scope or quality of a project is a major consideration. The scope is a reference to how wide or narrow a range the project will cast. Sometimes a project might entail a sudden change in the scope depending on a business' needs. The changes may lead to confusion within the workplace.

Physical constraints may include a lack of space for handling materials, although this is often caused by a company having too many materials to work with and not enough room. Policy constraints may also come about as the business is unable to handle certain tasks or functions. Understanding how a business is evolving and what can be expected out of the business at large is vital to recognizing what should be done to resolve issues in the value stream map.

Lead Time, Processing Time and the Lead-Time Ladder

The bottom part of the value stream map should include a lead-time ladder. This is a measure of the production lead time. The feature provides information on how long it takes to get items ready versus the amount of time necessary for processing. While it might be difficult to cut down on the necessary processing time, it's critical to review the lead time to ensure that there is less idle time involved.

The lead time in the value stream map is a measure of the time it takes from receiving a customer request to the time when that request is fulfilled. You start this by taking the order as soon as possible and then beginning to manage the request right away. You have to calculate the lead time accurately to ensure the customer knows when to expect the order. More importantly, the lead time has to be planned to where it will not take too long, thus ensuring the customer's satisfaction.

The lead time should be compared with how long it takes for an order to actually be completed. Identifying the difference between the lead time and the actual time you spend can help you with figuring out what changes should be implemented. You should focus on reducing the waste that you find in the value stream map. After that is lessened, you can enhance the processing time. You will also better understand the constraints that might develop.

Processing time refers to the effort required for moving items along. After the products are prepared in the lead-time period, the processing time begins when items are shipped out or moved elsewhere. The processing time can last for just a few minutes when compared with the days that the production lead time might take.

The lead and processing times are combined into a lead-time ladder. The two time periods alternate between one another. You may see that one stage takes a while to complete when compared with the others, for instance. You'll need to review the work that goes into each process to see if it's reasonable. This includes seeing that the time frame is appropriate and avoids any unnecessary delays.

The SMED Process

One option you can consider for improving upon what your Six Sigma work entails is the Single Minute Exchange of Dies (SMED) process. Many Six Sigma tasks struggle due to long setup times during the design process; the SMED routine helps with keeping those times down. You can review things relating to how a machine operates through internal and external forces. The key here is to keep the setup time from taking too long, possibly even reducing it to as little as ten minutes.

Eight steps must be utilized in the SMED process:

1. Review the difference between internal and external setup functions.

External setup functions work when the machines or other items in question are turned on. Internal setups work when the machines are off or down. You can compare the items that are involved in your setup to resolve any problems. For instance, you might need to run certain processes before a task begins. Much of this includes working with enough materials based on what you are analyzing.

2. Convert internal setup processes to external ones.

Look at what you can do when a machine or other item is operating. In some cases, the internal items that normally work when things are off may be adapted so they work while machines are on. This may help with getting the work process to run smoothly, thereby allowing a particular task to be executed much more quickly and efficiently. The key is to standardize all of the external functions in this process.

3. Document details on all external processes.

Internal functions may vary based on the quality of the machines or other items being used. You can use full documentation to record information on how external processes are being handled. This should help you with following up and resolving any problems or concerns that may eventually arise.

4. Look at how you change over from internal tasks to external ones.

Review how internal activities link to external tasks. Part of this might entail linking old processes up with one another to create a more thorough process for the task. You should not assume that something has to be prepared with the same shape. The functions between the internal and external tasks should be carefully managed.

5. Improve upon external setups.

External processes can be improved upon once the internal ones are functioning as needed. The external processes may work with an arrangement that features everything based on the functions of your items and how they link together. Create a map of the materials you will use in the SMED process. The map can illustrate everything regarding what works in a task and how well certain items might work if they are paired together. Getting your external tools ready reduces the risk of bottlenecks.

6. Produce an automated setup if you can.

This part of the design is more technical in nature and is not necessarily something that everyone should try. But this part of SMED gives you the option to create a link between any computer programs, machines or other items needed for work. The automation can be planned and tested to work at certain times or based on particular triggers. You can use the work in question to make your workplace more efficient.

7. Identify any problems that might occur in the changeover process.

The changeover from when you start the machining or manufacturing process to when you stop should be noted. Review how all parts work and how well they link to each other. See if anything is not functioning properly when switching from one point to another. Identifying such issues early on can save you time and resources.

The SMED process is clearly designed for when you have technical matters to work with. But the routine may also work well as a part of the design process and can be incorporated into your value stream map. Though the setup process and cycle time can cause the value stream map to become more complicated than necessary, you will have more control over the work if the SMED process is carefully planned out.

Chapter 21 – Options for Process Mapping

The value stream map is one of the top tools you can utilize when designing your Sigma Six process. But it is also vital for you to look at the other choices you have for preparing a process map. By creating an appropriate process map, you are fashioning a review of what you want to do when designing a Six Sigma process. It will help you determine what you have to focus on and will also clarify what makes your project so valuable.

Note: The options here are different from a value stream map in that the value map focuses on cutting down waste and making a process as lean as possible. The maps listed in this chapter are made for profiling processes and actions more than going lean. But you can use these maps to figure out what parts of your work are excessive versus what should be eliminated from your task. Be aware of your project routine and what you feel is right for the task so you can create a project that fits your business' work needs.

SIPOC

The first option to consider for the process mapping routine is the SIPOC map. The SIPOC layout has five factors. Each factor identifies the inputs and outputs that you will use in the SIPOC process. You can use the SIPOC map to figure out who is managing certain processes and how customers and suppliers all relate to whatever you are planning. You can also use this map to establish boundaries for what you are expecting to get out of your process. The five SIPOC points are:

1. Supplier

The supplier is the person who provides the input to the process. This could be an organization that supplies resources to your business. The customers or other clients who receive your end products may also be considered. The management in the workplace may also be a factor; this is especially the case for when management has an everyday say in what you are doing. You can use any party as the supplier in the SIPOC process.

Let's look at an example of a business that makes ovens. The business might need to contact a supplier that offers pilot lights and other critical oven parts. The SIPOC process identifies the supplier. The company will then send that supplier an order for oven parts. After the order is sent out, the company can start the manufacturing process.

2. Input

The input is the data that a process will entail. You may use the input to analyze what is happening with a process and how people in the workplace are being contacted. Scanned documents relating to processes or emails alerting people to their particular tasks may be factored into the mix. Any updates on a queue or any system reports may also be incorporated. The data that you gather must help you recognize what you have to do to obtain the optimal final input. In our example, the input may be the materials that the company needs to make its oven ranges.

3. Process

Process refers to the activities you participate in when trying to satisfy the needs of your customers. You may consider reviewing any input you take in while acting upon that data. You may discuss things like how input is processed, how that data is forwarded to certain entities, or how changes should be managed. You can move the process in any direction you see fit. For instance, you might have received input relating to what you need to make your business operations run. The process could then involve you purchasing something to facilitate the particular operations you are trying to organize.

The process in this example entails the oven manufacturer contacting the supplier. An order is created and the supplier is told about the parts that the oven company needs. The process can involve an analysis of the items that will be required, followed by the number of precise parts needed. The number can be calculated based on the needs the business has for manufacturing or the capacity that the business has for producing products without resulting in overstock or possible downtime.

4. Output

Output is the data or other material that comes out of a process. In this case, you might have used a process to order something for a task. The output could be the resources that you requested. You may use this process map to review what the output looks like versus what you needed and your general expectations for it. The output in our oven range example is the materials that the company ordered.

5. Customer

The customer is always the last step of the SIPOC process. The customer is the entity that will receive the output. This could be a person who goes shopping at a store you operate or someone who will buy services from you. Maybe a business partner might be a factor in the SIPOC process. Either way, the partner you work with should be someone who is going to receive whatever you have produced during the SIPOC routine. Using our previous example, this will be either the business that receives the oven parts it requires or the customer who receives the oven that he or she ordered. Either way, the process should end at this juncture.

Producing a SIPOC review is vital for ensuring your business can grow and operate with certain standards in mind. But in some cases, it might help for you to list specific needs surrounding the inputs and outputs of your routine. You can use these requirements in the SIPOC process to confirm what is happening with your work and to establish whether there are any problems with the SIPOC routine. You can always review the requirements later to determine if they were met or not. For cases where those demands were not met, you can analyze the system to see what could have caused that particular problem to develop.

The most important part of the SIPOC review is that this is just a brief shot of what your business is doing. This is not intended to be overly thorough. Rather, you are listing what everyone is going to do (and when) in the process. The information should be relevant to the task and give people an idea of what to expect. Keep the content organized and people in the workplace will know what is happening and what they can expect from your SIPOC work.

High-Level Process Map

Another process mapping choice is a high-level process map that identifies how a process is working. This solution does not require loads of technical data. You only have to produce a flowchart that illustrates how well your process is orchestrated while analyzing how the relationships between many people are organized. You should show where the inputs and outputs within your business are going.

A good rule of thumb is to keep all parts of your process map laid out with multiple colors. Use a different color for each entity involved with the process. One color is for the person requesting a process, another is for the accounting or purchasing effort, a third is for the receiving team and so forth. You can also add Xs or other marks on your map that illustrate the spots where certain problems are arising. You can use this to determine the issues at hand and possibly locate the root issues that are making a situation worse.

You can list about five to 10 steps on your process map. This should be enough to create a thorough map of what you are doing without being far too complicated for people to follow. You can also use this limit on steps to keep the process streamlined or to reduce the waste generated by the Six Sigma effort. The review of these steps may also help with establishing relationships between everything you want to do at a time.

Detailed Map

The detailed map is a solution that requires extra time for producing data. This map is all about illustrating every step in a process. You list one step at the start and then follow it up with the next step. You explain in the map why certain steps follow older ones. Everything has to be as progressive as possible as you illustrate to readers what makes certain actions so distinct. The question of "what happens next" will be resolved throughout the detailed map. The detailed map can also be called a process flowchart as it illustrates all the things that are going into your business and how it is moving forward based on the actions that take place within a certain process.

A convenient idea for a detailed map is to add a series of "yes" and "no" responses to what you are planning. You might state that one thing is being done in the workplace. But then you might ask if that event did occur. If the answer is "yes," you move on to the next phase. If "no," you go in a new direction. The answers can branch off in completely separate directions, but they are all supposed to link to each other as cleanly as possible.

The detailed map is a little different from a value stream map as the detailed layout focuses more on the content that might happen. The value stream map is more about things that add value to a task. You can use the detailed map to be as specific and unique as possible. Best of all, this can work for as many steps as you want. This also works for any field you want to highlight your work in.

You can also create the detailed map as an alternative-path flowchart. With this, you will aim to keep the detailed map moving towards the same goal, but you will have several alternative ways that people can get to the desire end result. For instance, you might have a process where a person in the workplace has to decide which customers can be called by telephone for possible orders. This may involve looking up purchase information to find the people who are most interested. Let's say that you want to sell microwave ovens to customers, but you are not sure about what to do when calling those people.

You might have a step in the map that leads to two options: you have to decide who to call and then look up information on how many products people have ordered from you in the past. If the total is above a certain total, you can call that customer because that person might be more likely to buy something from you. But if that person has not purchased enough items, you can go down a secondary path where you research the specific orders that the person has placed. Since you are trying to sell microwave ovens, you can use a research parameter relating to the specific types of items someone has ordered. These include specific kitchen appliances that might relate to a microwave oven. After you make the appropriate decision, you can contact a person by phone provided that person has spent enough money on kitchen items.

The practice should entail whatever parameters you wish to utilize. But you must keep the parameters relevant and realistic. Don't have too many alternative paths. Anything that changes too many times or which offers too many options might be a challenge to work with. You also have the option to use different colors on your map to further highlight specific paths and parameters.

Don't forget that while the detailed map can go through an entire process as needed, you have the option to keep certain segments of the map brief or limited in scope. You can introduce information that is broad in some parts and then go into the really specific aspects of the work later on as you move forward. The good news about the detailed map is that the reinvention of your work can be as thorough as necessary for your business, although you can always leave certain aspects of your work as they are if you feel they are good enough.

Swimlane/Deployment Map

Sometimes it is important for you to produce a flowchart that looks more at the specific parties involved in the Six Sigma process. This is where a swimlane or deployment map will come into play. The map gets its name from how it is organized into a series of lanes. Each of these horizontal lanes covers a specific entity in the Six Sigma process. One lane may cover the buyer; another, the agent; a third, the dealer; a fourth, any other entities like legal service providers and so forth. You can use as many lanes as necessary while applying any type of role to each lane depending on what you feel is right for your business. But as you plan out the map, you must notice how the chart runs from one end to the other.

Buyer		Answer		Converse		Accept Proposition		Finish Call		
Agent	Make the Call			Converse		Accept Proposition		Finish Call		Prepare Contract
Lawyer										Approve Contract
Dealer	Area Advantage									

Whereas the y-axis concentrates on roles, the x-axis relates to timing. The earliest parts of the process go on the left. As you move forward to the right, you will see how each group relates to each other. You will notice that certain people are working with your processes versus others. Arrows help let people know how the process is moving. A circle may also be added at the end of a process to let the reader know that the process is complete.

For instance, a manufacturing company might use a swimlane map that illustrates four parties: the requestor, the purchaser, the supplier and the accounting team. The map starts with the requestor asking for something, which leads to the purchaser sending an order out to the supplier. While the supplier gets that order, the accounting team gets information on the order and plans an invoice. The map should evolve to where the requestor and purchaser get the items that they asked for from the supplier. The accounting team should then record information on the transaction that took place and how it will move forward.

While the swimlane map holds many people accountable, this map might become complicated and can take up lots of space. Depending on how many events occur, it may also be tough to figure out which parties are linked to each other. That said, the swimlane map should help with organizing data and content.

Relationship Map

A relationship map is not necessarily designed to illustrate in full detail a process based on the work that has been completed. Rather, the map shows the process according to how information moves from one party to the next. You can use a relationship map to figure out how well people are to work together and whether certain changes should be made to allow the transaction process to be as organized as possible.

The map works best when there are many people participating in the routine. The information should be organized based on factors like how many people are participating in a program, how many steps they undertake and the number of parties those groups will get in touch with during the routine. A purchasing team might send a purchase order to a supplier, get a request for a purchase from the receiver and send details on that purchase order to the accounting team. You can use as many back and forth arrows on the relationship map as necessary, provided that the information is easy to identify and measure.

The most important part of getting all these features in a process map ready is to ensure you're moving forward with the right solution. Assess all of these map possibilities as you design your Six Sigma plan. Feel free to incorporate as many aspects of one map as you wish, but ensure the map you choose is appropriate for the task.

Chapter 22 – The 15 Most Important Details for Planning a Six Sigma Task

The design process for Six Sigma tasks is critical, but you must always be aware of how well the design works when planning your effort. The intent is to make your efforts easier, more efficient and more streamlined. As you get the DMAIC process to work, look carefully at how well that task is organized. Assess how well the DMAIC routine is run based on the details involved and what makes your work so unique and useful. The effort is thorough and can take months, if not years, to complete. Not knowing what will go into the DMAIC routine before you start can be dangerous. There are several points that may be incorporated into the effort for making the details in the Six Sigma plan work while ensuring the DMAIC process is created accurately.

Each of these points can be weighted in any way you see fit. But you should have realistic answers to all of these aspects no matter how greatly or lightly you value these details. There are fifteen things to be considered:

1. Will the customer find the quality of the product or service to be any better?

The Voice of the Customer should be used to identify what a person or organization feels about something. The VOC needs to be fully understandable and organized however you see fit. Regular reviews of what customers are thinking and how they are thinking about the work you are putting in should be carefully coordinated. You can use the analysis at this stage to see what people are saying about you and how they might feel about the things you are putting into your work at large.

2. How stable is the work?

There has to be a sense of stability involved with a task. The work should move steadily along without complications. This includes looking at how often you might have to change things within a task. You can make any changes that are necessary, but it helps to see how well the changes are laid out and that everyone involved agrees with whatever is being planned in the routine. Stability is especially critical when you're trying to assess the Six Sigma work without anything possibly interfering with whatever is being managed.

3. What are the defects and how can you define them?

The defect in the process can entail anything. Your defects might run the gamut from a small mismeasured value, to a different color used in the manufacturing process. Changes with a lead time or how long it takes for something to be completed or processed may also be factored into the process, although the changes can vary based on what you analyze. But the parameters for a defect can come in many forms. It might be a challenge to figure out what parameters are being used in any situation, but you should at least think about what is working in any given situation.

4. Is the data that works in the Six Sigma effort available? Can you access that data at any time?

You will measure how well the Six Sigma work is proceeding based on benchmarks and parameters you have generated. Are you able to measure the data that is produced? Do you know how that data is developing? Better yet, how often are you able to monitor said data? Data should be reviewed consistently to ensure that you understand whatever is happening at any given time.

5. What is the solution that you have in mind?

The solution you wish to utilize should be carefully planned. You have to think about the answer to the questions you have in the DMAIC process and how well they are to be answered. The final product, or at least what you feel is the best possible final product, should be defined. This is the goal for everyone in the effort to follow through on. Only then will it be easy to convince people to participate in the work you are planning.

6. What benefits can you expect?

Benefits should include more than just better sales or improved customer satisfaction. You can also look at benefits such as how your employees will have an easier time with completing their jobs. Maybe your business image will improve. Perhaps the business will grow in size. Any benefits you can think about should be cataloged as you find them. Share them with others in the Six Sigma or DMAIC effort so everyone will feel more confident in their work and likely to remain onboard with the project.

7. How is the Six Sigma work going to impact the quality of the service?

While the process of managing and running a business is important, it is also vital to see how the service is handled. The customers are always the final judges. They will determine if a business is worthwhile based on whether or not they are satisfied. When Six Sigma plans improve the quality of service, it becomes easier for a business to grow.

8. How well are people willing to support or sponsor a Six Sigma plan?

The Six Sigma effort being organized should be supported by the right people. These include shareholders who want to support the operation and who may even fund some actions. Managers who observe everything involved with a business should be noted too. Everyone should agree to work together on a Six Sigma process and to show support for whatever is planned out.

9. What types of goals are in the DMAIC project and how do they compare with the goals that the business has in general?

A sense of alignment must be produced within the project. The strategic objectives should be explored based on the things that a business wants to do over time. The task has to match up with whatever a business wants to do or else the task will not be funded properly or capable of running right. Also, the resources that are needed in the Six Sigma process might not match up with a particular routine. Check your business' goals to see that whatever you are using is suitable for the needs you have when managing a task.

10. How are the inputs going to be controlled?

The inputs in the work are the things that will contribute to the output and which will influence the results of the Six Sigma plans. You have to know how each of these inputs are planned out. Look at the inputs you will add while also seeing whether you can control them and analyze how they are working in real time. A Six Sigma task that does not provide the user with any control over inputs might not be all that easy to manage. Nor will it necessarily give you the desired results.

You may look at how individuals in the workplace will be responsible for managing many functions in your Six Sigma work. These include people who will handle different tasks based on factors like how much money you will spend, where you will switch things off to during the process and the general efforts involved with your task.

11. What are you expecting to get out of the work after a while?

The timeline should be realistic and suitable for the task. You might be expected to spend months on the Six Sigma work. This is due to extensive benchmarks or the need to prepare many resources for use. The work can be extensive, but it can make all the difference with the task.

12. What are the chances for a task being resolved the right way?

There is a chance that the Six Sigma process will not work as well as it should. You might find some cases where the task has a margin of error which is hard to manage. The risk can be significant depending on the significance of the task. Naturally, there might be a slight learning curve at the start of the task, but after a while the business should start to move forward with the work. You'll have to be aware of what might happen if the task does not work well and you need to make certain changes after a while.

13. What type of investment is required?

One of the main reasons why so many Six Sigma and DMAIC efforts don't occur is because businesses are not willing to spend money on the practice. There should be some kind of investment to encourage certain tasks in the Six Sigma effort to work to the liking of the business.

14. How accessible are the people who need to handle the task?

All the people in the Six Sigma process should be accessible. From the Champions to the Black Belts and even the Green Belts, all people should be open for anything that could happen. Everyone also needs to have a clearly established role so they can share information the right way. The people who are to be contacted for managing the task should be capable of doing what they can to make the work in question move forward. Having at least one person associated with the Six Sigma work on hand at all times is always vital for the task's success. The fact that the work will entail multiple people improves the chances that someone will always be accessible and able to help.

15. Is there going to be a need to redesign the work?

There are often cases where Six Sigma processes don't run as well as they could. While the DMAIC effort is needed for thoroughly proceeding through the Six Sigma routine, you should at least think about some opportunities for alternatives. Time frames for when those alternatives can be planned out may be of particular help. You need to plan alternatives and also figure out which ones might be suitable, not to mention what you can measure if you have to go down an alternative route. This is always a worst-case scenario that you never want to fall into, but you should at least prepare for what could happen.

Each of these criteria is vital to review before starting a Six Sigma process. It's not all that tough to get the project running once the proper details are addressed.

Chapter 23 – Designing a Communication Plan

The communication plan that you wish to utilize within your Six Sigma process is vital to the success of the work. You can get a quality communication plan up and running with enough details surrounding what you feel is suitable for making a routine work. You must remain in regular touch with the people at your workplace and with others associated with the Six Sigma task so everyone can stay on top of what is happening. Besides, the process will entail many complicated steps that are not always easy to follow on their own.

1. Question and Answer

A question and answer document should be included in your communication plan. This will be given to people throughout the workplace with a description of what you have designed and what you plan on doing with the Six Sigma work. You can talk about why you are going lean, what you will be doing with it, how the business might save money and so forth. Anything that relates to the lean process should be explored in detail here.

2. Regular Meetings

Meetings are important throughout the Six Sigma process. You can plan any kind of meeting that you wish to utilize, from a face-to-face meeting to a town hall or other presentation. Videos of any presentations or other efforts should be documented.

3. Emails

Emails can be sent to people throughout the process. You can send out new emails based on the stages of the Six Sigma process a project is entering. Emails can be great for keeping people updated, documenting progress, addressing questions etc.

4. Milestone Updates

You can prepare special updates surrounding your Six Sigma work when you get to certain milestones. These include milestones that entail meeting particular objectives or goals that you want to attain. Some milestones may also include points surrounding how effective and useful a task might be. The best part of working with milestones is that you can use them to organize your work based on particular goals.

The communication plans that you put into your work are a necessity. You must know where you are going with your work and ensure that the people involved are aware of what's happening. A regular line of communication will keep confusion and frustration at bay. It should not be hard to plan when you have enough team members on hand who can review your work.

Chapter 24 – The Cost of Quality and the Cost-Benefit Analysis

This next part of the Six Sigma routine can work in many parts of the process. It can work for the Improve stage, when seeing what values are coming about, but you can also use it in the control stage or even when you're trying to design the task. In fact, it is easier to use the cost-benefit analysis or CBA at the start so you can let everyone in the workplace know what makes your work useful. This includes explaining to everyone why the task will help the business grow.

The cost-benefit analysis entails a review of a project based on its design and whether the solution in question is worthwhile. While it is true that Six Sigma is about making a business more effective, it is profitability that is more important than anything else. The cost-benefit analysis looks at how profitable your work is and whether there are any problems in the business based on what you are spending.

Profitability is different from revenue in that profitability is about how well your business can manage the money it takes in. You might take in lots of revenue, but that does not mean that the business is growing correctly. You might have problems where the business is not growing for many reasons. The business might struggle due to factors like excess expenses or unnecessary processes that cost more to manage. The expenses involved can be high, but your work should help you with identifying what makes your work useful and efficient.

The Five Key Costs of Quality (COPQ)

There are five important costs of quality that must be analyzed if you're going to make the most out of your lean process. These points may be factored into the CBA and your task. These four points are known as the Costs of Poor Quality or COPQ. Some of these costs are preventable, but others are things that will occur if you are unable to manage the processes you wish to follow.

1. Prevention costs

The first part of the COPQ entails the costs surrounding your attempts to prevent things. You can use the prevention costs to analyze the extra expenses involved with preventing defects. These costs are controllable and are designed to ensure products and services without defects will reach the customer. Your Six Sigma effort is designed to reduce those prevention costs by looking at how well those costs are organized in order to keep a business from producing faulty materials.

2. Appraisal costs

Appraisal costs are also controllable and relate to identifying the things that might come along within your work. Appraisals can include general inspections of each of the products or services being provided to people. Your goal should be to keep those inspections from having to be too extensive. Six Sigma is about seeing that you can confirm quality products without going through lots of bothersome appraisal costs in the process.

3. Internal error cost

This next expense entails the issues that arise in your workplace, particularly some that you might have been able to prevent had a Six Sigma task worked. The internal error cost refers to when products do not meet their designs. This could be a result of defects. For instance, an orange juice concentrate factory might notice that the orange juice being produced is not appropriately concentrated. An excessive amount of water might be found in some orange juice products. This problem must be resolved before the products are moved out to the public. The internal error cost should be less than what you might bear with when the fourth expense is considered.

4. External error cost

An external error cost refers to a cost that arises after items have been sent out to customers. This could come from repairs on a warranty, product recalls or other legal concerns. An example could be a chicken farm. The farm might send out chicken breasts for cooking and then discovered that there was a possible E. coli outbreak. This error might have been caused by certain problems that a Six Sigma routine could control. The external error will result in a recall of chicken products. This will cause significant concerns where the farm will lose money, have to resolve the existing problem and possibly shut down production for a small bit of time, all while contending with negative publicity.

5. Poor equipment cost

This fifth expense is a mix of both a problem that can be found before and after items are sent out, plus a mix of controllable and resultant costs. The poor equipment cost entails the cost associated with trying to measure a product or service. The added costs might be hard to manage at times depending on how extensive a process is to resolve or control an issue. These expenses may be very high, so make sure you analyze how well the equipment is being used and have a plan in hand for ensuring your work's efficiency.

Indirect Costs

You may also come across some indirect costs relating to customers not knowing how to use certain products, being dissatisfied with your work or feeling your company's reputation isn't all that strong. The indirect costs may come from product downtime, repair costs that come from a warranty, travel costs and shipping expenses for returning and fixing items and any backups that have to be planned out. While you might try to show your customers that you care about them by assisting them after problems come along, it's best to prevent the processes that might cause such indirect costs to arise in the first place.

Planning the CBA

The cost-benefit analysis reviews the possible solution to your problem and how it can be implemented. The solution is analyzed based on the possible benefits and the cost involved. These costs may include issues relating to how much it costs to get a project started, how to maintain it and what resources are required. You may analyze factors like salaries and the costs associated with training people or switching to a new process. Expenses can entail anything in the work environment.

The CBA can be used as the Six Sigma routine is moving along and you need to see how well the process is going. You can analyze your business' productivity versus the costs involved and the end results. The CBA is mainly for use with the improvement stage above all else. You can use the CBA to figure out if certain changes to a process are suitable and affordable. After that, you can move on to the control stage and use the CBA to review whether the costs and benefits are consistent or if sudden changes have developed.

The steps for the CBA are as follows:

1. Identify the benefits of the project you are starting.

2. Review the benefits based on the variables you can measure. These include the dollar amounts involved, the timing for something and how long a benefit may last.

The effects or benefits should be analyzed based on the people involved. Look at what the business will experience or what the users or non-users of products or services might get out of the work. Any possible social benefits may also be analyzed. Such social benefits entail how a business' image may be improved or how a company may grow.

3. Analyze the cost factors in the workplace. Review the materials needed, any contracts you will operate, the costs associated with employees and other factors that may come into play.

4. Identify the dollar values linked to these cost factors. Add totals for employee salaries, contract values and so forth.

5. Calculate the net gain or loss on the project.

The gain or loss can be as high or low as it has to be. Be accurate in your review and identify the change in the value of something based on what you are using and how the funds you take in work. This is to give yourself a sense of control over the work you put in.

6. You may change the cost values around depending on factors like who is earning more money or the changing costs for resources.

To understand this process, let's look back at the hockey equipment example from earlier in this guide. The company might want to cut down on its expenses associated with producing equipment. The team may review factors like lightweight materials for use on some products or alternatives to certain fabrics. The company will have to analyze what it will cost to get those items versus the benefits of those items. Some benefits of the new resources will have to be explored, including possibly marketing these items as being more unique or useful when compared with other items.

Remember that the changes you make can influence what you earn and should be reviewed based on what is right for the business and what you are capable of earning within a given time frame. The cost-benefit analysis has to be monitored and analyzed to see how effective it is and what you are getting out of the process.

The most important part of the CBA is that it might require you to make a few trade-offs. This means that you may have to abandon something you might want because the CBA says it will not work. The hockey equipment manufacturer might want to add its logo to the front of its goalie pads, but that might cost too much extra money. In other words, it's difficult for a company to have everything it wants.

Controlling Accuracy

The cost-benefit analysis may be wildly inaccurate if you are not cautious. The CBA has to be organized to where the content is easy to review. But there is always going to be a risk that the data is inaccurate. The inaccuracies can come from your subjective impressions or from being too reliant on past data. A few things can be done to keep the CBA accurate:

1. Avoid being reliant on prior studies.

Prior CBA reports or other studies in your field may be outdated. Some of these may be based of old values of items. Others might be based off prior procedures that are no longer relevant. Any changes in your workplace should be analyzed based on what you find is helpful in the current moment.

2. Ask for people's viewpoints.

Getting enough viewpoints is important. Check with others about the benefits you are working with. Ask about how whether there are any problems that might be dangerous or otherwise risky. This is to ensure the efforts you incorporate and use are handled right and that there are enough ideas around about what may work. Having some plans on hand for your content is vital to its success and the work you take in.

3. Avoid heuristics.

Heuristics are processes that are practical. These are not related to logic or realism. You might use heuristics to try and reach a goal. But those ideas may be irrational depending on what you incorporate in your work and how you plan it out. Avoid adding any heuristics to your work in order to maintain consistent control of your work.

Looking at Your Image

The image of your business can make a difference when it comes to what you wish to do. Your image may be influenced by factors like how well you respond to certain negative stories or events. While you might consider cost-effective measures for making your business stand out, that does not always mean that your image will be positive. You should look at how well you are managing your costs and expenses while thinking about the possible risks that may develop if you do not manage your work right.

Consider how Ford Motor Company responded to issues surrounding the Ford Pinto. The vehicle was notorious for having a substantial design flaw where the car could burst into flames following a wreck. While Ford could have issued a recall, the company decided against it. The recall would have been worth more money than the wrongful death settlements Ford had issued. But because of this move, more issues arose, thus causing the settlements to rise in value. Furthermore, Ford's brand and image were damaged.

This is an extreme example, but it suggests that there are often problems that come with the cost-benefit process. While you might think far too much about the finances of what you are doing, you also have to look at what is going on with your business based on the image you are projecting. Showing a sense of care and concern for the public and your stakeholders is vital. Be aware of this when planning your work.

Remember that the particular costs you might come across within your work will vary based on the task and how far along you are with your process. Ensure that costs are not creating a burden on the workplace. The charts and other layouts you use may help you identify some problems or costs. These costs can be reduced over time while you keep the profitability in your workplace up. Keeping that profitability steady is more important than getting lots of money only to end up having to use that money on managing problems.

Chapter 25 – Choosing the Y Between Effectiveness and Efficiency

As you read earlier in this guide, the Y variable in your work is the point where you will measure the success of your Six Sigma work off. You have to measure the Y based on what you know will influence a project. Whether it entails the amount of input in the workplace, how many errors are made or even how much time it takes to finish tasks, you can use the Y variable as a gauge for how well the effort you put in has been organized. But you have to look at two points that make the Y variable distinct. These refer to effectiveness and efficiency, the two measures that are often the basis of various Six Sigma tasks.

Six Sigma practices can use either efficiency or effectiveness as a standard. While many people use effectiveness as the ultimate guide for measuring data, efficiency can be used when aiming to produce a lean or streamlined environment. But whether you want a lean environment or a more effective one, you need a Y variable that fits in with what you wish to do. In fact, you can attempt to incorporate both points into your Six Sigma work if you wish. This will require a bit of extra effort, but it can all work to your liking if you know what you're going to get from the Y variable that you wish to utilize.

Efficiency

First, let's look at efficiency. This is a measure of how well the resources in a process are going to be utilized for the needs or efforts that you want to take on. Efficiency is a measure of how resources are not only used but also how well the work moves to your liking. The cost per transaction is a good example of this. For instance, you might try to reduce the cost associated with handling certain tasks. This could be controlling how many items are produced, adjusting prices or even figuring out things that should be done to resolve costs. Whatever the case may be, the efficiency has to be measured correctly to produce the result that best fits your needs.

Effectiveness

The effectiveness of a task is important to notice as well. Effectiveness is a measure of how well the process meets your specific requirements. An example may be how a call center is orchestrated. You can measure how effective that call center is based on who is answering the calls properly and whether there are any problems associated with people not taking in calls the right way. A business that is effective will be handling all calls correctly and on time.

Which Is More Important?

Both the effectiveness and efficiency of a Six Sigma project are vital points to consider as you plan your analysis. In fact, neither one of these is more important than the other. Effectiveness and efficiency are equally valuable, but the specific results that you will get all depend on your particular goal. For instance, you could use a large truck if you need to carry large amounts of cargo from one spot to the next, but that truck won't be efficient if you need something that can save fuel. On the other end of the spectrum, a smaller vehicle would be efficient as you won't have to waste lots of fuel, although it would not be effective at carrying cargo.

You have to look at a particular situation to give yourself an idea of what is best for your work. You might find that a truck will work better when handling more items, but a smaller car is efficient if you don't want to use lots of fuel. Your final goal will determine what you should be doing and whether something that you wish to plan out is appropriate for your work.

Sometimes you might find a solution where you can be both effective and efficient. For the car example, you might find a truck that can not only handle large amounts of cargo but which also operates on ethanol or an electric battery or something else that is cheaper or easier to supply. A call center might also be effective by answering all its calls properly and efficiently by answering more of those calls within a certain time frame. You will require extra effort to get everything to be both effective and efficient, but the work can be worthwhile if planned carefully and cautiously.

Helpful Tips

Some tips may be used when you're working with a Y variable:

1. Review the perspective of the customer.

The customer has to see that what you are doing is effective and useful. The work must be interesting to the customer. That party must see the final result of whatever it is you are doing while also being appreciative of what you have planned out. That customer will potentially recommend you to other people.

2. The work should be repeatable.

Any measurement that you plan should be for something that can be repeated over time. This includes getting results that can be produced many times over. You can always plan those goals as you move along, but you can change them around if need be. The most important thing is to see that the measurements you use can be measured while confirming that what you are doing is correct. Being accurate and correct every time is a necessity for allowing the Six Sigma task to work.

3. You must think about the benefits above the cost.

You will surely have to spend money to measure the Six Sigma task . But whatever you do, you must look at the benefits that will result from whatever you are spending. The benefits have to outweigh the costs associated with a project. You'll still need to assess how well a task is managed so you know what you are putting into your efforts and keep costs organized right. The last thing you want to do is spend so much that you put the finances of your business in jeopardy.

As you look at your measurements, you need to look at how the Y variable is planned out. This includes identifying what your overall objective for making a task work is. Are you going to make the work efficient, or do you wish to head down a road where effectiveness is the key to your success? Whatever the case may be, you have to plan your work based on what you feel is right. You can use the right measure to give your business the help it requires while moving forward in its effort to be efficient, effective or both.

Chapter 26 – Musts and Wants

You will always have different ideas for what solutions should be utilized in the Six Sigma routine. In many cases, you might have certain things that you want to do. But in other cases, you'll have some requirements that must be followed. In order to make the most of your efforts, you have to analyze the musts and wants.

This part of the process works well for the measurement plan, although this is less about quantitative analysis and more about the qualitative data you want to work with. You can use the process as desired, although the musts and wants should be carefully identified. You can review the musts based on what your business can afford or handle, but you must be careful to ensure there are no problems with the work you're aiming to manage.

Musts

Your solutions should be organized based on the musts and wants that you will use. The musts will focus on the things that are essential and valuable to your work. You have to plan enough of these musts as is suitable for your Six Sigma plan. Part of this includes manufacturing items correctly and ensuring that all items are made within a budget. The specific standards that you must follow are critical to the success of a task.

Returning to the hockey example—you might need to work on producing safe, sturdy goalie pads. Your musts may include things like being able to produce those goalie pads within a certain budget while also using a specific number of threads or fibers that will ensure a goalie's safety. The standards must be met or else the process will not work right.

Wants

Wants are the things that you would like to have in the Six Sigma process but are not necessary. You must review the wants based on what you might be interested in while considering whether they are critical to the task. Spending too much time on your wants instead of the musts could be dangerous to your process. Also, some of those wants might be difficult to obtain when your finances are considered. The good news is that the wants can be handled after your musts are met; this is provided that you have the funds needed for managing those wants and a plan in place.

Going back to the hockey equipment example, you might have some wants for the goalie equipment. You might want the equipment to come with your company's logo printed directly on the front. You may also want to get the pieces to come with washable surfaces. These are convenient features that you might like, but they are also things that you might not necessarily require.

The Weighted Rating Sheet

Your needs and wants can be organized on a rating sheet. This sheet lists information on the things you want to do with your content. The weighted rating may be planned based on a number from 0 to 10. The 0 is for the least important things, while 10 is for what you know you want the most. You can use this with as many employees or factories as needed. You can get enough opinions to figure out if the things you want are attractive, are not necessarily important or cannot possibly be obtained.

Each item is also weighted on the sheet. That is, some items might be worth more than others. The items are weighted on a scale of 0 to 100 with each of the items totaling 100 in the end. The factors are then cut down into numbers based on what is important and then analyzed with each other to figure out how valuable these things are. The comparison ensures that the most important wants are the ones that will be followed in the work routine. This can entail as detailed and specific a support system as necessary.

You can use the weighted rating sheet to produce as much information on what you are interested in as desired. You can also ask many people about what they feel is important for your work environment and how you want things to run, although the end result should be based on what you are most comfortable with and what you feel is appropriate for your use.

Here is an example of a weighted rating sheet. This is based on a consulting firm working to determine what people think about governmental affairs. The team gathered a few people (listed as X, Y and Z) and included some things that people were asked to review on a scale of 1 to 10. The individual items were weighted based on how important they would be in the process. Here's how the measurements were gathered:

Category	Weight %		Rank (1 to 10)			Score	
		X	Y	Z	X	Y	Z
Economic Growth	25%	9	8	9	2.25	2	2.25
Government Debt	5%	10	5	9	0.5	0.25	0.45
Foreign Policy	5%	7	5	8	0.35	0.25	0.4
Education	15%	9	9	9	1.35	1.35	1.35
Government Role	5%	5	6	6	0.25	0.3	0.3
Women's Rights	10%	6	6	6	0.6	0.6	0.6
Medical Care	10%	6	6	5	0.6	0.6	0.5
Immigration	5%	6	5	5	0.3	0.25	0.25
Freedoms	10%	9	6	8	0.9	0.6	0.8
Leadership	10%	8	6	5	0.8	0.6	0.5
Total	1				7.9	6.8	7.4

Note how the people in this example had different attitudes about factors like economic growth around the country. The scores were higher because they found that want to be more important, not to mention the weight associated with it was higher. By combining the scores for everything, people can identify how important wants are in general. Those who had a higher score for the wants, or in this case Person X, felt that those needs were extremely critical to the success of the work environment. Having enough of these items on hand was vital to helping the business to grow and thrive over time. In general, the concepts about developing an educational program and managing economic growth were extremely important, while concepts relating to health care and the role of government were not all that high in terms of people's priorities.

You will also notice that the many factors that go into the equation will add up to 10 at the most. This is because of how the data is weighted throughout the process. When you look at the weighting total, you will see the value of each point. For instance, the Leadership option has a 10 percent weight to it. The person who put in eight would have that total reviewed when compared with the weight. Since eight is 80 percent of the maximum total, that would be considered versus the 10 percent standard to create a total of 0.8. This would be a smaller number than some of the more valuable or highly-weighted materials, but that number might make a difference depending on how intense it is. You can also round the numbers to the nearest tenth if desired, although you might not want to do this if you have too many weights at five or 15 percent or any other number ending with five.

In your analysis, you'll need to think about the people who are giving you these results. In the above example, the idea of women's rights was not all that high on the list. This might have been because the people who were interviewed were men. Either way, every person has certain attitudes and values that have to be analyzed. You can check the results of your analysis to see what considerations have to be met.

You can use as many items as you wish on the weighted scale. The key is that all the items have to total 100 percent in weight. You must balance everything out based on value and importance and then let people tell you what you should get out of the task. You can ask about anything that is relevant to your work. The review will help you with identifying how well a task is considered and what people feel might be most important to include (or exclude.)

Chapter 27 – Brainstorming

Brainstorming specifically involves getting many people in the workplace together to think about unique ideas and to be as creative and thoughtful as possible. The work can go in any direction that the people involved want it to, although plenty of effort is required for helping to make the practice work right. This chapter will look into the many types of brainstorming solutions that may be utilized for your efforts.

Mind Mapping

Mind mapping is a practice where you produce a visual representation of the ideas and concepts you want to use in your work. The practice focuses on identifying relationships between the ideas you want to use and the solutions you might consider planning. People can add ideas and then layer them with issues and possible solutions. The visual data will create connections between ideas, problems and solutions to those said issues.

A mind map is similar to what you might see when planning a book or other piece of school work. The task entails looking at many major points you want to utilize alongside details on what you feel is suitable for your use. You can produce a map based on things like processes, tools you will use, uses for anything and what you will define in the Six Sigma process. You can plan as many details in your map as possible. Everything should be organized accordingly while being simple enough for use.

Reverse/Anti-Solution Brainstorming

While brainstorming is normally about finding solutions, reverse or anti-solution brainstorming goes the other way around. In this case, you are coming up with ways to create problems. You will look at how the results of a Six Sigma review have come about and find ways to make those results more problematic or hard to follow. For instance, you might produce a reverse point where a manufacturing company's processes become less efficient. After coming up with that problem, you will figure out a way to resolve the issue.

The practice is useful for identifying cases where specific ideas might work. You might find that certain ideas are easy to follow when preventing future problems. In other cases, the new ideas you have come across could be easier to follow and use. You can work with as much data as you wish. The goal is to ensure the content is not hard to follow or utilize. Be careful with this when planning a solution that fits your use needs.

Nominal Group Brainstorming

A nominal group brainstorming method involves bringing people together to come up with useful solutions based on the Six Sigma findings in the measure and analysis processes. But while a traditional brainstorming session involves people who work together sharing unique ideas, a nominal group process involves others who are not familiar with one another getting together to find answers for certain problems. The people in a nominal brainstorming group will not engage in as much interaction with one another as they would elsewhere. The people will narrow down ideas and create a list of priorities for their brainstorming efforts.

Each person in the nominal group effort will share ideas on how well a process is to be run. These people will talk about their ideas based on factors like what they feel is appropriate for work and how content may be handled. Each person has an input to share with the intention of ranking the overall result being produced. Everyone can participate in the discussion and share the solutions they want to use based on priority. Since the people in the nominal group are not too familiar with each other, it becomes easier for a practice to be handled right while giving an idea of what can be done in a situation.

Brain-Netting

The interesting thing about brain-netting is that it is a practice that focuses heavily on gathering ideas online. Sometimes it's called online brainstorming. Think of brain-netting as though you are placing a large net out and are working to gather as many ideas from people around that net as possible. The best part is that the practice can be done anonymously if desired.

Brain-netting works by using a private system where you share ideas privately and then collaborate with others publicly. You can use a program from Slack or Google Docs among other sources if desired. You will present a solution to other professionals online. Those people can then anonymously provide ideas for what you can do to reach your benchmarks. In some cases, you might talk with someone in person by reaching out to someone who came up with a particular idea.

Role-Playing

Role-playing is a process for brainstorming that entails looking at various unique situations. The process works through various methods, but the goal is to think about what might happen in a simulated situation. You could create a new problem or look at a focus that might arise following your Six Sigma analysis and measurement. You can then review what you will do based on the subject matter or content you are working with. There are a few forms of role- playing that may be utilized:

1. Role Storming

Role storming is a practice where you look at the roles that one person in the Six Sigma process may follow. Think of this as a process where you are putting yourself in the shoes of someone else. You will act out a scene where someone is in a situation that has to be resolved. Review why that person is unhappy with a situation. Look at what can be done to make that person happy once again.

    2.   Reverse Thinking

Reverse thinking is where you ask what someone might do in a situation. You then look at the different things someone could do that might be different from the usual. What would someone do that is different from the usual approach? Ask what someone could do and how those ideas might change after a while. You can ask someone for help with getting an idea ready.

    3.   Figure Storming

This approach focuses more on historic examples. You can talk about things like what someone has done in the past versus the results of what that someone did. You can review this content based on what someone has been doing and whether those efforts have been working as well as hoped. Review the philosophies of other people to see whether or not their beliefs will work well in your situation.

Analogy Technique

You can produce analogies during the brainstorming process to help people understand what they should be doing with their ideas. The analogy technique works by producing a series of concepts or ideas based on certain analogies you come up with. An analogy can be planned out in many ways, including comparing a procedure with something from a different industry. You can produce an analogy in any way you see fit, including a style that is attractive and appropriate for use. You have to make sure the analogy you produce is simple and easy to follow so you won't struggle with producing an answer.

For instance, a fruit cannery might look at how it is producing suitably filled cans of fruit. An analogy can be made stating that the business is looking to fill as many bathtubs as possible with warm water. The key is to get those tubs filled so a person has enough water to relax in. The cannery will have to look at how it is filling its cans with enough fruit and water to ensure they meet mass standards. In particular, enough water has to be added to each can to ensure the fruits are preserved and that they are a texture customers can enjoy. This is a simple type of analogy to follow, although you have to look at how reasonable or sensible the analogy might be based on what you plan on working with in any situation.

Channeling

Another technique for brainstorming entails channeling. You will look at the results of your Six Sigma review and then produce a series of categories dedicated to specific ideas you want to utilize. These categories can be produced in any way you see fit. You can plan different ideas based on what you feel is appropriate for your plans. The fruit cannery can prepare categories for ideas like how to manage employee interaction in the manufacturing process, how to review machines and what to do with harvesting the foods that will be prepared. The team can review these segments and eventually produce ideas for each one. When people have finished producing enough ideas in one segment, they can move to the next segment or channel.

The cannery employees might look at ideas for how to improve upon their machines' functionality. The employees will then move forward to the next channel, a review of how the employees themselves are acting and what they can do to improve upon how the business works. The employees have to not only come up with plenty of ideas, but also figure out those ideas based on the channels they want to work with. Coming up with as many ideas in each channel as possible produces a thorough approach to finding ideas for the brainstorming effort.

Prioritizing the Ideas You Come Across

You can organize the ideas produced in the brainstorming session as you see fit. You can produce a task based on factors like what ideas were most popular among the people you brainstormed with. You can prioritize those ideas to get a clear idea of where you are going with your task.

Multi-voting is a practice that may help in this case. This is called N/3 voting in that you take the number of ideas, or N, in your setup and divide them by three. You can use this to figure out the total number of ideas in the brainstorming segment that should work. The key is that by using a third of the ideas, it may be easier for a task to work. You will have to get many people in the group to vote on which ideas should be incorporated into the final project.

Chapter 28 – Identifying and Managing the X and Y

Before you get into your DMAIC routine, you have to look at the two key points that will be measured and utilized throughout the lifespan of your Six Sigma effort. The story of your Six Sigma plan should be told through the X and Y that you use on your plot. While the X is the time frame or other duration for the process, the Y is whatever it is you plan on measuring in the setup. But to make the task work out right, you have to recognize what you will do when analyzing the X and Y. The best way to review the Six Sigma routine is to look at this equation:

$$Y = f(x)$$

In this equation, Y is the main point that is being measured. Y is interpreted as a function, or f, of X. The outcomes listed on the Y axis are determined based on the drivers produced by the X axis. You will look at the processes illustrated on the X axis and then figure out what influences the changes in the Y axis to develop. As those changes move along, it becomes easier for you to go forward with the process. You can get carefully orchestrated measures based on what you feel is correct.

To understand this a little more, let's think about a basic chart. You might have seen a time-based chart that illustrates a line moving from left to right, like a typical stock report. The X-axis is the time frame for trading while the Y-axis is a reference to how high or low the value of a stock or index is. The Y-axis is what is being measured in the long run, and the X-axis is the measure at which something is being analyzed. In the stock example, you measure the value of the stock from one point in the day or month to the end of that day or month.

This chapter focuses on how the five parts of the DMAIC will work with the X and Y variables that have been introduced. You can use these points to determine how you can best prepare your Six Sigma routine. You will start with developing the Y variable. After that, the X variable will come into play. Knowing how to organize the data will be vital to your success.

1. Define

To start, you must correctly define the process that you will be starting. The Y should be defined above all else. In short, it is the thing that will be measured throughout your effort based on what has been most valuable and useful. You can also use this definition to figure out the benchmarks that you want to use on the Y axis and how low you are willing to go. Part of this can entail the development of sensible limits and rules.

The Y is produced as you state the problem in the business or the process. You must explain something that can be measured. A SIPOC diagram can be used alongside the VOC readout to figure out what is needed for making the definition work to your liking. You will notice the requirements of the customers and the plans that you need to orchestrate for the Six Sigma effort to move forward.

You may still come across several choices for what will go onto the Y axis. You can use the VOC and other voices in the design process to figure out what the specific point for the Y axis will be. You can produce anything very distinct at this point, although you have the option to use something that is a little broader in its reach if you prefer. Eventually, the Y axis should have a measure that is defined and easy to follow. More importantly, the content should be attainable and realistic.

2. Measure

The X axis is introduced in the second part of the Six Sigma effort. The X axis entails the thing that you are measuring the Y axis with over time. You can use this based on factors like how much time has elapsed in a task, how much money is being spent, the number of customers taking in items, how many products are manufactured and so forth. The X axis will move progressively from one point to the next and the Y axis can change in value depending on the things that occur within that point. But you must look carefully at the specific X axis that you will use.

You can look at possible cause and effect relationships when figuring out what X variable should be used versus the Y. The cause and effect should be as realistic as possible while maintaining an appropriate measure or range for your review. You can use a research process or use any of the voices for studying the work to see what cause and effect links are best for you to work with. More importantly, you can use this to figure out patterns based on events, time periods and anything else that shows up on the X line.

3. Analyze

You can use any kind of graphic tool for the analysis point. Whether it entails a pie chart, a line chart, a frequency plot or anything else you want to use, the graphic tool should be reflective of the X and Y variables you are introducing. But you must also look at how you are going to manage the content at this juncture. You have to ensure that the data you are working with is either discrete or continuous. For discrete data, ensure that content is coming about at one point without much repetition. For continuous data, ensure that work is consistently moving with no real stoppages when that content will be made available.

You can choose a certain measurement for analyzing the X and Y variables depending on whether the content in question is either continuous or discrete in nature. The proper measurement standard works in cases where the content being handled is consistent.

Here are some standards to consider:

1. When the data entails a singular discrete event, a bar chart or pie chart can be utilized to measure both factors.

2. A frequency plot works best when the Y variable is continuous but the X measure is specific or discrete.

3. A probability curve can be incorporated for when the Y variable is discrete but the X point is continuous.

4. A scatterplot helps for when the data is continuous on both axes.

Using these points in your measurement for the DMAIC process is vital for confirming cause and effect. You can use this information in the Six Sigma task to get an accurate idea of what to expect out of the content being managed. Best of all, it should be easier for the content to be measured properly and with enough of an idea of what to expect. Review each plot to see what fits in well, but also look at the nature of each measure you are working with. This is to give you a clearer idea of what to expect out of your work.

4. Improve

Take a look at the X points. Whether they entail specific events, inputs, times or other measures, you can use those points to find connections that help you determine how to organize your work. That can then help you to improve upon how the Y variable is working in your routine. But the analysis should look particularly at how the Y will improve and how certain X points are analyzed and measured based on your particular requirements.

A failure-mode effect analysis may be used at this juncture to identify how the Y variable is moving along. This will be discussed in another chapter later in this guide. But the general measurement here is to see what can happen that might cause the Y to fail plus the causes that are influencing the issue. Your goal is to keep such failures under control. More importantly, you have to know how to resolve issues and questions before they worsen.

5. Control

The control stage requires you to monitor the Y axis all the way through while also still watching for any highly important parts in the X line that make a difference. Identify X points that are changing the work more than anything else, while monitoring the Y based on how the program moves. Notice the connections between X and Y throughout the work while using what you have learned throughout the process to see what can be done to fix the issues that may develop.

Figuring Out the Qualitative and Quantitative Data

As you work with the X and Y variables, you will analyze how to get qualitative and quantitative data to work for you. This is an aspect of the X and Y variables that can be used throughout your Six Sigma task, although it is particularly vital for the general measurement process.

Qualitative

First, you should review the qualitative data that you will utilize. The qualitative data refers to subjective data that cannot be measured with numbers. For instance, you might notice a call center's functions being managed well. The call center might have people who are courteous, friendly and prompt in answering their calls. This is an example of a qualitative review that does not measure specific things, but rather assesses key workplace elements.

There are three kinds of qualitative data that you can use.

1. Nominal

Nominal data involves variables that are not measured with a ranking order in mind. Gender, race and other demographic factors may be incorporated. In most cases, you will only use a few choices in this setup. Think of nominal data as something you might find in a report that can identify some of the people you will come across. The details can be used mainly to identify different elements you want to utilize.

2. Ordinal

An ordinal set of data entails a list of variables that can be arranged in order based on how they relate to one another. As an example, consider a medical report that shows specific blood types of people in a hospital or other area. You might also see some reports that discuss how well a person performs a task based on how often he or she is working and the kinds of effort that person is putting in.

3. Binary

Binary data involves two options. True/false, yes/no, wrong/right and other related types of questions are binary. These questions relate to very limited data, but they can help you with analyzing opinions or certain events that are limited in nature. You can gather a certain number of responses over time, but you have to watch for what you will get out of this so you know what to expect out of the work in question. Some binary solutions may also come with three answers, although that is uncommon. In such cases, you will need to work with only those three specific answers without any outside data getting in the way.

Your qualitative data can be as thorough as necessary. You can use the qualitative information based on what you are finding that works for a task and how effective your routine is. For instance, a project that entails a review of how well something works after an adjustment will require an ordinal analysis. However, if you have variables that have extremely specific or strict answers, a binary option is better.

Quantitative

Quantitative data is a form of data that involves content that can be easily analyzed and attributed. This involves something that you can directly measure. The content is objective and therefore makes it easier for you to make precise decisions. You can use this kind of data to figure out whatever might be running right within your workplace or to make the data you are using easier to follow.

1. Discrete

Discrete data was mentioned earlier, but it should be discussed in further detail. This is a form of data that can be attributed to a very specific event or occasion. The data can be categorized and placed into one particular field. A count may be used to figure out the discrete data you want to use. The data should be finite and capable of being measured once again for added clarification.

For instance, you might look at a call center's actions based on how many people are being served. You might create a discrete measurement of how many people were served within a certain day. You can also measure how many times people were served within that period and then use that measure to assess how well organized the call center is. The discrete measurement lets you see what is happening at a specific time and how well things are being managed.

2. Continuous

Sometimes you will have to measure consistent, continuous data. This involves measurements based on the very specific types of actions you wish to take when determining the content you want to work with. Continuous data can be measured through a scale. You might measure a shipment based on its size, weight or volume. The measurement can be divided into the smallest increments you require.

A warehouse might measure its shipments based on volume or weight. You might use a continuous measurement that focuses on a certain shipment. This will be used as a standard that you want to attain for Six Sigma measurements. You can also measure a total down to the ounce or gram if you wish. But the goal is to create a continuous measurement that can be identified while also using a process that makes it easy for the data to be appropriately measured in some form.

Understanding the Difference Between the Two Choices

Discrete data is all about something that is happening right now and which might not change all that much. Meanwhile, the continuous process entails anything that will work permanently and which will therefore only have to be monitored on occasion. You can use the continuous review to identify anything you want to work with in your task. Depending on what you find in your work routine, this might lead to a few changes.

The data measurement process should be planned out during the DMAIC routine's measurement process. This is to give you an idea of what you will measure and analyze throughout your Six Sigma process. You can use the measurement to get a better idea of what is working within your business and what can be changed over time.

How Many Variables at Once?

The good news about working with a plan for identifying X and Y variables is that you can work with as many of them as you wish. You can use a multi-vari chart if needed to identify many X and Y variables at a time. This can help you with identifying variation based on the things you are working with.

But you must only produce a review based on the number of variables that you feel will be appropriate for your use. The variables should be planned based on what is more important for your task.

It is typically best to stick with many X variables if you have a line chart or bar chart among other things that may be easy to measure. You can use different Y variables, but that requires a more complicated review. You will place one Y variable on the left end of the chart, plus a second Y variable on the right side. The added variables allow you to organize the data and distinguish the points. This works best if you keep the variables distinct from one another and use different colors that help people to tell measurements apart.

Chapter 29 – Variations in the Measurement System

The way you measure content in your Six Sigma process is important for the success of your plan. But to make the most out of this and to gauge what is acceptable, you have to look at the variation that will come about. Variation entails the leeway that you will utilize when handling particular measurements.

As you work with your tasks, you need to establish a sense of variation. This can entail anything within an acceptable range so long as you keep your measurements within that total. You can use this with any layout or plan for information that you see fit.

Your goal for variation is to attain a state of central tendency. The central tendency refers to the ability to get your results in a single space. For instance, you might throw darts at a board. Your goal will be to hit that bullseye. Central tendency entails getting as many shots on the bullseye or as close to it as possible. You need to attain that central tendency in your Six Sigma process to ensure you maintain precision and consistency in your work.

What Type of Analysis?

As you work with your data, you can utilize one of two types of analytical points:

1. Measurement System Analysis (MSA)

The MSA is a measure for variation based on how often things can be repeated and reproduced. A study such as this can be done based on many factors you explore within your work, including a tolerance percentage and a percentage for contribution. These totals are based off a number of categories that you may plan within your work. The MSA may work based on how often measurements vary, although you have the option to use this to identify whether the data you are working with is precise or accurate.

2. Discrete Data Analysis (DDA)

The DDA is all about accuracy. You can use the DDA to post details on how accurate readouts are, how often those results repeat and whether they can feasibly be reproduced. You can use this to see how the variation of results change based on outliers, how long you get the same results and whether or not those results are easy to work with. The data you produce can be as thorough or simple as necessary.

The MSA may work for helping you to identify how measurements are working so that you can manage your data the right way. But the DDA may also be used for cases where you need as little of a spread as possible while aiming towards that central tendency you want to use. You can use either option to your preference based on the resources you have on hand and the particular you are trying to complete.

Variation Based on Actual Processes Versus a Measurement System

You may review the variation of your Six Sigma routine based on the changes that come from the process itself. You must look at both the factors you can and cannot control. You might find that the data you are trying to work with is easier to control based on certain parameters within the work environment. But there may also be seasonal changes, outside economic factors and underlying laws that your business cannot control. Each of these factors should be considered equally as you aim to produce results.

Variations from your measurement system may also be put into play. Such changes may include variations from an appraiser who analyzes how what you doing when measuring your output. You may also use a gauge of individual actions. Accuracy, stability, repeatability and reproducibility should all be examined.

You have the choice to work with any of these variations, but it is best for you to obtain a variation from the process itself. Although a variation from a measurement system might seem effective, every appraiser treats the situation differently, thus resulting in possible changes in whatever may be handled. The instrument or standard for measurement may vary as well, thus resulting in some substantial changes in whatever you have planned. Working with the process itself and identifying factors inside and outside of the workplace may be the best choice for when you're aiming to review what is happening in your environment.

You may be at risk of errors in your measurement system. These errors may arise due to factors such as:

1. Accuracy. There is a difference between the values you observe versus the standards you are trying to maintain.

2. Repeatability. There may be changes based on who measures the items in question.

3. Reproducibility. Multiple people may work with the same unit many times over with an identical measuring tool. However, not all people will measure things in the same way.

4. Stability. The measuring tools utilized can be mishandled by some.

5. Linearity. All ranges of measurements can vary by intensity among other qualities.

Observed Variation

The observed variation in your setup is an analysis based on the actual variation in your field versus the variation in your measurement. As you work on your task, you may come across a greater variation based on what you have found in measurements. The actual results may vary and therefore could influence the measuring process. Therefore, the observed variation may be a little looser in value than the actual variation. The bell curve might be wider for the observed variation, although you can still keep the upper and lower levels the same based on what you find appropriate for your task.

Aim to utilize some standards when reviewing your observed variation. See that everything is at least 90 percent accurate of your planned readout and that the work can be repeated at least 90 percent of the time. Your goal should be to mitigate the risk of significant problems ever arising. You can also use accuracy standards to get a closer idea of whether or not something you are working with can be supported or if there are other issues that might persist.

The observed variation may be as widespread or narrow as it has to be. You can use the variation to look at many outside factors, not to mention any changes in the operators. You can also look at individual points that may have contributed to your variation changes. Anything that might make an impact on your work is always important to assess. You can use the review to figure out if you need to change anything during the measurement process, thus helping you make the analytical aspect of your work a little easier.

The Concept of Conformance

Conformance is an aspect of quality that cannot be ignored. The best way to describe conformance is with an archery bullseye. You want to ensure that every shot you make hits that central spot. That middle space is the standard that you want to attain; conformance is all about actually getting into that middle spot.

The bullseye comparison gives the impression that variance may be minimal. To get your Six Sigma routine to work within certain parameters, you have to attain the smallest possible variance range. Having the narrowest possible bell curve is always best as that ensures you are managing your work appropriately. Conformance is all about gearing your work towards the central tendency that you are trying to attain.

Regardless of the results you encounter, you need to look at how well organized, consistent and useful your measurements are. Having an idea of what measurements you wish to work with and how they will be organized can help you with growing your

Six Sigma plan while planning out your work. This is to give yourself a better idea of what you will do for your marketing needs.

Don't Forget Capability

The capability of a task focuses on how a process handles the work you are putting in. While control focuses on how well something can work for a while, capability works differently. You have to keep things capable to see that there are no problems with the work in the process and that things are working well within the limitations of the machines or people you are relying upon. Everything involved must be able to work within the standards you wish to incorporate.

Capability can be a measure of anything relating to how well a task is being run versus what makes that routine useful. You can figure out the capability of a process to determine how well a task is being run and whether or not everything is moving smoothly. You might also have some restrictions as to how well you can manage a task. These include restrictions concerning how much content you are trying to handle. Every measurement and plan you put in place must be arranged according to what you feel is appropriate for the task and how you intend to forward with that work.

Chapter 30 – The Sampling Process

Sampling is a critical aspect of the Six Sigma process that cannot be ignored. Sampling makes it easier for a business to gather information on what is happening in the workplace. The general concept is that a small number of items in one grouping are studied to ensure that the work routine in question is functioning smoothly.

For instance, you might have 100 repetitions of a process in the workplace. You can gather a sampling of about 15 to 20 of those repetitions to measure and assess how the process is operating. While this is not as comprehensive as going through each repetition, the process still gives you extra help with identifying many things happening in your working environment.

Sampling is especially important in cases where you only have a certain number of resources to work with due to limitations on what is happening in your market or what your business can handle at a given moment. Maybe you have time constraints and need to get a few items in a grouping right now. You may also have financial concerns regarding what you can and cannot afford. Don't forget about times when it might not be as easy for you to capture an entire population as you might think.

The most important part of the sampling process is that whatever you are testing has to be something that can be repeated many times over. A manufacturing process can be measured many times because the same process or routine is used in every instance. But when every process is unique and works with several parameters or things that might quickly change, you have to watch for what you are getting yourself into. Planning your work in the sampling effort is vital to helping you see how well your business can work and what you might expect to get out of it in the general process.

But, while gathering the processes or persons you wish to analyze can be a useful endeavor, you also have to be aware of how a process works in any situation. Biases can arise when you are choosing the right sample size for your work. This chapter will help you recognize such instances so you have more control over a sampling effort. But before this, you have to look at your plans for what you will be sampling and how you expect to move forward in your efforts to produce the most distinct and thorough samples that you can work with in your project or task. Having a better idea of what to expect in such a situation will go a long way towards giving you the help you require.

Probability Sampling

The first type of sampling option is probability sampling. There are four types of probability sampling standards that can be utilized. Each option focuses on gathering segments of a population in different ways:

1. Simple Random Sampling

Start your work with a simple random sampling process. Give every item in the population an equal opportunity to be chosen. You might have to use a computer program or a random number draw. Either way, for the best results, all items you choose should be anonymous. This is to prevent any possible biases.

The concern with this option is that it is often difficult to figure out what you might pick. You might be random, but you could also produce something that is far too consistent. The data might be the same all around. The key is to ensure the task is managed with as much of a random process as possible. This process may also work well if you have a larger population or are going to take in a significant number of items at a time. A larger sample size might be easier to manage depending on what you are planning.

2. Stratified Random Sampling

Take the population and divide it up into a few groups. Select an equal number of items in each of these groups. For instance, you might divide a population of 200 items into four groups of 50 and then select 10 items from each of those four parts. The process will be random after you divide up those groups. But you will have to decide the particular groups that you are going to work with. You should make each of the four groups as different as possible to produce a more dynamic approach to sampling while also determining which of the four groups in question will be the best all-around performer you can choose.

The best part of the process is that it can work with many segments and can give you data that is more representative of your task. You can use this if you know of certain items that are distinguished by certain variables or concepts. This helps keep data simple to read and largely unbiased.

3. Systematic Sampling

Another option is systematic sampling. This works as you gather items and pick certain items based on numerical order. You might pick every third, fourth or fifth entry among other things. Let's say you have 200 items in your sample's population. You could pick every seventh item, thus leading to numbers 7, 14, 21, 28, 35 and so forth being chosen. You can use this to get several items in your sample size while still maintaining a sufficiently a random layout. This works best when you have something that is random enough and is not too hard to choose.

4. Cluster Sampling

Cluster sampling is a valuable part of sampling that focuses on items being sampled after every couple of events. For instance, you might see in a factory that a machine handles specific processes throughout the day. In the cluster sampling process, you might include events that take place at the top and bottom parts of the hour. You can use this to get an idea of how a process works throughout the day and to analyze whether or not the quality of that process changes.

The cluster can be a challenge to handle. There is a chance that the sampling might produce some skewed results because of certain items working within the same demographic or point. Even so, you can use the cluster sampling process to identify any problems in your work and determine whether you need to fix things before they become harder to manage. In general, cluster sampling is simple and easy to carry out.

These sampling choices are based mainly on what you might find to be useful while also producing a sense of fairness in the sampling effort. You have the option to add a few extra parameters into the sampling fold if desired. But the options you consider in any case have to be planned such that you have an idea of where you want to go with your work. The samples should be arranged evenly and with enough control based on what might be useful within the task.

Non-Probability Sampling

Another choice for your sampling needs entails non-probability sampling. This is a practice where you gather information on purpose. You use several parameters to figure out what you will use. Whereas the stratified random sampling process entails a combination of random and specific, the non-probability sampling process focuses on an extremely specific point without being so random. There are four other things that can be utilized when getting the non-probability sampling process to work for you.

1. Convenience Sampling

As the name suggests, convenience sampling is about finding the right items that you can get immediate access to. You can use convenience sampling to find something that works for your study as soon as possible. You will intentionally choose something based on what you know works for the test even if the standards or parameters for that item are different from what you expect. The general goal is to just immediately get the things you need, so this technique might be best suited for when you have no other options.

2. Judgment Sampling

Judgment sampling works in cases where you feel that certain items are going to fit the characteristics of whatever you are interested in managing. You should look at your beliefs and then make a choice based on what you feel is appropriate or useful for your needs. The judgment you use can be as specific or broad as you want it to be; that is all up to you.

3. Quota Sampling

You might need to produce a representation of enough parameters in your study. For instance, you may have four different machines in the workplace that all do the same thing. You might want to get as many samples from each of those four machines as possible so you can get a clear idea of how everything in the workplace is running. Quota sampling helps you to get a proper sense of representation in your studies. With this, you will gather a certain number of items within your working environment, ensuring that those items are representative of each parameter you want to use.

4. Snowball Sampling

Snowball sampling occurs when you respond to the referrals that others have for certain items or concepts. You will get referrals for other items that feature very specific types of characteristics or qualities, thus giving you extra help with obtaining items that are somewhat related to one another. You should ensure that all the items you want to use are alike and carefully calibrated to your liking.

Figure Out the Size of Your Sample

You have the option of making a sample as large as you want it to be. However, it is best to keep that total within limits based on what is practical and what you know you can afford. You can also utilize an equation to help you figure out how large your sample will be. Part of this includes a look at the deviation of whatever you can handle in your work. Remember that having too small of a sample size can be inefficient, while having too large of one might cost you more money to implement, thus impacting your budget.

1. Measuring Continuous Data

Your first option is to look at how the sample you use for measuring continuous data works. You can produce a sample of the right size by using the following equation:

$(1.96\sigma / \bar{X})^2$

In this equation, σ is a measure of the standard deviation in your population. $\bar{X}$ is the amount of uncertainty that you will accept. The uncertainty should be listed in a percentage total.

Use this equation to determine how well the sample will work based on the types of people or processes in your sample population alongside the margin of error you want to work with. You will get more items when the uncertainty increases, what with you showing that you can accept more items. But when the total declines, you will have to work with fewer items in the sample. You have the option to change this point around as much as you wish.

2. Measuring Discrete Data

Your other choice for handling what you are working with is to look at the discrete data that will enter into the process. Discrete data can be as specific and for a certain time period as you want it to be. The equation that you can use here is:

$(1.96 / \bar{X})^2 \times P(1-P)$

In this case, you eliminate the standard deviation. The P used here is the proportion of defective items in the population that you estimate may arise. You can use any proportion that you wish and round it as needed, so long as you are realistic.

Avoiding Sampling Bias

One reason why it is so important to gather anonymous content, if possible, is so you can avoid the risk of sampling bias. This is a concern where you are influenced by personal beliefs or thoughts when gathering items from a sample population. You might think that you should stick with certain items within a population. Knowing how sampling bias can occur will help you to figure out what you should do to avoid the possibility of this happening.

1. Convenience Selection Bias

The most common form of bias entails what happens when you gather the items in your sample that are the easiest to gather. These include items that are more accessible. This can be useful for when you need to get as much data as possible, although that does not mean that the process will be as useful as you hope. The bias produced here suggests that you might be taking in more content than what is necessary for the task. Then again, you might have no way to avoid this type of bias due to concerns about how the bias works and what you might expect to get out of something of value.

You can avoid this bias by allowing for a more wide-open time period during which you gather items from the population. The effort you put in works best when you have a better idea of how well the content you are gathering is organized and know what to expect out of your work at large.

2. Systematic Selection Bias

In some cases, your selections will all be based off a specific platform. A certain structure will be laid out in this bias. You might stick with specific parameters that relate to whatever you are interested in. The bias that arises can be frustrating at times, but it is through that bias that you might experience some sizeable changes over time.

The use of a computer program or random number-generating machine may be recommended in this case to help you arbitrarily select items when preparing your sample.

3. Environmental Bias

An environmental bias will develop when you have particular environmental conditions that arise. These conditions may change from when the sample is drawn to when that sample is used. Such environmental details may include things like the economy changing, the number of resources you have to work with changing and even literal weather changes. Whatever the case may be, some of these bias points should be carefully examined to give you an idea of what changes might come about.

4. Non-Response Bias

This fourth bias occurs in cases where you are working with other people. This is something that the people in the sample population will generate and not you. A non-response bias occurs when you only have a certain number of people, such as from a certain demographic, who respond to a process. Other people may not respond because they are simply not interested. There is no real way how you can avoid this particular bias.

Acceptance Sampling

The acceptance sampling process occurs when you are trying to sample things but have limitations over what you can handle in your work. The acceptance effort is for when the testing process might be risky and could hurt efforts in your workplace. It works when the cost to inspect something is too high. An acceptance sample is also suitable when a full inspection process takes too long.

The best way to think about the acceptance sampling process is that it involves a sniper-like setup that focuses on extremely particular processes or actions in the workplace. You can use this if you want to target specific items in your efforts. This includes when you want to concentrate on minimal concepts within your work while not going too far in the effort. This might also work for when you have materials for testing that are too dangerous to handle on their own and which have to be controlled before any problems develop.

Essential Questions to Ask in the Sampling Process

Sampling can be a challenge to handle if you don't ask the right questions. The following are useful questions to consider when planning a sampling process:

1. Who will collect the data?

Look at who is going to gather the data for your sample. That person should have enough time to collect a sample while also knowing what parameters are involved. That someone needs to have the appropriate resources on hand. Any definitions of the data and content being handled should be noted as well. The definitions should be planned based on whoever is collecting the data and how that content is to be managed. You can use as many people to collect your data as necessary, but those people should be selected based on what they can do for you.

2. What will be measured?

You must have an idea of what you're going to measure. The process should include a look at how you're measuring something based on its important characteristics or qualities. The most important thing is to measure only things that are relevant to the task, thus keeping you from wasting time and money. A definition can also help with identifying specific populations that you might plan on working with. You can use as much data in the measuring process as needed provided the work in question is properly organized.

3. Where are you going to get the sample from?

The sample can come from one of many locations. You can prepare the sample from many points in a process. You should determine how well the process is run and ensure that you can get a stable analysis of what is in the sample when working. This is to help you get the task working to your liking and without any risk. The way the process has evolved at large should also be noted so you can get a better idea of where you are going in the process and how your work is to be managed.

4. When are you going to gather the sample?

A sample should be planned at the right time. That time can include any point involving the process based on how smoothly it is running and how much time you are putting into your work.

A good idea is to plan your samples in between shifts. For instance, you might have two shifts at your workplace dedicated to manufacturing a product or service. You can use a sample size based on the first shift and then a new sample size based off the second shift. This can then help you to determine whether people in different shifts are following the same processes.

5. Why are you taking the sample?

Every sampling process has a rationale. What might make the sample work for you? Look at why you're planning your sample, whether it entails designing a process or finding a way to control particular work. You can use any kind of question in the process, but ensure it is geared toward specifying why you are spending time collecting a sample and how that will ultimately move your task forward.

6. How are you going to collect your data?

You can collect your data in any way you see fit. You can produce a survey, analyze data from a manufacturing process or review what customers are saying about your products or services. An automated source may also help you in the process of gathering data. Look at how you're going to gather your data based on what is appropriate for your work and what you are finding to be most useful in the research process. Anything that provides a simple approach for gathering data is always a good possibility.

7. How many samples are to be gathered?

Look at the number of samples you will utilize in your work. A task with more samples might be easier to analyze and review. You need enough samples to give yourself an accurate readout of what might be working in a routine. The overall measurement you plan on using should be assessed based on what you feel is both consistent and right. Also, any cases where you're going to work with several samples should be carefully planned to keep yourself from running into inconsistency errors and other common problems.

You can always categorize samples as you wish. Such categories might entail specific points relating to certain things of value in a task or routine. You can prepare any kind of sample so long as you recognize where you are going with your work and how many types of entities are going to be reviewed.

Your ability to gather the right type of sample in your work effort is important to your success. Look at where a sample is coming from and ensure that you know where the content or concept is moving toward. You can use a full analysis of the process at hand to figure out how your work is proceeding. No matter what you hope to get out of it, ensure that your sample is easy to follow and understand.

Chapter 31 – A General Measurement System

As important as it can be for you to collect data in the Six Sigma process, it is even more important for you to ensure that the data you are gathering is prepared and gathered consistently. You can use measurements to help you see how that data is coming along. The measurements have to be planned through a system that identifies how well your work is being managed. Anything you can do to get your work organized right and ready for use is critical to your success.

The MSA

The main measurement standard that you can use for your Six Sigma work is the Measurement System Analysis or MSA, which was briefly discussed earlier. Your use of the MSA helps you to experiment with different parameters in your workplace.

As noted earlier, MSA works for both continuous and discrete data. For continuous sets of data, you need to look at the repeatability of your work and the reproducibility involved. You can also analyze the tolerance that your sample has for certain results or events. A contribution percentage may also be analyzed to see how well the content works. You can produce as many distinct categories for your measurement needs as necessary. The goal in any situation is to produce a result that is efficient and gives you the best results possible.

You can also use a Discrete Data Analysis (DDA) or if you prefer. This is for discrete data and focuses mainly on the accuracy of a review, how well you can repeat data and your ability to reproduce the content you wish to handle. These points should be carefully analyzed to see how consistent or useful your measurements might be. But the DDA is only for cases where you have very specific information to work with and are trying to get a more accurate or useful result.

Five Measurements in the Process

The MSA or DDA helps you to review how well you are preparing a study. You can use the MSA or DDA to figure out if you are doing well with your measurement efforts or if you need to change things around. There are a few important measurements that have to be explored in the process to make the system work right.

1. Bias

You have to watch for biases that can cause you to get inaccurate results in a task. The bias may arise because you are working with the wrong ideas for how data is gathered and used. You might prepare an unfair assessment of various tasks when you are working with a certain bias. It's important to minimize biases as much as possible so as to lessen their impact on your work.

2. Linearity

A trend will always arise in your work. The linearity of the work you put in can relate to how detailed the content you are managing is and whether there is some sort of relationship between the two. A change in one process might result in changes in your measurements. You can get the analysis to work with as many changes in the variables as you wish. But the goal is to produce an end result that you can identify and measure to your liking while getting an appropriate answer every time.

3. Stability

The answers that you get in the process have to be stable. Stability refers to how consistent your measurements are. When something is stable, you will get the same results every time. This is appropriate if you are trying to plan out specific processes where things have to always proceed a certain way for it all to work right.

4. Repeatability

Repeatability refers to how well you can complete the same kind of measurement many times over. You have to be capable of repeating the same things many times over for the best results. You can also measure the same processes to see if identical results are being derived.

5. Reproducibility

It is one thing for you to repeat the testing process. It is another for you to reproduce the same results. Look at how well the results vary based on how many times you complete the same testing process. You need to use a good standard for managing the process so you know what to expect out of the test results and ensure that you are putting in the right effort for making it all work. Anything that can be planned out the same way every time is always something worth noting as it helps with a task's overall organization.

Three Key Terms

There are three terms must be utilized when planning your measurement system for Six Sigma. These are points that may be analyzed in the MSA routine to help you see what might be changing at any given time:

1. Accuracy

You need to produce results that are accurate, although it might not always be easy to do this. Accuracy is a measure of the difference between the true average and the observed average. The true average can be calculated based on the original measurements that you had planned based on the different items you are measuring. You can plan those measurements to be as specific as you need.

Watch for how the true and observed averages change in value depending on what you are working with. The average value should be as close to the true average as possible. A system where the observed average is too far off from the true average is a sign of inaccuracy and an indication that you need to fix the error in your system.

2. Stability

Stability is a measure of how well two sets of measurements remain the same in value over time. This includes reviewing one procedure, person, machine or other item you are measuring and seeing how well that single point changes. Your goal is to see that the same result occurs every time or that you are close to that total. Any cases where there is a radical difference should be examined.

3. Discrimination

Discrimination refers to the smallest possible increment between two values measured. This is different from other measures in that you are focusing on something that might change over time. When discrimination arises, the total changes in value, but there is a possibility that there is a smaller total. You might have to measure two items together many times over to see how much of a discrimination occurs between the two.

Errors in Measurements

There are times when you might come across a margin of error in a measurement. The margin of error is a measure of how far off your official readout or analysis might be. The error should be measured based on the difference between the measured value and the true value of whatever you are assessing. The measurement error will vary based on the type of instrument being used and the person who is using that instrument..

But how much of an error in your measurement is acceptable? A good rule of thumb is to allow for an error in your measurement of under 10 percent. This is enough to give you a loose idea of what is working in your business without being far too inaccurate or unreliable. A 10 to 30 percent total suggests that there is some kind of error, although that might be based on a machine not working properly or an employee not following the right work standards.

Any margin of error that is greater than 30 percent in value should not be accepted. This is a sign that there is a sizeable problem with the measurement process. In such cases you'll need to use different instrumentation or a new process to take the necessary measurements. You'll also need to change the person who is completing the task.

As for discrete data, as discussed earlier, you should look for the accuracy, repeatability and reproducibility of your work to be at least 90 percent all the way through. Anything underneath that 90-percent threshold should be considered unacceptable. You can use these measurement totals to have an idea of how certain trends may influence your work.

You might have to complete the measurement process a few times over to confirm a sense of consistency in your results. This may also be done with some base examples to help you see what problems exist.

Accuracy vs. Precision

Two terms that you might come across that are relatively similar to one another are accuracy and precision. Accuracy refers to a measurement being around the center of the actual value of whatever you are measuring. Accuracy occurs when there is minimal deviation between a reported value and an actual value. Precision is more about the actual measurements only differing from one another minimally.

Your goal should be to be both accurate and precise. If you are precise but not accurate, there might be some error with the measurement process. If you are accurate but cannot remain precise, that means you need to analyze the process you are working with to see what changes might need to be made.

Variation

An important part of working with your measurement system is to look at the variation in your work. Variation occurs when you notice some sizeable changes in whatever it is you are working with. The variation can occur due to many factors, some of which are easy to manage and others which you cannot correct on your own.

A general measurement can be completed by taking the actual variation and adding it with the variation that you measured to get the observed variation that you have come across. The observed variation should include a much larger bell curve, but the measurement will work alongside the true process you are working with.

The lower specification limit (LSL) and upper specification limit (USL) can also be factors in your measurement. You want to get as close to the middle of those two as possible. The bell curve that you produce should guide you in figuring out where those limits are to be situated. The variations that you produce will fall in between those two points to give you an idea of what might work best for your purposes.

Causes of Variation

There are two causes of variation to note:

1. Common Causes

The common cause is also known as noise. This occurs in a stable environment. You may come across sudden changes in the workplace, like materials not being handled right or employees not following designated procedures. The good news about common cause is that the problem can often be easy to find. Once identified, proper changes and tests may be utilized to see if the noise is now being kept in check.

2. Special Causes

A special cause is also called a signal. There is no way you can predict when a special cause or signal will arise. There might be a lack of resources in the workplace or a disaster that occurs that keeps you from completing your regular work as normal. Anything involving a vendor, such as a strike, may be a concern of note.

While you might have some control over common causes, the same cannot be said for special causes. It's impossible for you to predict special causes. But you can reduce your risk and establish a contingency plan if the need ever arises during the course of your Six Sigma efforts.

Knowing what you will get out of your measurements is important when aiming to get the most out of any process. Be aware of how you are going to review your data and ensure that you have an understanding of how the content you are handling works. The general goal is to gather only the information necessary to make your task work to its best overall potential.

Chapter 32 – Key Factors for Data Interpretation

As you work with your data measurement process, you will come across many different data display features. You will find many types of data that show certain trends or commands. You will need to review the ways data might change as there are times when that changing data can make a sizeable difference in your work. Your business must look at how it can interpret data to help with understanding which direction your Six Sigma plans are moving.

The data interpretation process is vital for your success. You can use one of five interpretation patterns to help you recognize how your content is organized. Each of these patterns can be measured or identified through specific measuring tools. These should provide graphical displays of how well your content is handled so you can make the right decisions when making the most out of your Six Sigma routine.

Stability

Stability occurs when data remains largely consistent over time. There might be an extremely minimal amount of variation before and after a period of stability, but nothing that will affect your task.

A median line is utilized in a stability review. The median should be in a straight line and can be used as a bellwether view of the measurements you are trying to attain. You may notice certain stability trends.

Your period of stability can entail one of many measurements:

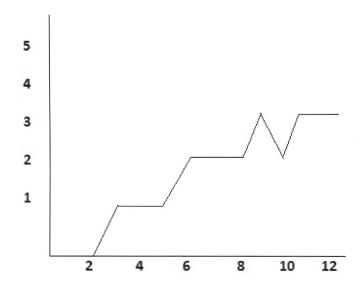

1. **Same value.** The listed value is the same within a trend and will not change. Any period can qualify, but any point with at least seven consecutive measurements should be analyzed well. A few shifts may be found here and there, but the chart may continue to run with the same value for as long as needed. Some charts, like the one above, include cases where two or three consecutive measures are of the same value, although this might only suggest a sense of stability before or after certain shifts arise.

2. **Clustering.** The data in a clustering pattern includes multiple data points that are bunched together on one side of a median. You may see about three to five consecutive points together. However, then you will get a bunch of points on the other end of the median. The same three to five points should appear on that end. You might also come across one point in between each cluster.

3. **Mixture.** A mixture develops when there are responses found on both sides of the median. In this case, at least ten points will go up and down in alternating order. There may be times when two consecutive points appear above or below the median line, and there the measurement should be analyzed well. In the chart listed above, the 80 may be used as a median. You will see that the value is close to that median, but there is no telling what side of the median the measurement will be listed on. You may also notice some resistance lines at the top or bottom of the mixture plot to see how intense some measurements might be.

4. **Oscillation.** With oscillation, the data points on your chart are moving on both sides of the median, but there is no distinct trend. Those points are higher or lower than the median at varying intensities. Sometimes, two or three consecutive points will show on one side of a line. As the chart above shows, there are many cases where several items might be grouped on either side of the median over time. But there is no general way to determine whether something will be higher or lower in value. The totals should still be near the median though.

5. **Trend.** A series of points on the chart will move up over the median line and then move down below the line. Those points are arranged in consecutive order; you may find five or more points gradually increasing at the same rate and then a few more points that decrease at that rate. The trend is like what you might find on a stock market report. You might see a trend where something keeps going up or down over time, thus giving the impression that something will keep on moving in that direction.

6. **Shift.** At least eight points are on one side of a median. The move suggests that there is a shift in the process to where the functionality might move in one direction for a while. Sometimes that total might progressively move up or down based on where things are going.

You will need a run chart to assess how stable your results are. The run chart may include a measurement of a variable over time. You might determine that a machine should be measured based on how many widgets it can produce in one day. If the machine produces from 35 to 38 widgets per day, that total may be stable depending on your acceptable level of variance. You'll need to check on the measurements before and after that period of stability to see how well the task is proceeding.

Normality

Normality or normal distribution refers to the ways data is distributed. In this scenario, a bell curve is utilized. The curve is measured based on the mean and standard deviation. Such a layout predicts the behaviors within a sample. The testing process should move as close to the middle of that curve as possible.

The frequency distribution must feature a higher frequency of values around the mean. That is, the mean or average of measured values should be as close to the top part of the bell curve as possible. Meanwhile, the lesser values will appear further from the curve. These include the unusual values that are unpredictable. But, no matter what happens, the values are not going to touch the X axis on the bell curve layout.

Normal distribution can be measured based on the number of Sigmas that come along within the curve. The Sigmas can range up to 99.999998 percent in value, meaning that the measurements need to come within that precise of a total. But the lowest value that can be utilized is 68.26 percent. The key is to ensure that the totals come closer to the top part of the bell curve for the most precise and accurate results. Either way, the Six Sigma total will remain at that 99.999998 percent value, thus requiring specific support for ensuring that a large amount of materials that you are planning will meet the standards for manufacturing that you wish to attain or utilize.

It is the first three closest standard deviations or Sigmas that make the most difference. The first of these is listed at 68.26 percent, while the second is at 95.44 percent and the third appears at 99.73 percent. This may be interpreted as the Empirical Rule for how a normal distribution of data may work. The most commonplace data, or at least around two-thirds of that data, will be arranged in the middle of the bell curve. This is to create an idea of what is normal.

The setup that you utilize in the Six Sigma process should work with the assumption that a false positive may occur. A confidence level of 95 percent should be utilized during the process of producing your readout. You will have to make substantial alterations to your Six Sigma effort if the confidence level is any lower than this. Also, the mean should be calculated before you produce the normal readout. The mean will help you get an average idea of what to expect out of your work.

Sensitivity

The sensitivity of the data in question should be explored. The data may be highly sensitive to the smallest influence. A measurement process should be as precise as possible with as little of a difference between measurements as possible. You might find differences in a measurement that can be about 0.1 percent or less of the standards you are working with. A measurement should be reviewed with as little of a percentage point interval as possible so you can be ensured the most precise results possible.

How Can the Data Be Distributed?

The data in your normal distribution layout may include a review of your bell curve. A symmetrical shape may identify cases where a certain range arises, but there is always the potential for a false positive. In a symmetrical layout, each standard deviation will lead in the same way. You will have an expanded range of materials that can be accepted at this point.

You may also come across positively or negatively skewed shapes. A positively skewed shape entails the data leading towards the left. The right part is closer to the X axis. For a negatively shaped design, the bell curve leans towards the right. These points suggest that the standard deviations will be much closer to that top measurement. You might want the data or measurements you are planning to be as close to that top part as possible. The positive aspect of these skewed shapes is that you might have fewer false positives, but you will also have to be more precise when trying to get certain things ready.

A long-tailed shape may also develop. This is where the bell curve is present, but the design is very narrow. The standard deviation states that you need more items to get within the standards you have imposed. The standard deviation is small to where you need more items to fit within your parameters or measurements. The risk of a false positive is minimal in this case.

What to Do If Your Data Is Not Normal

There may be some cases where multiple bell curves are found on the same readout. These are cases where you might have to modify your data. You might find there is a testing error involved, whether it entails the process itself or any possible issues surrounding how the data was measured. You should also look at how high up the bell curves are laid out so you recognize how well they are organized and whether there are certain problems that need to be fixed in your work.

You might have to revise your specification limits to ensure a more accurate readout. The new data you gather off those limits will transform the results you plan out. Be sure you use this when planning a full analysis of your data. These limits should only be configured if you have exhausted all the other solutions to the problem, including options like validating your data for consistency or adding more data as necessary.

One way to make your data normal is to raise your measurements by one power. You can use this to possibly increase the values of the data to get an idea of how well the content is organized and to determine whether there is a sensible range worth noticing. A reciprocal of your measurements may also be produced; this includes taking a y measurement and turning it to 1/y. Either option should entail the base data of your information being gathered at this point.

Shape

The shape of your data should be analyzed. The shape can have a specific appearance where results are arranged in a distinct layout. You can use the shape analysis process to get an idea of what you are coming across in your research and to know what to expect out of your study. Trends may be explored based on different totals that you come across. Take a look at the following examples of how shape can make a difference in your analysis.

Exponential

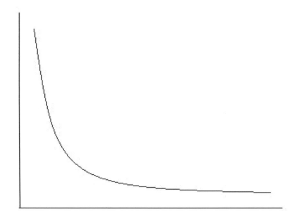

An exponential distribution in your data is a measure of your content based on time or other parameters. This entails a line chart with the data being measured based on time elapsed, the number of people or resources involved and so forth. In most cases, the exponential distribution will entail a line curving to where it eventually becomes a straight line. The line should be defined well enough to give you an idea of what the optimal amount of time or resources for something may be. You can use this to also see when the cut-off for timing or resources may be, as you can figure out how many of those resources are too much.

Lognormal

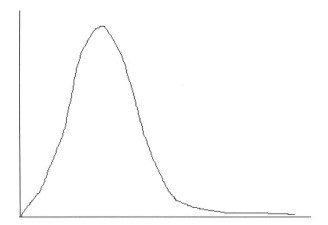

The lognormal distribution layout entails an asymmetrical layout, although there is a chance that data was skewed. In this, a value rises up to a certain total, only for that value to progressively decline after a while. You can also use this layout to identify how well the measurements are organized. You can use this to identify intriguing phenomena in the workplace, although this might work best if you measure efforts based on the time frame involved. The lognormal shape is more likely to be noticeable when the range of values in question is very large.

Geometric

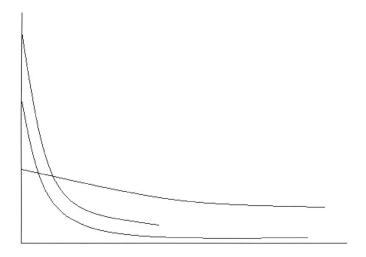

The geometric distribution layout comes in a shape where the highest data values appear at the start. For instance, a machine might make more widgets at the start of the day, but that total will taper off after a while. You may use the geometric shape to figure out what can be done to control the production of the machine and to see that it creates the widgets that you want the right way. Remember that this solution is best for time-based measurements.

Spread

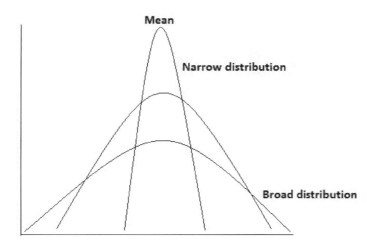

You may also interpret your data based on the spread in question. While the bell curve or other measurement has to fall within the proper standard deviations, you must be aware of how well the data is spread out. Sometimes the results will spread out to where a process is producing a diverse array of results. Your goal is to corral those results and to reduce the spread in general. A spread review will help you identify if there are problems with your work that must be resolved.

You will notice in the spread that you might have a narrow distribution of something. This means that the mean is located closer to the ends of what you have analyzed. Meanwhile, the broad distribution focuses on the values being spread a little further out from the mean. You can use your bell curve to notice how intense the values might be; the extreme between the mean and the ends will be greater if you have a narrow distribution. You can use these totals to confirm a sense of consistency or other value in your work.

Centering

The last part of data interpretation entails a centering process. In this, you look at the data that is produced at the start and see if it is as close to the middle part of the curve as possible. Anything that falls within the middle part of the curve within the first or second standard deviations is always welcome. But any instance where a majority of items are within those center points will show that you are carefully planning your work while focusing on intense accuracy and detail in your work.

Centering should be monitored based on what is working in your task. The centering might be challenging to manage, although the centering work should be noted based on how thorough the process might be. You must see that the center line is organized right while thinking about the general range of the work. You can prepare the center line with the intention of calculating the standard deviations that you wish to utilize. You can also use as many of these Sigmas as you wish, although this will require some extra control over how the task is organized.

You can utilize all of these methods of data interpretation to help you with analyzing many factors relating to your Six Sigma task. You must analyze these with the proper data charts and other features as necessary. Be aware of any trends that may arise over time. This includes a review of how well your Six Sigma process is working based on improvements or changes in certain trends.

Chapter 33 – Using the Right Measurement Chart (The Basic Tools of Quality)

In the mid-twentieth century, a new concept relating to managing the troubleshooting and analytical processes in the workplace was developed. This concept was known as the seven basic tools of quality. The tools were utilized to identify statistics while also being simple enough for people to use without lots of technical knowledge. These measurement points were produced as alternatives to the traditional quality control standards where statistics were reviewed with more complicated efforts. The intention was to provide a simple approach to identifying data that may be used at the start of a research project. The number of measurement options that you can utilize has expanded beyond seven, so the choices you have to work with are diverse and can provide you with the answers you need when figuring out how well your measurements may work.

When working on a Six Sigma project, you'll need to measure your data. You have to both analyze that data and figure out which items in your work are the best to utilize for that task. You have the option to work with one of many measurement tools to produce a fair sense of representation in your Six Sigma routine. You can use many types of charts in the layout of basic tools of quality to illustrate data that you gather through your Six Sigma process while also using those illustrations to review trends and connections. Your goal in finding out how these connections work should be to help you move forward with your work. It will also assist you with explaining your content and work efforts to other people.

To have an easier time with completing your task, you should look at each of the measurement chart options that are available for your use. The type of chart that you utilize will vary based on the type of data you are going to measure. Review whether you are working with continuous or discrete data sets. A discrete set may work when you have a set amount of data to work with. This includes work where only certain integers may be utilized. A continuous chart is for any type of value you wish to utilize.

You should also look at any time-based variations that may arise. Such variations include points where the values of items will change over time. Again, you must look at the difference between discrete and continuous data that you wish to utilize. You may review these points to see what the influence of certain points might be. This includes a look at how well you can control certain data at a given time and how you can make it all work to your liking without being hard to follow.

Charts for Discrete Data

Bar Chart

Your first option for a chart for discrete data is a bar chart. This is a graphical layout of data based on certain attributes. You can produce a bar chart based on details like how individual machines or employees operate, how many items are produced or the general quality of items generated. You take an attribute and lay it on one axis while the number of items involved with each attribute is on the other. You can use this chart to compare items and help you identify what might work best in your situation.

For instance, you might have five machines that you are trying to analyze based on how their performance within one month. You can measure the number of widgets each of those machines generated in that month. You can use the following steps for this chart:

1. Title your report: "How many widgets were produced by x machines within x month"

2. The X axis will include a listing of the five individual machines. You can use identifying numbers or names for each.

3. The Y axis will feature a series of numbers. You can use numbers reflective of how many widgets were produced by those machines.

4. The machines producing the most widgets will have longest bars. Whoever has the largest bar will be the machine that has done the most.

The bar chart helps you when you're looking to compare things between individual items. The process here can entail as many details as desired. The process works best when you have access to individual items that are easy to measure and review. But you have to ensure that the content being handled entails items on the X axis that are similar to each other. This can help you to compare individual items. More importantly, you can figure out if machines or other items are successfully carrying out specific processes, or whether certain gaps exist in the production process.

Pie Chart

Your next option for measuring data is a pie chart. This works for cases where you have one particular item to measure versus various types of attributes that an item can entail. The pie chart is a circular representation of different sets of data. The goal of the pie chart is to list the relationship among many quantities. This includes a review of how often certain results may be found in your research.

To create a pie chart:

1. Take a look at the object that you will measure. Specifically, you might have multiple objects that produce the same result, or a machine that might produce different items of varying results.

2. Determine the parameter for the object that you plan on measuring.

3. Analyze each of the items in the set.

4. Take a look at the number of entries linked within the set. This includes entries that are different from one another.

5. Add together the total number of entries that you have in the set.

6. For extra points represented on the pie chart, divide the smaller number by the total number of entries. This will be the percentage of the pie chart that the point will be represented by.

7. Round all the items you measure. You can produce whole-number percentages if you wish, but the full layout must total 100 percent.

Let's say that you have one machine that makes a series of widgets. You might want to analyze whether the widgets are of good, fair or poor quality. You will then measure 200 total widgets being produced by that machine in one day. In this sample, 140 of the widgets are of good quality. This means that 70 percent of the pie chart are filled in by the "good" marker. Meanwhile, you might have 40 fair items and 20 poor items. The "fair" segment is 20 percent of the chart, while the "poor" section is the remaining 10 percent. The full pie chart gives you a clear idea of what you will find in the testing process.

The pie chart will help you understand how often a certain item or a specific population fits in with certain standards or measurements. That allows you to determine what opportunities are available for you to work with so you know what to expect out of the content you are handling and where you want to go with it. The pie chart can work with as many items as you wish, but it works best if the plan is managed to where you have a defined series of points.

Pareto Chart

You can use a Pareto chart with both lines and bars to produce a readout that includes more data all around. The values in the chart are represented by bars to show the number of items being represented and the percentages on the line. The line shows a series of percentages based on the number of items represented on the chart. The chart illustrates types of item with many parameters or objects involved. The following steps can be used for making a Pareto chart:

1. Determine the items that you are going to measure. These include items that are similar to each other or which work with the same general objective in mind. The items in question go on the X axis.

2. Review the number that you will utilize for measuring items. This should be a measurement that is relevant to the different items you are working with. Place that number on the Y axis.

3. The items on the X axis should be organized based on which ones are the most prominent. The ones with the highest number on the Y axis go on the left part of the X axis. The bars will then be aligned from largest to smallest.

4. The right-hand side of the chart will have a second Y axis label. This is a measure of the percentage of items.

5. Add the sum of the Y axis readouts for each of the X axis items.

6. Divide the number of each bar by that total value. You will get the percentage of whatever you are measuring.

7. Draw a line that moves upward from the first bar to the last. The percentage for the first bar is added to the second bar and then to the third bar and so forth.

The design helps you to identify how well the measurements you are planning are organized.. The X axis items should be arranged evenly so the content is easy to follow. Don't forget to see that the line you produce has the right arc. The curve should move up gradually; any case where the curve is sharp suggests that one item will dominate the rest of the set.

Remember that the Pareto chart is designed to work in the same way as anything else you might review in the Pareto measurement. A small number of items are going to cause a majority of the concerns or issues in the workplace. This might include one variable or event being the most prominent issue. In the chart above, the layout shows that traffic and child care issues make up most of late workplace arrivals . The Pareto layout will confirm that these are the most prominent issues that require the most attention.

Charts for Continuous Data

Histogram

In some cases, you might have data that can be organized based on parameters that are consistent with one another. The data in this case is produced in a histogram. You will place class intervals on the X axis while the frequencies of those intervals are on the Y axis. You can use this to produce a bar chart that identifies certain data. You can especially use this when getting an idea of demographics. The goal is to identify certain actions and functions in an environment and to potentially create a new measurement for the data being generated.

To create a histogram:

1. Review the parameters surrounding the items you are measuring. Place those parameters on the X axis.

2. Analyze the frequency of each of the items you are working with. The Y axis will reflect those frequencies.

3. Organize the data based on the parameters and frequencies and create a bar chart.

4. The top parts of each bar should include a numerical value featuring the frequency that you wish to work with.

An example of this entails what you might do when you are getting a layout ready stating the number of employees that are working with a machine at a time. You may list identification numbers for each machine and place them on the X axis. The Y axis will reflect the number of employees dedicated to each machine. You can prepare this to get an idea of which machines are receiving the most attention at a given time.

The histogram can also be used for demographic purposes. You might utilize a histogram based on factors like the ages of the people in the workplace or the number of hours they work in a week. The measurements you use should entail different parameters that are based on the qualities of the people you are working with or anything else you are producing.

Box Plot

Another unique option for your measurement use, the box plot is similar to something you might notice when you read information on stock value changes. Like the stock market candlestick, the box plot uses a vertically organized bar with some lines coming out of the top and bottom. The box plot is unique in that it summarizes details on the process data. You will figure out the range of production coming from the data, how that range is dispersed and the center of the data that you are working with.

The box plot features a box that can be as tall or short as needed. The box includes three points:

1. Median

The median appears in the middle part of the box as a representation of the midway point for the data being handled. For instance, you may be measuring the value of widgets produced by a machine per day while using a 25-day sample. You can gather the values of widgets produced during each of those 25 days. The median value, or the one that is directly in the middle of that 25-day sample, will be the bar that cuts through the middle of the box.

2. First Quartile

The bottom end of the box is the first quartile. This marks the 25-percent mark where data is being reported. For a sample population of 25 items, you would use the sixth or seventh number in the layout.

3. Third Quartile

The third quartile is the 75-percent marker. This would be the eighteenth or nineteenth item for the items that you are working with. The third quartile can be far from the first median in some cases; any instance where the third or first quartile is very far from the median suggests that the results may be top-heavy on one end.

4. Lines

The next parts of the box plot feature some lines that go beyond the first and third quartiles. These reach the highest and lowest parts of the range. A number will be found at the top and bottom parts of those lines to list the highest and lowest overall values. The lines will help you identify how much of a range may be found on whatever you are measuring. You can also use the lines and numbers to get an idea of any significant outliers in your measurements.

5. Asterisk

In some cases, there might be an extreme outlier in one of the items you are measuring. An asterisk should be applied when there is an outlier that is at least 1.5 times the value of the box and the spots between the first and third quartiles. An asterisk is unlikely to be produced often, but you might have to use one in cases where an extraordinary event takes place. The asterisk may also be kept out of the original measurement for the box plot and the lines if desired; this may be for cases where you want to keep the readout being utilized in your work somewhat fair and sensible.

The size of the box produced in your box plot can go a long way to showing you how precise the measurements or functions in a process are. When the box is smaller in size and the lines are not too far off, you will be precise with similar values all the way through. But when the box is large, that means something may be off with a process.

The results may be incredibly sporadic; the range may also be intense depending on how well the lines are organized.

You can use a box plot in any way, although a good idea is to create a box plot where data is organized by time. You can take on a series of machines that make the same type of widget and compare each of them over a specific time frame. You can measure six machines based on how many widgets they produce in one day over a 28-day period. Each of those six machines will have its own box plot, complete with the lines outside their boxes. Your chart will compare all these box plots to figure out what changes might have arisen over time in each of the machines. You can use this to figure out which machines are working the best, thus helping you to identify what machines the rest of the factory should duplicate.

The process may also work for other procedures that are supported by people. For instance, you might be looking at how a call center works. You will review individual people and see how well they handle the calls that they receive. A box plot for each employee can be produced to help you figure out how quickly or slowly they manage calls. You can see how those employees respond to their calls and assess any problems.

Charts That Work for Both Forms of Data

Run Chart

A run chart features details on data that has been collected over time. You can use this to identify data over time to find trends, shifts, cycles and other changes you might come across. You can also use this to review data, implement a change as a part of your Six Sigma routine and then measure how well the data changes after you plan that routine. You can use the run chart to identify the changes that have taken place while avoiding the natural variations that might develop in the work you are putting in.

You can create a run chart by following these steps:

1. Determine the data that you are going to measure on your chart.

2. Gather the data by collecting a series of data points. Try to use about 15 to 25 points if you can, although you can change that total based on how much data you want to use.

3. Create a graph where you will plot your data. Use the X axis to list information on the time frame involved. The Y axis should include the numbers that you will measure.

4. Keep a measure of the items that you are going to analyze. After you go through the selected time period of interest, add the data to your run chart.

5. Take a look at the chart based on how a process has evolved over time. See what changes have come about thanks to recurring or consistent changes seen in the chart.

6. You can take an average of all the points on your run chart and produce a thicker line that goes along the X axis to show the general average of your results. This is an optional feature that can be added to your chart if desired.

Your run chart can help you to find cases of variability. You might find some irregularities where there are problems with a routine or process to the point where the work might be either weak or strong at certain times; you can use this information to figure out what problems have developed. You can also find shifts in your process and then determine trends. A trend should include an increase or decrease in data that lasts for several points in a row. The changes should be gradual; anything where a change is far too dramatic from one point to the next may be a sign of concern.

Control Chart

On the surface, a control chart is similar to a run chart in that both work with a single line of data that changes over time. But a control chart is different in that the control layout includes upper and lower control lines with a centerline in the middle. The lines are arranged to identify how well the process is working and whether it is stable. You can also use the middle line to figure out if the process is working or if there are issues.

There are three lines in a control chart. First, there is the Central Line or CL; this is the average measurement that you are working with all around. Second, you have the Upper Control Limit or UCL, which is organized based on the highest averages you are getting out of whatever you are measuring. Third, there is the Lower Control Limit or LCL, which identifies the lowest value of the measurements you are working with. The UCL and LCL can both be modified to feature some slanting or changing positions based on the moving average of the items you are measuring.

Your goal for the control line is to see how well the design on the chart works. You can see if the process is consistent and the materials are around the same value. In other words, the data that you are working with is in control. But there may also be times when the data varies far too much. In that case, the data is unpredictable due to multiple causes of variation. But the most important key is that the data is managed with a review of both the average of your measurements and the width or range of whatever it is you are handling. The average is where your data is coming through on and the range involves how tight the content is.

The control chart is designed mainly to identify how stable the content you are working with is. Getting a proper measure of the content is vital for ensuring that the content being produced is managed as precisely as possible. Keeping the range involved as minimal as possible is important for your success in the work. The control chart may also help you identify when you should leave a process alone instead of making changes. A comparison between the change you make and what happens in your process as a result of said change may be utilized.

Variable and Attribute Data for the Control Chart

The control chart can work with details on the variables or attributes that you feel are appropriate for your analysis. The data can be planned out in any way you see fit. To start, let's look at the variables that you can measure in your effort. The chart may include a review of the standard deviation being handled in the Six Sigma routine. You are using an extended X variable to see how the Y changes over time. You might notice some dramatic changes when the Y becomes unsteady and moves out of the standard deviation you are trying to manage.

The attributes in your work may also be noticed. You can work with the following attributes when monitoring how well your content is being handled and where you are going:

c = the defects you have found

u = defects when normalized based on your sample size

p = the proportion of items that are defective in your research

np = the proportion of what is defective when multiplied by your sample size

You can use any other variables that you find useful. But you must also look at where those variables are going and determine whether they are appropriate for use in your situation. Remember that you have the option to use software to get the control chart working, although a manual review of that data may be used if you prefer to go that route.

Other Choices for Measurement Needs

Scatterplot

You might have two variables that will need to be measured. There may be a link between the two. In this case, a scatterplot may be utilized. You can incorporate a scatterplot to figure out if there are certain changes that might come about based on how one variable changes. The plot will feature several dots or marks aligned up with the two variables. Here's an example of how a scatterplot would work:

1. Figure out the two variables you will use. One variable might be the number of years of experience a person has at a factory, and the second could be the number of widgets that person can produce in a day.

2. Align the two variables on separate axes. The experience factor may be on the X axis, while the number of widgets is on the Y axis.

3. Review the number of entities in your population. This includes an analysis of experience versus widget production.

4. Each entry should be listed with a dot or other marker. Produce as many of these markers for your entry as possible.

5. Review where those markers are placed. See if there is a sizeable change in how those markers are laid out.

You might discover some interesting trends in your review. This includes a look at people in your workplace or other factors in that environment. The key is to figure out if you need to make changes to certain variables. For instance, you might find that the workers with more experience are capable of producing the most widgets. Therefore, you might need to educate your less-experienced employees about what they can do so they can catch up to their more experienced colleagues.

You can create a line on the scatterplot to see how those variables have changed over time. A straight line means that there is a definite correlation between certain variables. You can change your work process around based on what you feel is relevant or suitable for the work you are putting in. The line will illustrate the functions in your task and can help you with identifying what trends are arising.

Cause and Effect Diagram

You have to look at the possible causes and effects of many things that you might come across in your work. A cause and effect diagram can be utilized when you're aiming to get an idea of what is happening at a given time. The cause and effect diagram can also be called a fishbone diagram because it has a distinct fish shape to it. The head is the effect or problem that you are looking at. As you work with the diagram, you will use several methods and concepts to figure out what the issue in the workplace might be. This measurement chart is mainly for identifying individual events that take place during a process.

The cause and effect diagram is used for cases where you are not aiming to measure any quantitative data but are instead looking to analyze things that are changing in the workplace. The cause and effect analysis will help you to explore the issues surrounding your content, but this will require you to work with specific points. The diagram requires immense detail for it to work. To make the cause and effect diagram work, you need to use six particular points for a measurement that can be utilized.

1. Machine

The first part of the process entails machines. The machines are the tools required for getting a process to work right. You might have machines that are not as functional as you wish. Servers might be down on occasion, while a workstation may not be fully functional. You can use a machine analysis to figure out how well your business is working.

2. Materials

Your machines might require the use of certain materials. You may also need forms to run some processes or to load up data depending on what you are using. In either case, you have to look at how the materials you are working with are planned. Some problems may include a lack of documentation, materials having defects or a lack of education regarding how materials work. Sometimes you might come across cases where you don't have the appropriate materials on hand.

3. Measurements

The root problems may relate to the measurements that you utilize. Incorporate any problems surrounding your measurements in this section. You might come across issues like the collection process not being consistent. Issues surrounding a possible bias in the process may develop. You may also find problems like certain measurement standards being too vague.

4. Nature

The nature of the business should be analyzed. 'Nature' in this case refers to the time of the year, the weather conditions or any regulatory concerns. For instance, your business might do better at certain points in the year or when the weather is a little nicer. You might also thrive when other businesses in your field move forward, what with your market possibly having ups and downs. Regulatory issues may include new laws that inhibit what your business can do when trying to make money.

5. Method

Some root causes entail methods that you try to utilize. Such methods might involve problems with staffing, training, approving procedures or processing items correctly. Other instances may include previously existing problems that have worsened. Prior design processes can be utilized to help you figure out how your methods are working.

6. People

The people involved with your processes are the last things to consider when planning your cause map. Look at the skills that those people have. Consider whether you are staffing your business correctly or are struggling to make it work. Review how the people in the workplace understand the processes you wish to follow. If people in the workplace don't know what they are doing, that needs to be studied and rectified.

Flowchart

The flowchart is a concept that you might have seen earlier in this guide, but it is important to discuss it further. Flowcharts will help you to identify the actions and inputs that take place throughout a process. You can use a flowchart during the analytical process to get an idea of how well any processes you have planned out are working. You can take any process charts that you produced earlier and then align them alongside a new flowchart that illustrates what you have been doing.

Your flowchart must show how processes relate to each other. Contingencies may be included within the chart as well. The details included should be thorough and provide you with the support you demand for making a task work. More importantly, the steps that you produce should be logical and easy to follow.

An interesting part of a flowchart is that it will include different shapes based on what tasks take place. An oval shape illustrates the start and end of a process. A square or rectangular box shows a step. A triangle can illustrate a point that might lead you to a different process or an alternative means of resolving something.

Check Sheet

A check sheet works as a prepared form that includes several categories of data that you will collect. You can use a check sheet if you ever need to analyze your data based on how often certain activities are taking place. You can also use this to identify defects, cases where certain actions are working better or when any changes in the production or work process might make a difference in your routine.

To create a check sheet:

1. Figure out the operational definitions of the task you are working with. These will be measured throughout the check sheet.

2. Review the number of entities you will review and how long you will review them for. The check sheet can only work for a limited time.

3. Place a checkmark for every time a certain action takes place.

For instance, you might have five machines, with each them being tasked to make the same widget. You can review the widgets produced and identify any problems in the assembly line. One part of the check sheet will include labels for the specific errors that those machines produced. Place a single checkmark in the appropriate boxes for every time an error takes place. At the end of the time period, you will analyze the results of the check sheet to see how the machines are working; this includes finding out if there is a specific problem with a machine or if there is a definite error in the process as a whole.

Spaghetti Diagram

This next choice for your use is a little different from what you might expect, but it can make a difference if planned out right. The spaghetti diagram lists information on how well your physical processes are working based on where people might be moving about in the workplace. Using the diagram, those movements can be studied and analyzed based on how well your tasks are working depending on where people go.

You can use the spaghetti diagram to analyze how well the movements in the workplace are run and what people are doing when trying to correct themselves or handling various issues. You may review where people are moving around a warehouse or other space and then keep notes on how often people make those movements. You might notice that people are traveling more than necessary within a task. This includes moving too much to complete just one task. This can be a tough chart to review, so it is best for when you're trying to calculate information on how well a task is laid out in any situation.

You can always use multiple colors for the items you are trying to measure. These colors may be used for when you're trying to manage individual employee paths or processes. Those colors might be easier to read and distinguish. You can plan a spaghetti chart for figuring out the specific trends and motions that are taking place in the work environment. This, in turn, can help you determine a more conducive approach to handling your materials the right way.

Choosing the Proper Measurement Tool

Although all of the tools that you can utilize in your Six Sigma measurement efforts are useful, you cannot assume that just one particular tool will work for every situation. You have to look at your data to see what is most appropriate. While you have already read about how certain ideas may work for continuous or discrete data or both, you still have to be careful when organizing your content. There are a few steps you can use for figuring out what you should utilize when getting a measurement tool to work for you:

1. Are you looking to find a relationship between certain variables in your work? A scatter diagram may work.

2. Are you trying to figure out how the content is divided up and what parts of your work are linked? A histogram is recommended.

3. Are you trying to figure out frequencies? A pie chart or bar chart can work, although a check sheet may also be appropriate.

4. What about the particular changes that might come about during a significant change in your routine? A line-based chart may work as it gives you an idea of how the changes you are making are creating an impact.

Your goal for handling measurement tools should be planned accordingly. Getting measurements under control is a necessity to achieve your goals. The best part of working with these tools is that they help to make the information you gather in the Six Sigma process as detailed as possible.

Chapter 34 – How Capable Is the Process?

Process capability is a measurement standard that involves whether the Six Sigma process is consistent and can work even when there are no outlying factors or causes that might influence the work at hand. You can review the capability of the project for the short- and long-term. The short-term review entails the true capability of the task, although the long-term analysis may consider noise and other factors. The review tests both how well the machines or people in the process can work versus whether those resources can last for a while.

Process Sigma

The Process Sigma is the main measurement you will utilize when reviewing the capability of your task. Process Sigma refers to how well the output works versus a standard of performance. Your goal is to attain the highest Process Sigma possible; a higher total, particularly the Six Sigma measurement, means that the process is highly capable of working and staying consistent. You will have to measure this based on various parameters, which is where the next point in the review comes in handy. You should use the defects per million (DPMO) measurement to get an idea of what is coming in your work.

Figuring Out the Data Being Calculated (DPMO Measurement)

You will have to analyze the data that you will calculate when figuring out the capability of the process. You must identify the units being measured or processed and what the defects for each unit may be. Defective items that are produced or identified should be monitored and avoided if possible. Your goal is to avoid defects and to increase opportunities, which are products or services that meet the standards involved and can be measured. As you plan the data, you can get a measure of the number of defects per million opportunities with the clear goal of keeping that number of defects down to the Six Sigma standard.

DPMO can give you the most accurate depiction of the efficiency or accuracy of the process you are working with. The review will help you recognize everything you are doing in your work and what makes the task valuable. A review where the DPMO is too high might suggest that your work is not going to be effective. More importantly, you might hurt your relationships with your customers because the DPMO will be too high and people will therefore notice the problems in your products and with your work.

You can use the following calculation when taking a look at your data:

1. Figure out how many units you're going to sample.

You need to use the largest possible sample unit for your task. The sample layout can include thousands of items based on what you are naturally producing. You can use a massive total, close to a million, if you make lots of things, but sometimes a few thousand is good enough. Either way, the total you will measure should be planned cautiously without expending too much effort on more extensive or convoluted processes.

2. Look at the defect opportunities for each unit.

A defect opportunity is a problem that might arise. For instance, you might work for a company that makes basketballs and other pieces of sports equipment. You can review how well your company makes its basketballs. The defect opportunities for the basketballs might include issues like the basketballs not weighing enough, not handling the optimal amount of air pressure, discoloration, a change in the number of grooves on the surface and problems with how thick the lines connecting the panels on the ball are. Those are five defect opportunities that you might come across. You can add as many of these opportunities as needed provided you know what they are. Anything realistic within your work helps too.

The defect opportunities should be things that the customers will care about. Anything that negatively influences how products or services are used might be analyzed here. Only routine defects should be included, rather than anything rare. When finding ideas for what to incorporate in your work and research process, focus on steps or processes where things can go wrong

3. Review the number of defects you come across.

You may come across many items that are defective in the sample size. Include the proper number of items based on what has defects in general. This is regardless of how many of these defects something might have. For the basketball, you can include as a defect something that is discolored. An item that is not of the proper circumference and which cannot inflate to the right pressure level can also be a defect.

4. Divide the defects by the product of the opportunity for defects per unit and the number of units being measured.

For instance, you might have produced 100,000 units within a certain machine. But 25 of those units are defective. Your opportunity for defects per unit might be around 15. For this, you multiply 15 by 100,000 to get 1,500,000. Divide 25 by that 1,500,000 total to get 0.0000167. This gets you closer to the Six Sigma standard, but you still have to attain the Six Sigma goal of 3.4 defects for every million opportunities.

The total DPMO needs to be as close to 3.4 as possible. You can always go a little under that total if you have certain limitations in what you can handle in the process. Be sure to also look at how effective the system for work is depending on the layout you want to utilize in your general process and routine work.

Yield

One helpful measurement for the capability of the Six Sigma process is the yield that you are producing. The yield, which relates to the rate of production, has to be consistent but firm. You may have some units or processes analyzed and tested to see if they meet the standards you have set up. When more of those items pass, your yield becomes greater. Your goal is to create a yield where almost every item being produced or every opportunity meets your standards.

The Classic Yield or YC can be analyzed in the process. This is a measure of the approved units or processes divided by the number of units that were tested. For instance, 76 of 85 units that were tested passed your standards. Your yield would be 0.894. Your goal should be to get closer to one, or at least to 0.95 or greater if possible.

The first time yield or Yft may also be measured. This is a measure of how well a routine is working at the start. The calculation is the same as what you would use for the Classic Yield. You take the units passed and divide them by the items you are reviewing in that first-time review. You might have analyzed 92 units the first time around and only 85 of them passed; your first time yield would be 0.9239.

A rolled throughput yield or Ytp is another choice for your measurement needs. The Ytp is a measurement of many yields produced at varying times. For instance, one yield will entail 95 of the 100 items passing, a second yield will have 85 of 90 items working and a third features 92 of 95 items. The equation looks like this: $(95/100) * (85/90) * (92/95)$. The overall yield is 0.8685. The decimal number will often be smaller than the totals that you calculated, but this is utilized to help you find corrective measures for making your work more consistent and capable.

One useful idea for measuring the capability is to look at how you will change your process around. You might plan at least three testing processes for your items. While you might come across many items that pass the first time around, you might refine your test to add new parameters and eventually discover that more items failed your test. You might have 100 items in the first process with nine of them being rejected, thus resulting in 91 items in your first yield. After that, a second test of those 91 items will cause six items to be rejected, thus leaving you with 85. A third and final test with new parameters will cause 11 items to be lost, thus producing a passing grade of 74 items. While you are cutting out many of the items that do not meet your standards via extensive testing, you will also have to review what you are doing with those items so they can be fixed.

Calculating the Data

The key part of reviewing your data is to see that it appears normal. You can use a large sample size here to increase your potential for obtaining normal data in a report. The data should be placed in a consistent line that moves upward. For instance, the X axis may include details on the time spent with your data. The Y axis will then feature the number of processes that were generated. An upward line should show that your production is capable and that it will continue at the same rate during the course of your work. But in other cases where the process is not capable, you might come across lulls or changes in how well your content can be prepared or planned out.

The Z Value

One parameter that may be calculated when looking at the capability of your Six Sigma project is the Z value. The Z is a measure of the standard deviation from the mean in your work. You can use this to identify how far your data is from a mean and how much work you need to attain to reach Six Sigma status. You can figure out the Z value by using the following equation:

$$Z = (Y - \mu)/\sigma$$

Y is the data point that you are looking at; this may include anything that appears in the middle part of your bell curve. μ is the mean of your data points and is therefore the spot where the bell curve should reach its apex. The σ is, once again, a measure of the standard deviation of the other two variables. You will get Z, the standard deviations between the mean and Y, after you complete the equation.

For instance, you may have a machine that produces a mean or average of 300 widgets in a day. But you might see that the standard deviation is around 22, which is a general measure of how often something might be off. You might look at the probability of the machine possibly producing 350 widgets in one day. With this, Y will be 350, and the mean 300, thus resulting in a numerator of 50. Divide that by the standard deviation of 22 to get 2.273.

Now that you have the Z value of 2.273, you can figure out the probability of the machine producing 350 widgets in one day. To do this, you must look at a normal distribution table. To do this, review the Z value and its tenth position on the Y axis. After that, match up that value with the hundredth position on the X axis. In this example, you are looking at the value 2.27. You can review this by looking at the two normal distribution tables and subtracting that total you get from one to see what the probability is:

Z	0	0.01	0.02	0.03	0.04	0.05	0.06	0.07	0.08	0.09
0.1										
0.2										
0.3										
0.4										
0.5										
0.6										
0.7										
0.8										
0.9										
0.91	0.81859	0.81859	0.81859	0.81859	0.81859	0.81859	0.81859	0.81859	0.81859	0.81859
1										
1.1										
1.2										
1.3										
1.4										
1.5										
1.6										
1.7										
1.8										
1.9										
2										
2.1										
2.2										
2.27	0.98839	0.98839	0.98839	0.98839	0.98839	0.98839	0.98839	0.98839	0.98839	0.98839
2.3										
2.4										

For 2.27, the number will be 0.98839. Therefore, there is a 1.161 percent chance that the machine can safely increase its productivity from 300 widgets to 350 in one day. If the Z value is any higher, you will have a much harder chance of your project being capable of producing that set value you wished to attain. You can use the charts above to give yourself an idea of what might work when preparing your tasks.

Another solution is to figure out a probability total for a certain range based on the Z value you generate in the process. Let's go back to the machine that makes 300 widgets a day as its mean, with the standard deviation of 22. You might want to see what the probability is of that machine making between 290 and 320 widgets in a day. For this, you will calculate the Z value for those two totals separately. For 320 widgets, the Z factor is 0.91, which is 0.81859 on the chart. For 290 widgets, the total is -0.45, which is -0.67364. (When the Z value is negative, the total you find on the box should be converted to being negative as well.) The sum of the two should be incorporated; in this case, take 0.81859 + -0.67364 to get 0.14495. At this point, you have an 85.5 percent chance that the machine will produce those widgets within that 290 to 320 range.

The key part of the probability is that it helps you to see how capable your process is when all is considered. Be aware of how the probability in your setup works and have a plan in mind for making the most out of your content.

More importantly, look at everything you are getting out of your manufacturing and production efforts. You must see every opportunity for a problem that might come along. Don't worry if the problems you are looking at seem unusual. The goal is to identify the issues that might develop and which could change what happens with your work. Knowing where to go with your work and how you're going to fix it is a necessity. This will also allow you to recognize the faults and flaws in your work and prevent such problems from developing or causing chaos in your work in the future.

Cp and Cpk – Specific Points for Capability and How to Measure Them

The greatest concern surrounding the capability of your task entails when you are focusing on more than one voice. While working with three standard deviations from a central point to produce six Sigmas helps, there might be cases where you concentrate on many voices that have different ideas of how something works. You might produce a chart showing the process and how the voice of that effort works. This includes how well you are capable of producing things. But that voice might be radically different from what you would get out of the voice of the customer.

The VoC is all about sticking with some limits over what the customer finds to be acceptable. This may include sticking with the standard deviations you have created. Sometimes the voice of the process might be radically different to where you are producing more things outside of what the customer wants to utilize. You have to keep the voices from being a threat by looking at how you're going to work with four specific measurements. These are measurements that identify how capable your task may be.

There are two measurements that you have to notice when getting the VoC to work for you— Cp and Cpk.

Cp

The Cp is a measure of your capability. The Cp may also be recorded as the ET/NT or Engineering Tolerance and Natural Tolerance. You will measure the ET as a width between specification differences. The NT refers to the data from the process in general. The NT is often about six times the value of the standard deviation produced. The Cp is a measure of how capable a process may be if that process is centered between your specification limits.

Here is an equation to use for calculating the Cp:

$$C_p = \frac{USL - LSL}{6 \times \hat{\sigma}}$$

In this equation, the SLs are the specification limits, the upper and lower ones specifically. Those are the standards that you must follow for the Six Sigma process. These are not things that you can allow to have values surpass like with the control limits. Rather, you must ensure the results fit within the specification limits that you have set up so they will not fall apart or be harder to utilize. The difference between those two limits is divided by six standard deviations. You can use fewer standard deviations if desired if you're trying to get in a little more leeway before moving into the stricter Six Sigma standard.

A Cp value of one means that the process is capable of meeting the needs the customer has. But the Cp value should be as high as possible. When the Cp is higher, the variability in your work regarding your specification limits will be minimal. For Six Sigma, a Cp of two or higher is optimal. The total may be lower if you are working within fewer standard deviations. Look at how many Sigmas are to be utilized as you're planning this aspect of the process so you will have a sense of control over the work.

Cpk

The Cpk measurement is another valuable total to review. The Cpk is a little harder to work with, but it focuses on how the process is capable regardless of whether the mean is centered between specification limits or not. The Cpk has a total similar to the Cp measurement and is all about the capability in general. The big thing about the Cpk is that it is about centering the process. You might shift your control barriers depending on what you get.

The Cpk is about what the process can generate within specific limits. The Cp is about seeing if the functionality is capable. The Cpk goes one step further to find details on how well the task is run and whether any sizeable changes might develop within the task.

To calculate the Cpk:

1. Take the mean and subtract the lower specification level or LSL from the total.

2. Take the upper specification level of USL and subtract the mean from that total.

3. Take the smaller of the two numbers you just produced.

4. Divide that number by the product of 0.5 times the NT.

Due to the width of the distribution on your chart being consistent all the way through, the Cp should be the same. But the Cpk must have a logical value. The Cpk will be zero when the process mean is equal to a specification level. Meanwhile, the Cpk should be under zero if the process goes beyond one of the specification limits. You should aim for the Cpk to be higher in value so you can confirm the security of the total. Of course, anything higher in value will be more secure and easier to predict, just like what you would get with the regular Cp measurement.

The ideal Cpk total for a Six Sigma task should be 1.5. This is a good enough total that shows you have a logical process in place for the work at hand. You can use the Cpk total to produce a firm result chart. Be sure to look at the Cpk total to get an idea of where your work is going and what you might be planning when trying to make the work in question more effective.

The task is harder to handle, but it gives you an idea of how well the design can work for your use. You can plan this based on anything you wish to utilize, although it helps to note how well the routine is managed and to have a plan in mind for your use. You can use the Cpk to see how well the process runs and whether anything has to be shifted around. Be prepared to review your specification levels as well.

Chapter 35 – Root Cause Analysis

When it comes to Six Sigma, it is critical for you to analyze what you can do to make the most out of your business. Part of this includes looking at how the problems that you have developed. The problem with a business is that such problems can occur at any time.

You have to analyze the root cause of any problems. Specifically, the root cause analysis reviews problems that are preventing the desired result from occurring; any problem that is directly responsible for preventing the result is the root cause. It is more important for you to remove the root cause than it is to address superficial issues. You are only resolving small aspects of your business' ongoing problems when you target such issues.

On the other hand, the root cause is specifically the issue that has triggered the problems you are dealing with. The detailed cause must be something that is triggering all the other issues in the workplace. Failing to resolve the root cause may keep you from being capable of moving your business forward.

The process of finding the root cause requires extensive documentation. The support you put in for analyzing the root cause will help you to fix the issues that have developed in your workplace. You can produce a full report on the root cause and use that to analyze what your business needs to do to move forward. You can gather information surrounding the root cause based on statistics, although in most cases the root cause analysis will focus more on the problems in the workplace that are causing an issue to develop.

Explaining the Event

The first thing to do when working with a root cause analysis is to identify the event in question. You must explain the event based on the problem that is hurting the business. You have to be as specific as possible. Examine who was influenced by the problem, how people were affected and who might have found the problem. The date and time of the event can also be listed as needed. The explanation has to be thorough enough to figure out what can be done.

To make the root cause analysis easier, you have to name specific processes. Every detail in whatever you are listing should be included in the introductory part of your root cause analysis.

What Was Expected?

One part of the analysis is an explanation of the event. The explanation can include a review of the events that were regularly planned. The events may be part of a one-time occasion or something recurring. A flowchart can be prepared to list information on all the things that were to take place. The description should be as detailed and thorough as possible.

The expected actions might have been listed in a policy program or other directive given to the employees and managers. This includes the staff training process that might be provided to people as they start working somewhere. The support offered in the manuals or orientation points that people receive should help with explaining what is expected. Any documents or actions that are conducted to help people learn things should be discussed in the analysis report.

Deviations from what was expected should be listed. Each deviation should be discussed in detail. The deviation should also be discussed based on whether or not that issue could have contributed to the result. The deviations can be as far from the original planned event as needed; all deviations should be listed as accurately as possible.

The expectations should also be discussed based on the regulatory standards that a business is required to meet. The plans should fit in with what is asked of a business for its operation. You can talk about the references or literature that the team has reviewed. The analysis should give you an idea of what caused the expectations to be as they are. Remember that, sometimes, improper events may be radically different from what a business is supposed to meet based on regulations.

This process works best when the documentation involved is fully up to date. A business will have to keep its documentation updated regularly to ensure that the content being listed is fully accurate and easy to follow or use. You must make sure the data is handled accurately and that employees are using the right processes or terms. More importantly, the processes should be explained clearly enough to be easy to follow. After you look at these details, you can go deep into the background of the event to potentially get further answers on what you can utilize.

Reviewing the Event Background

You will have to ask many questions surrounding the background of the event in question. The event should be analyzed in detail based on not only what made the event different from expectations, but also on what could have caused it to develop. You can use the event background analysis to ask questions on what could have happened and why certain actions occurred. You can ask as many of the following questions as you want, so long as you are thorough in your answers:

1. Did a worker or other person do something specific that could have contributed to the issue? This may include inactions. The action or inaction should be discussed based on how the concern developed.

2. Were there any issues relating to the equipment being used? This includes possible defects in the equipment or a malfunction in the materials. The improper use of the materials should also be discussed. You can talk about how the improper actions differ from what is expected. Describe the equipment in this situation alongside how the equipment contributed to the issue..

3. Did the issue develop in the same location that it usually takes place in? This includes an event that is normally situated in one spot in the workplace. For instance, a machine might be positioned in a new spot separate from where it usually operates. Explain where the issue developed and whether it was different from issues in the usual location. Explain why the new location was used.

4. Was the person who completed the action familiar with whatever had to be done? A business should have a person who is familiar with a machine or other equipment to complete a particular task. The business may also have a person interact with specific customers pertaining certain actions. Explain any cases where the regular action was not completed by the person recommended for the task. Talk about who completed the activity and why the regular person responsible was not involved.

5. Did the staff members who took care of an action have the proper credentials? The root cause may entail a person who is not skilled enough to complete a task attempting to handle that work. The inadequacy of the situation may be discussed if the staff member or members in question do not have the right credentials.

6. Were there enough staff members on hand when the problem developed? Explain why there were not, if that was the case.

7. Explain other staffing factors that might have contributed to the problem. You can talk about any particular staff member provided that the staff member in question is relevant to the process you are trying to support or utilize.

8. Was the information clear for everyone? That is, was anyone confused or uncertain about the information relating to the event? Explain any information that led to the issue and how it might have influenced the problem that developed. Talk about the information that the people involved should have received and assess whether those details were too complicated.

9. Was there a lack of communication involved? If so, explain who failed to provide communication and what that person should have explained to workers. Discuss how the issue contributed to the problem at hand.

10. Were there any outside factors that might have contributed to the issue? Explain the factors that arose and how they contributed to the problem.

11. Were there any organizational problems relating to the event? These include problems where leadership did not recognize what could be done. Any factors relating to the leader's struggles should be discussed. How those problems specifically contributed to the issue at hand may also be discussed.

12. Had there been any assessments or other tests that contributed to the issue? A test might have resulted in an improper or inaccurate result. The test could also have entailed complicated information that was skewed in some way. Talk about the factors that influenced the situation and how those problems contributed to the situation.

13. Explain any other factors at the end of the review. Every factor should be listed, with the most significant event listed first. That first event may be the proximate issue that might have directly led to the issue. Anything else that is explained may be problems that link up to the original root cause. Use as many contributing factors as possible; you can always organize them on the list as you go along.

Planning a Timeline

A timeline should be planned in the next part. The timeline is a listing of events that took place before, during and after the problematic issue. The timeline will help with determining any possible issues that developed. All parties should be identified alongside the dates and times of the event. The timeline can be as long as necessary.

Have Any Actions Been Taken?

In the next part of the root cause analysis, discuss any risk reduction actions that were taken. The actions should be described based on the problems that developed. You can discuss the actions and how they relate to the root cause in general. The dates for when these actions were implemented should also be listed. The information produces an idea of efforts that took place to fix certain problems. You can also report on the estimated cost for each risk reduction action, although that is optional.

Some other actions that might have been completed are preventative. These are to prevent the root cause from developing once again. You can review these actions by organizing them based on those that are the most valuable or those that directly relate to the root cause or which are as close to that cause as possible. The new strategy being planned and the estimated cost for each strategy should be included. Any special considerations surrounding the preventative actions should also be listed.

The Cause and Effect Link

It is critical to look at the cause and effect that comes with a certain action. The cause and effect in the root cause analysis may be gathered for the analysis process. As the cause is identified, the events that occur after the cause develops can then be reviewed. The review can be as deep as necessary provided that the content is handled the right way. The setup ensures that the source of the problem may be identified and the problem may be kept from recurring.

To find the specific cause relating to the effect, it is vital to review the steps involved with the action in question. Any cases where the action changes dramatically could directly influence the quality of the situation at hand. The relationship between the cause and the effect can be as vast or limited in scope as necessary. The goal is to figure out the link to produce the proper solution or to at least gather ideas as to what may be done. Knowing how to handle the cause and effect is vital for organizing the content in question.

The Five Whys

One way to review cause and effect can be to use the Five Whys process. The Five Whys assists in analyzing the cause of a problem. The process involves asking the question, "Why did this happen?" After that, the group asks, "Why did this problem that caused the event occur?" The process entails the use of five "why" questions being asked, although the number of questions that may be posed can vary. The business can use as many of the questions as necessary.

The process of using the Five Whys routine entails the following:

1. Define the specific problem.

2. Address the primary cause of the issue. Why is this happening?

3. Ask questions on why something happened. This may be done for as long as the business has to analyze the concern.

When you look at the primary cause and ask why something is happening, ask, "Why is that?" For instance, you might say a cause for a factory's lack of productivity is that its supply chain schedule is out of control. You can ask, "Why is the supply chain schedule not working right?" You will then figure out an answer to that question; in this example, it might be because of a lack of a set day of the week for when shipments are supposed to happen. After this, you will ask, "Why do we not have a set day of the week for getting shipments handled?"

4. Keep on asking why questions with the intention of getting to Five Whys, although a few extras may be applied. The root cause should be evident when you get to that last why.

Every why will be about the same thing—some action is taking place because of something that occurred in the past. Knowing how to identify something that occurred in the past is vital to understanding how certain actions take place. Having as many Whys in the line as possible is vital for seeing what the true root of the issue is, what with workplace processes often being complicated. The root cause should be found at the very end of the line, as this is where the process or other action in particular should have been formed. The root cause will be removed from the basic point, but the Five Whys will link them up.

5. Add other contributing problems if needed. Apply the same Five Whys to those problems as required.

The Five Whys process should entail an analysis of a primary cause at the start, but can then move on to other problems. The contributing problem may be a concern that either encourages the root issue or which is a product of that said issue. You can use the same Five Whys process on those contributing issues to go further in the process to find a cause for the problem in question. You can also use a second contributing problem or even a third or so forth if necessary. But you must ensure that the Five Whys for each of those problems are separate from one another so you can get a clear idea of the issue.

To fully understand the Five Whys process, it helps to look at an example. Let's say that you are driving your car, but it is no longer able to start up. You might try to start the car in your garage but discover that the battery is dead. You can use the Five Whys to figure out what the problem with the car is. Here is how this would work:

1. Why is the car not starting? (Because the battery is dead.)

2. Why is the battery dead? (Because it has been used for too long.)

3. Why was the battery used for so long? (Because I forgot to change it.)

4. Why did you forget to change the battery? (Because I didn't have the time to get my car inspected.)

5. Why didn't you have time to get your car inspected? (I'm so busy with life that I never think about that kind of thing.)

This example shows that the battery died because you used it for too long and did not consider the battery over time, let alone getting the car inspected, given how busy you are. You might have to reconsider your priorities for maintaining your car to keep the problem from repeating itself in the future. Long story short, your lack of care for the car has caused that car to stop working, thus creating an extensive amount of inconvenience.

What If the Final Why Doesn't Have an Answer?

There may be times when you are unable to come up with an answer to the final why in your Five Whys process. If that is the case, you will need to go back to the previous why in the chart (probably the fourth, unless you used more than five).

That fourth why might have to be analyzed further and even broken off into a new contributing factor if needed. You will then have to go through the entire process to confirm the data being managed.

Planning Corrective Actions

After you go through the Five Whys, you must describe the action that you feel is necessary for fixing the problem that you discovered at the end of the Five Whys. This includes details on the party responsible for managing the fix and figuring out the date when the action is to start and end. You can use as much detail in this section as possible, so long as the content is logically organized. You can also use this point for as many concerns or issues in the workplace as needed. The only goal is that you recognize what you are doing with fixing the problems you are coming across.

Let's go back to the car battery example. You can correct that problem by planning a better schedule for maintaining your vehicle. You will require resources like a battery tester, a tire air pressure tester and pump and added fluids like engine coolant or vehicle oil. These items may be used over time to keep your car running. Therefore, the car will be safe to handle and capable of starting up. Getting your car inspected regularly is vital to its operation; the Five Whys process will have helped you to recognize what should be done to keep your car from breaking down.

Control Impact Matrix

Another measurement tool that may be incorporated into your work is the control impact matrix. The matrix is arranged in a box to help you identify how well you are working with cause and effect functions. You can use the matrix after the causes that you know exist have been appropriately captured. The matrix is organized based on factors and impacts. The factors are the causes that you can control, and the impacts are the extents of the factors on the problems in question or the effects that are being produced.

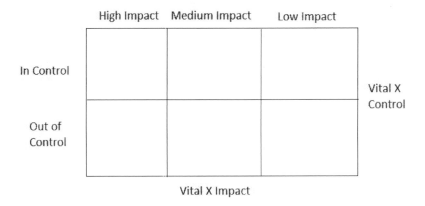

You will have to review the following questions:

1. What types of actions were outside of your control? Also, which ones were in your control?

2. How much of an impact did each point in the work make? You can sort the impact out by high, medium and low levels of intensity.

3. How far removed are these points in the matrix from the root cause?

You can use this process to get a clear idea of what to expect out of your work and how you will plan it. You may also use the Five Whys process to review many additional concerns surrounding these causes. But the control impact matrix is designed to focus more on things that you can control versus what is impossible to control on your own. You can use this to give yourself an idea of what you can do to change your plans in the future.

What Are the Incidental Findings?

The incidental findings that may develop in the work environment are actions that have developed due to the root cause. These are not things that were directly caused by the root factor but are things that occurred in response to it. This could include cases like people behaving differently in the work environment or people avoiding certain procedures or items to try and resolve issues. The incidental findings arise as a result of some changes that take place due to a root cause. You can talk about these incidental points if needed and figure out if they are things that can be resolved with corrective actions. Be as detailed as possible when listing information on those incidental findings so you know more about the surrounding factors that are getting in the way of your work.

Discussing Solutions

You can discuss any solutions that you feel are sensible for resolving issues in the workplace. The solutions can be as detailed as they have to be, so long as they entail proper resolutions to the problems you come across. As you plan these solutions, you have to work with a few points for getting the work organized:

1. Discuss how the solution is to be implemented. The solution should be related to the root cause.

2. Explain the risks that might develop. These include risks surrounding any problems that may develop. Discuss the likelihood of certain problems coming along. The likelihood may be high or low depending on the issue. Talk about any modifications you will make to your plans if needed.

3. A measurement of success should also be planned. The measure will include certain settings that developed. You can explain anything that might have to work for your efforts to be successful. The results that occurred in any situation may also be explained in detail.

You can use any kind of solution you wish to utilize. Review how well your task will work versus how efficient and thorough the process might be. You can use this to identify how well a task is run. This, in turn, improves upon how well the process works.

Chapter 36 – Cause Mapping

It is vital for you to recognize what is causing certain problems to develop in the workplace. Every issue comes with some kind of problem that is making the situation worse. Identifying the issue and figuring out the root of the concern is a necessity for the Six Sigma process. You must see how well the concern has developed and what you can do to fix the problem before it can become worse. You can also use the answer you come across to find a solution for how to resolve issues that may be too persistent or hard to resolve in some situations.

One solution that you can utilize in the analysis process of your Six Sigma effort entails cause mapping. This is a practice that combines several aspects of the diagnostic concerns in your Six Sigma work. You will move the root cause analysis alongside the general DMAIC template, not to mention the Five Whys analysis. The following chapter focuses on the steps you should take when completing the cause mapping process. This includes an emphasis on how you will explain the problem, complete analytical steps and would manage incidents or other concerns in the workplace.

Explaining the Issue

First, you must look at how the issue in the workplace was formed. The issue should be analyzed based on an individual incident. The event may be a problem that was caused by a certain defect or issue. You must explain when the issue took place, the specific details on the defect, the number of defects involved and how those defects occurred. At the start, you will analyze the issue surrounding the defect. You can review the concern based on the larger picture that you come across. After that, you must use a few additional steps for reviewing the concern:

1. Define the problem. This is the incident you are investigating.

2. Map out the process for the procedure if you can. This is not always necessary, nor is it applicable. The process mapping effort will be discussed in the next section.

3. Gather the data surrounding the incident. Review as many details as possible on where it took place, when it occurred, who was involved and any other data you can obtain.

4. Complete a cause and effect analysis. Review the data that was produced to see if a root cause was found. You can use the Five Whys analysis process at this step if you wish.

5. Develop a series of steps for identifying the problem and finding a solution.

The solution should be based around the things you might have noticed in your work. The steps should be utilized for not only finding solutions but also to prevent any future problems. Prevention entails identifying what causes issues to occur. This includes controlling those problems before they can become harder to manage.

6. Produce a pilot stage where the solution is implemented.

The pilot stage involves taking the data you have gathered and testing it out in the field. You can test the ideas you have come across and figure out if those ideas are relevant to your work success or if some additional changes have to be made. The pilot is intended to be a test stage. This may be corrected if needed, and you can go back to the start of the cause mapping process if you have to. Keep on completing the pilot stage until you notice a significant difference in what you are completing.

7. Compare the pilot effort with a control stage.

A control stage operates with the same content you are working with in the workplace. The control stage can be interpreted as business as usual. You can compare the pilot and control stages together to see how your efforts in operating business functions are handled. The control can work for as long as necessary based on the plans you have for managing your content.

8. Document anything you have learned in the process.

The pilot stage should be analyzed to see how it improves upon a process versus the control stage. The pilot stage should show some improvements, or at least some changes that make the operational process in the workplace a little easier to follow. Discuss with others in the workplace how well the new changes have helped the business with its operations and what you wish to get out of the task. Be aware of what you are doing with the pilot stage and record all the necessary information so the documentation process can work well enough and with the content you need to analyze.

Process Mapping

Processing mapping, as discussed earlier, is a practice that entails a review of a certain procedure that will take place. You can use processing mapping to review how well a procedure is planned out and how you can get this ready. You can use any kind of process that you want, provided that you look at how well a routine is to be planned out. The process that you currently use can be mapped out, followed by a new map that illustrates something else you are planning in the workplace. You can produce the map to be as detailed as desired.

Process maps are created based on how certain actions are to take place and what steps will go into a process. Refer to the earlier chapter on process mapping if you need extra help with the practice.

Chapter 37 – Managing Hand Offs

No one likes it when they have to deal with hand offs. Let's say that you are trying to run a manufacturing site, but you have to move content between parties. A hand off might require you to move one task in the manufacturing process to others. The hand off would entail someone who is not fully familiar with certain functions being told to handle a new routine or effort. As a result, it becomes easier for a defect to develop.

As you plan your Six Sigma effort, you have to look at hand offs that might occur. Hand offs can arise at any time, including in cases where you are trying to improve upon a task. A hand off can be frustrating to everyone involved. The customer does not appreciate getting something that wasn't taken care of by someone who understood the task, let alone a group not fully aware of the parameters of an assignment. Meanwhile, employees do not like hand offs because they are being forced to do things that they are not comfortable with.

You must look at how your business can keep hand offs under control. The best Six Sigma plans are the ones where hand offs will be kept to a minimum and the risk of those hand offs developing will be minor. But at the same time, there might come a time when a hand off has to take place. In such cases, you need to keep the effects of hand offs in check.

Where to Find Hand offs

Hand offs can occur at any point in the Six Sigma work. The hand off is likely to be found in the receiving or inspection process. At this point, one party is moving the data and content in the Six Sigma work off to another person. The action is often frustrating and can keep people from being on the same page. This is especially true if the people involved don't communicate enough about what is happening in these hand offs and don't explain why the hand offs need to take place.

Review the points in your Six Sigma effort where the duties involved might change. These are times when hand offs are likely to develop. Be advised that in some cases, it might be impossible for you to keep hand offs from developing. You might have to get these hand offs working because people in the work environment have different duties. One party responsible for producing a product might have to send the item out to someone who can package that product, for example.

Here's an example of what you can find in hand offs. A soda bottler might have a routine where a few people are responsible for measuring and mixing the contents that will be produced and sent to the market. They mix all the parts of the soft drinks they are preparing while measuring the bottles or cans to ensure they are filled the right way. After a while, that first team will hand the products over to a packaging team that will support the production of labels for each item. Next, the packaging team will hand off the finished product to a shipping team that will move the products out to stores around a local area.

Needless to say, it will be impossible for the bottler to operate without those hand offs. The team has to work with many parts to allow the product being handled to move forward. But at the same time, the bottler should also look at how well it can manage those hand offs and ensure that they are running as smoothly as possible.

Identify Signals

Every planned hand off should be explored based on the signals being produced. What signals are being sent between the people regarding how content is to be moved? You must see that the hand offs are managed with all people being fully aware of the process. For instance, a sender might tell a receiver about the products being sent out. The sender may also send out signals explaining what has to be done.

Going back to the drink bottler, the manufacturing team might have a signal sent out to the packaging team explaining that the soda products being handed are a specific brand. The packagers needs to produce labels or other printouts that are reflective of the branded products they are receiving.

There might also be times when a hand off is unplanned. One segment of a manufacturing team might send a product off to a different part of that larger team. Each team might have different standards and rules. An analysis of these is in order and can include a review of why an unplanned hand off is occurring and what has to be done to stop the problem from happening again in the future. Sometimes this might include different parties in the same group having specific ideas of what to do in the workplace. You may have to retrain some of these groups.

Review the Middlemen

There are times when a middleman might be involved with your work. A middleman is a secondary person who makes sure the hand off proceeds smoothly. That middleman is not necessarily someone who is going to move forward with the rest of the task. You must look at what that outside person is going to do and whether he or she is necessary to the task. There is always the chance that the middleman in the situation is not someone who is fully required for your work.

You need to ensure that the middleman is not going to modify the product or service being distributed, and this also includes seeing that the distribution process works correctly and that everyone has an idea of what should be handled.

What the Outgoing Sender Must Do

There are generally two parties of note when managing hand offs—the recipient and the outgoing party. The sender is the first one to look at. This party is incoming and is ready to move an item to the next party. The hand off should be scheduled appropriately with a plan for moving the content as desired. The incoming entity must be ready to move items in the hand off. Plan the incoming process by using a few standards:

1. Have the sender look at the materials being handled.

The sender should notice how well the materials being sent out are organized and have a good plan in hand for the procedure. The sender cannot afford to manage a product without noting what it is or what it might be used for because that sender might have to convey some of that information to the receiver.

2. The sender should not try to tamper with or change anything in material that is being sent out.

The description of something has to be as accurate and thorough as needed. The sender should not try to adjust anything. Rather, that person should focus on moving the product out based on the appropriate established procedures.

3. Review the time frame for the sender.

The sender has to get the product out to the recipient as soon as possible. In your Six Sigma effort, review the things that are keeping the sender from being able to move something out to a receiver. Look at anything like shipping problems, transport issues and even any policies in the workplace. You can use the time frame for the process to analyze what needs to change and to assess whether certain problems might get in the way.

What the Recipient Must Do

The entity that receives the hand off must ensure that the product being handled is of the right standard. This includes confirming that whatever has been delivered is safe for use and will not be any harder to incorporate or use in the process. The recipient also must contact the delivery entity about how the product or service was made and what has changed while in transit. The proper review is necessary for seeing that there are no problems.

The main point of this chapter is that hand offs can be frustrating but also easy to control. You can manage the ways hand offs operate so you will have an easier time keeping your work in check. But it is also important to watch how your Six Sigma process works and ensure that you are training your workers to where unplanned hand offs are less likely to develop. Everyone has to be on the same page regarding their duties and efforts.

Chapter 38 – Hypothesis Testing

One good idea to consider for your Six Sigma project is to produce a hypothesis. As you analyze your work, you can come up with a hypothesis that will help identify how well your task is working. You can use any kind of hypothesis regarding your task as you wish, but the key is to ensure that the hypothesis in question is carefully planned out and that you have an idea of what you want from it.

Hypothesis testing is necessary for helping you to explore the statistical points that might come about between different data sets. These data points may represent data that is distributed in many ways. A difference may be noticed within your hypothesis. In that case, you will have to analyze both the continuous and discrete data that you wish to work with. For continuous data, the hypothesis testing process can entail a review between the difference in the average or mean and how different the variance in your work is. For discrete data, there may be a review in how the proportions vary.

The continuous data that you may work with could include a situation where your bell curve is not in the right spot. The mean or central part that the standard deviations emerge from might not be in the middle of your current space. You have to review how well you can move your data to the desired limits while getting the middle of your bell curve right. The point here is that the means are different from one another at the start. The results are precise, but not necessarily accurate.

For the discrete data, you might have the middle part of the bell curve listed at around the total you want it to be. But while you might have everything well prepared, the bell curve might be taller or shorter than you want it to be. The variances between the data are different at this point. The information is accurate, but not precise enough to where you are getting more of your output to work within the same limit levels. Your spread will then have to be adjusted.

How to Test a Hypothesis

You can use the following steps for testing a hypothesis:

1. Figure out the specific hypothesis test that you wish to complete.

2. Review the null and alternate hypotheses that you wish to use. These are both optional choices for your use. The null hypothesis states a lack of difference between two groups, while the alternate hypothesis states that there is a sizeable difference between those groups.

3. Review the P-value or test statistics versus the general values that you wish to utilize.

4. Review the results of your test. You might have to reject the hypothesis. This includes not only the basic hypothesis you are producing, but also the other two that might have been produced in the effort.

How a Null Hypothesis Can Work

You have the option to produce a null hypothesis in your work. A null hypothesis is a prediction stating that there is no relationship between two particular parameters in your work. You may conclude in your review that certain actions in your work are not relevant. For instance, you might come across the belief that a machine's widget product is not related to environmental factors like humidity in the room that the machine is in. You could state in your null hypothesis that even when humidity levels change in a spot, the machine will continue to produce the same number of widgets.

The null hypothesis is designed with speculation in mind. This is to be incorporated into the practice, although it is also something that should be realistic. You might want to review the null hypothesis while putting in a rate of about five percent for the hypothesis being correct. You may use this with planning a task. But the null hypothesis works best when you use it with the intention of identifying possible changes or impacts that might develop.

Type I and II Errors

Depending on your task and how you plan out your null hypothesis, you might come across some Type I or II errors.

A Type I error develops as the null hypothesis is found to be true but is eventually rejected. You are asserting something in this error that is absent. The error may be considered a false positive to suggest that a condition is present even though that condition is not actually occurring. For instance, you might produce a hypothesis stating that added humidity in a workplace will cause machines to produce more widgets, but your null hypothesis will state that adding humidity will not make a machine more effective. A Type I error in this case will occur when an effect that is not present is detected; this may include a case where the added humidity in a room causes a machine to be more productive. The original null hypothesis may appear true, but it is rejected due to factors like bad data in the testing process.

A Type II error is different in that the null hypothesis is false, but it is not rejected. This is a miss as it is not asserting things that are present. This can be interpreted as a false negative as a condition is not found when it is supposed to be there. Going back to the last null hypothesis example, a Type II error will develop when the effect of humidity making a machine productive is not identified. The null hypothesis is incorrect, but the data you gathered in the experiment suggests that the null hypothesis cannot be rejected.

You have to be aware of the errors that develop as they might make it harder for you to get the accurate results that you demand in your test. For equation purposes, you may place the null hypothesis as *Ho* while the Type I error rate is α and the Type II error rate is β. You can use the following points:

- When *Ho* is true but it is impossible to make a decision about *Ho*, a correct inference or True Negative can be attained. The probability of this is $1 - \alpha$.

- When *Ho* is false but you fail to reject *Ho*, a Type II error will develop. The probability of the error or False Negative is β.

- If *Ho* is true but the *Ho* is rejected, a Type I error or False Positive will develop. The probability here is α.

- If *Ho* is false and you reject *Ho*, a correct inference or True Positive will occur. The probability in this case is $1 - \beta$.

Such errors can occur in many situations. For instance, a spam filtering program might come across a Type I error when it identifies a legitimate email message as spam even if that message is not. The null hypothesis of "The email is not spam" is true, but the program will reject that hypothesis, thus keeping the non-spam email from being sent out. For an inventory control process, a control system might reject certain goods in a Type I error, but a Type II error will involve the system accepting poor-quality goods. Your statistical test will have to work with an appropriate measurement between what you will accept regarding false positives and negatives. Keeping these numbers as minimal and in control as possible is vital for your task's success.

P-Value

There are often times when the variation you notice is from a random source. In this case, the original hypothesis or projected distribution that you want to work with is not functioning as well as it should be. For this, a P-value may be noticed. This variation that you can measure is the chance that you might be wrong as some random changes have occurred. The P-value will be higher in value when the risk of being incorrect is greater. Your P-value measurement will help you to identify how well certain things are laid out in the Six Sigma process while recognizing what works in particular. The best way to see the P-value is that it is the probability of your Six Sigma process committing a Type I error.

The P-value will appear between zero and one in total. The P-value should be less than 0.05 if possible. When the P-value is less than 0.05, the null hypothesis can be voided.

213

The alternate hypothesis may be accepted. The number means that the confidence level in a project will be 95 percent. As the P-value drops, the confidence level grows, thus giving the impression that the results are true and that the hypothesis can be confirmed. In addition, the risk of there being a false positive or negative will be minimal at this juncture.

You have full control over the amount of certainty that you wish to utilize in your task. You can prepare a defined total for the data you wish to utilize, although you have to be cautious when organizing that total. The good news is that the process you use can be as flexible as you want it to be. You can allow for a bit of extra leeway at the start of your Six Sigma process, and you can then close up that total as you move along and the process starts to improve. Your significance level can be as high or low as needed, but the P-value will change as that project moves along.

Alpha and Beta Risks

An alpha risk may develop as you test the hypothesis. The alpha risk is the risk of incorrectly rejecting the null hypothesis. The alpha risk may be subtracted from zero to get details on the confidence level of a task. The best way to describe the alpha risk is that it is the likelihood of whether you will get a Type I error in your work. You can use this measurement as you see fit to identify how much certainty you want to have in your work.

The best alpha risk should be as low in value as possible. The risk can be around 0.05 or 0.10 if needed. The smaller risk should provide you with more control over the task. This may assist you with creating a more efficient setup for handling your content. The design can particularly do well if you're going to manage your content carefully enough and without issues.

The beta risk is a measure of the likelihood of a Type II error being committed. This may also be called the consumer's risk. The power in your test should be controlled to keep the beta risk from being high. In this case, you will increase the sample size of the test to allow for a more definite result. You may also change the measurement gauge to focus on some of the more minute changes or variations that you might come across within your work.

Hypothesis Testing Options

Note: The following segment treats the output as Y and the input as X.

For Continuous Data from the Input and Output Alike (Chi-Square Test)

When the input and output data are both continuous, you can use a chi-square test of independence. The output Y will be different from two or more smaller X groups. For instance, you might find that there are certain defects coming from a machine in the early part of the day. Meanwhile, added defects may develop during the later part. Your goal here is to figure out if the defects from the early part of the day are different from the defects that occur later in the same day.

The chi-square test works when you have two variables in one group and want to figure out if there's a link between the two. The test can be found in many situations such as in a polling center when people find that those of a certain demographic lean towards one particular voting choice. The process helps to take a sample of the data in question and figure out what might be coming out of the work process involved. The process for the chi-square test is as follows:

1. State the hypotheses.

You will utilize two hypotheses in the chi-square test. The Ho one states that Hypothesis A and B are independent of each other. Ha states that A and B depend on each other. A null hypothesis may also list details on how knowing what Variable A is will not help you with predicting the level of Variable B. The best way to state that the hypothesis works is that the alternative is not causal but that one variable is going to cause the other.

2. Prepare an analysis plan.

An analysis plan is used to review sample data. You can use this to accept or reject your null hypothesis. In this case, you might look at the values of Variable A while looking at whether or not you can predict the other variable. You might be able to scrap the null hypothesis depending on the results you find. After going through a null hypothesis, you can plan a routine based on a significance level.

The significance level used in this process is an analysis of how well the value can be handled and that the null hypothesis is not going to be deemed true. The significance level can be anything from zero to one. Most people use 0.01 to 0.1 as a value. After that, you can get the total test to work.

3. Review the sample data. Start by working with the degrees of freedom.

Check on the sample data to find the degrees of freedom and will entail a look at the expected frequencies and statistics involved. You can use the sample data to find the degrees of freedom involved. The DF will be equal to (r-1) x (c-1). The r is the levels for one variable that you can categorize. The c is the number of levels on that other variable listed on the same item. The process can help you recognize how far removed items might be. The one is subtracted by each point to make for a confidence interval to produce a more accurate readout. The total number of degrees of freedom will equal the independent observations that can be made in a sample when compared with the parameters that can be estimated off the sample data being used.

4. Look at the expected frequencies.

Review the expected frequencies of r and c by using the formula (Nr x Nc) / n. The Nr is the number of observations at the r level, while Nc is the observations at the c level. In other words, you are working with Variables A and B at this point in the research. The n is a measure of the sample size. You can use this to produce a carefully organized layout.

5. Prepare a test statistic.

A test statistic can be reviewed by getting a random variable or X^2 defined by using the equation:

$$X^2 = \Sigma \left[(O_{r,c} - E_{r,c})^2 / E_{r,c} \right]$$

The O is the observed frequency count on the two levels for the separate variables. E is the expected frequency count for each level.

6. Calculate the P-value.

The P-value is needed at the next point in the process. The P-value refers to the probability of seeing what a sample statistic may be and if it is up to the test statistic that was produced. At this point, you will require a calculator to identify the chi-square distribution level. Also, the degrees of freedom you produced may help you with the process. You can find an online calculator for the P-value.

7. Review the results.

You can reject the null hypothesis if you notice that the P-value is at or above the significance level. The design ensures you can confirm how well the variables are related to each other. That is, you will find that the variables can operate independently from one another and that you cannot tell if something is correct just by looking at it. You can ensure that the variables are working as uniquely as possible while remaining simple to plan out.

For Normal Continuous Input Data and Discrete Output Data (Multiple Regression)

Logistic regression is needed when the x is continuous and the Y is discrete. Logistic regression is designed with a predictive approach. You will analyze the relationship between the two variables with the intention of looking at how data might change on one variable. For instance, you might use logistic regression to analyze how the potential for a machine to work will vary based on each change in the percentage of humidity in a room. You can get as many humidity readouts as possible and modify them in many tests to figure out if there is a change in how the machines are working. You must ensure that the data you are working with fits the standards you have established.

A multiple regression analysis may be conducted to identify any concerns that have developed. For the best results, the dependent variable should be measured on a continuous scale. Also, the review can include two or more independent variables that will directly predict the value of that dependent variable. You'll need to produce a full chart to illustrate how the variable you are measuring looks and to assess whether there are any substantial influences upon the work being produced.

As the above chart reveals, the process of the analysis can help with identifying many factors that might directly influence certain functions. In the case of the chart above, the species type will directly influence the test results and analysis.

For Discrete Input Data and Normal Continuous Output Data (ANOVA and HOV Tests)

A T-test may be conducted to identify any sizeable differences between the means of the two variables. You can use a single-sample T-test where you compare one variable versus a standard. For instance, a call center might have its calls measured to see if the center is answering those calls within a specific time frame. You can also get a two-sample T-test ready where two populations are compared with each other. You might look at the morning shift at the call center and see if the calls are being answered at the same rate as those being handled by the evening shift.

An Analysis of Variance (ANOVA) test may also be conducted. You will test the difference between multiple means that have been measured or analyzed. The mean answer time of the morning shift at a call center may be compared with the mean of the afternoon staff. The evening staff's mean answer time will be added in and compared. You can use the test to figure out how well different groups in the workplace might be functioning.

A Homogeneity of Variance (HOV) test is another choice for the discrete X and normal continuous Y. You will compare the variance of at least two separate groups. The variation of the morning staff at the call center will be compared with the afternoon and evening staffs. Each group will be measured independently. The test will review how well certain staff members might do and assess whether there is a trend where the call center works better during a specific point in the day.

The main consideration between these two tests entails how they measure different types of items. The ANOVA test is suitable for comparing the means of at least two populations. The HOV test is for when you're testing the variance of those populations. You have the option to test as many populations as you wish in each of these tests.

For Discrete Input Data and Non-Normal Continuous Output Data (Mood's Median)

Mood's Median Test may be conducted at this point as X is discrete and Y is continuous and non-normal. The test involves comparing the medians of two or more groups with each other. The median of the morning staff at the call center can be compared with the other two staffs at that same center. The comparison helps to review how well the groups are managing calls while figuring out how far off their bell curves are. You will have to plan ahead to figure out how to get those call centers to the point where they have the same medians all around. You can also use the HOV test at this point.

Mood's Median Test is for when you're going to measure the cycle time, or Y, and the production lines, or Xs, on the chart. You can also use this test to review the Y ratings of X customers over time. The test process helps you to figure out how the distribution being produced for the median while also analyzing the content that you are working with. The process for executing Mood's Median Test is as follows:

1. Gather the total measurements produced from a series of items you are trying to compare.

2. Analyze the specific measurements, cycle times or other Y values that you are trying to compare.

3. Create charts showing the results that you calculated.

4. Review the totals together within a chart that lists the mean and standard deviation that you are using. N is for the sample size. P is for the P-value.

At this point, you should have an idea of how well a bell curve is to be formed. You can use the median to make a decision for how you're going to handle that bell curve. This will result in a setting of the standard deviations you wish to use. The results should produce a clear design that illustrates what you might be working with and how the content is to be used to your liking.

For Discrete Input and Output Data

A chi-square test of independence is recommended at this juncture. The Y from two or more smaller groups should be compared versus the X totals. In this case, you are looking at how defects in one group are different from the defects produced by a separate group. The testing process should look less into the number of defects and what is causing those defects to grow. You may find that different plans should be utilized based on the time of day when the defects occur.

The important part of testing your hypothesis is to get a clear idea of how well your work on the Six Sigma task is going. This is also to produce a more efficient result that entails the right value being generated at a time.

Chapter 39 – Producing Solution Parameters

At this point in the Six Sigma process, you should understand how to define your problem, how to measure it and what you can do when analyzing the issue at hand. But now you must look at how you are going to resolve the problem in question. An appropriate solution is required for helping you to move forward with your Six Sigma task. You can change the inputs in your work based on the parameters you have found and what you feel is appropriate for your work. In short, you are entering the Improve stage of the Six Sigma process.

To start, you have to determine the answers to the issues at hand. You must be aware of the solution parameters that you will utilize as you work on your Six Sigma task. After you analyze your data, you will need to find a way to improve upon how you are planning your work efforts while remaining sustainable and meeting the established requirements. You will have to review the analysis stage of your Six Sigma routine at this point while recognizing the cause and effect among other factors. The detailed effort you put into your work at this juncture will help you plan a specific solution to the problem you wish to fix.

Planning a Decision Statement

The basis of your solution should be planned according to a decision statement. The statement is the purpose of the decision that you wish to make. You can plan this based on the expectations that the customer has. Parameters can be established based on what solutions are right as well as any possible alternatives you can use if necessary. In the decision statement, you need to explain how said parameters will be established. Optionally, you can also reflect upon the reasons behind your overall decision statement.

Planning Criteria for the Solution

You can come up with a solution that fits in with many types of criteria as necessary for your work. The criteria should be organized based on the results you are working towards and the restrictions you are trying to manage. The availability of various resources associated with the task will also be a factor. In particular, you can plan your criteria based on what is necessary versus what you feel is acceptable.

You may start working with the general mandatory requirements (the "musts") in your work. The measurements have to be realistic and must fit in with any regulatory standards you wish to utilize. More importantly, the data must be refined to where you know there are no possible alternatives.

You can also use some comparative forms of criteria in your work if desired. These forms are the "wants" that you have. You can use these criteria for the basis of comparison purposes.

For instance, you might be working at a call center with the goal of trying to keep the response times for calls down. You can look at general requirements like employees working with a specific script for their calls or ensuring that calls are forwarded to the correct employees, those who are experienced with specific tasks or questions that the caller needs addressed. Meanwhile, you might have comparative forms of criteria like rerouting as few calls as possible. Additional call center criteria could include ensuring that callers get their answers in as few steps as possible or that proper sales promotional efforts are made during each call.

The SCAMPER Process

As you work with your criteria for your solution parameters, you can use the SCAMPER process. This is a seven-part process for figuring out the content that you will use in your solution parameters. The goal of the process is to clarify the goals that you wish to use while also preparing a sensible platform for how your work will be organized. The seven parts are:

1. Substitute (S)

You can replace any criteria or parameter you want with another choice. A call center might want to minimize how many calls are rerouted between employees. But you might also substitute the criteria with something like employees doing a maximum of one reroute per call. The key is to keep the calls from bouncing from one agent to another. The main goal will be to have no rerouting, but a substitute may be used if that original plan is not feasible.

2. Combine (C)

Some criteria might have to be combined together to create a new parameter. In some cases, you might combine one goal to create a completely new goal. In other cases, talent from many departments may be combined to produce one larger group of people. The combine attribute should be planned based on what assets you have in order to maximize their use.

3. Adapt (A)

As you work, you must look at how you can adapt your plans over time. The adapt criteria involves adapting one goal to serve a new purpose. You may use this to make your goals more flexible. This includes producing a new context or being inspired by another concept in the work routine. The call center listed above can adapt a goal for managing rerouting processes to create new criteria like producing new definitions for what it takes to make rerouting efforts more efficient and acceptable in the workplace.

4. Modify (M)

After a while, there comes a time when some criteria have to be modified to fit certain needs. The modify stage of the process involves the existing goals being shifted with certain ideas possibly being highlighted. Some elements of the work in question may also be strengthened to meet certain standards or to make processes work better. You can use the modify stage to change or magnify some of the things you are doing in cases where you know certain goals are more important and need to be better emphasized.

5. Put to Different Uses (P)

You might find that some products or services are better suited for use in different industries. For instance, a company that makes a glass cleaner might discover that the cleaner can also work on tiled surfaces. A testing process may be planned to see how well the cleaner can work on tiles, thus changing how the product is made or marketed. The P part of the SCAMPER process should be planned for cases where you know something can be used differently and you want to try the process out.

6. Eliminate (E)

After a while, you might find that some criteria don't meet the necessary standards for your work. In this case, you will have to eliminate those points in order to streamline the effort. A call center might find that a goal like totally eradicating rerouting can be eliminated if too much of a variance is discovered.

7. Reverse (R)

You can use the reverse process to assess how a product or service can be reorganized to produce different parameters or concepts that might work a little better for certain standards or goals that you wish to attain. In some cases, particular roles can be reversed. You may also try to complete the opposite of an initial idea if you find that might be a better solution.

You can use the SCAMPER process on as many of your goals as necessary. The key is to allow the process to work with all those steps to see how well your criteria works. In some cases, you might come out with fewer or more criteria after the process is run. But you will be using SCAMPER with the intention of producing a realistic and accurate review of all the things you want to do with your work.

Using the Likert Scale for Your Wants

In some cases, you might have many wants that can cloud the efforts you put into your work. You will have to review how important each of those wants is so you don't weigh your task down too much. A Likert scale readout can be used for each of the wants you wish to utilize.

The Likert scale is often utilized in many studies as a measuring scale. You can use the Likert scale to identify whether something is important or insignificant. Specifically, you will list all your wants on a scale from 1 to 10. You might list 1 as being less important and 10 as being the most important. After you review those wants, you can see how your Likert scale answers compare with one another. You might decide that certain wants are more important than others and that it's best to drop others because they are not all that important. The scale will eliminate the unnecessary clutter in your work and help streamline efforts.

Chapter 40 – Generating the Best Possible Solution

As you consistently review how effective your Sigma Six work is, a few techniques can be used for helping you to generate the best solution for the task. Each option should be utilized based on what you feel is appropriate for your work. Some of these concepts may also include finding ways to resolve problems that have emerged during the Six Sigma process.

Brain-Writing

Brain-writing involves reviewing the ways you might come across new ideas or concepts. The focus is to produce as many unique ideas as possible within the smallest possible time frame. As many people in the workplace as possible should be included. Within a five-minute span, each person will write down a few ideas.

A.6-3-5 Brain-Writing

You have two choices to work with when handling the brain-writing process. The first is a 6-3-5 approach. The process is named for how it entails six people, three ideas for each person and five minutes to come up with ideas. The effort can include more people if desired, but the 6-3-5 approach should be enough in most situations. The steps are as follows:

1. Six people in the group will work on coming up with new ideas. These six people should be shared within the same community.
2. Each person in the group will produce three ideas.
3. The group has five total minutes to produce those three ideas.
4. After the five-minute period ends, the people in the group will pass the notebooks that they wrote those ideas in to the next person.
5. A new five-minute period will begin. People have to write down three new ideas. These may be based off the ideas that were previously generated.
6. The process will be repeated four more times so every person will have an idea of what each person in a group is thinking or planning.

This means that 18 new ideas will be generated in a five-minute span. Since there are six sessions, that means the process will generate 108 new ideas in 30 minutes. The process ensures that everyone in a group can come up with unique concepts for how to resolve a Six Sigma issue. Each person can work off feedback or produce new concepts based on original ideas. The process identifies new concepts that may work while planning special efforts that might be easier to operate with.

Sometimes the same ideas might arise a few times within the work task. Maybe people in a group think alike and therefore are considering the same solution. But the people in the group may also have some minute differences in their thinking. They might want to stick with certain concepts or values. A discussion may be held among all people in the same group to figure out what can be done for a solution.

The 6-3-5 brain writing process is easy to follow and is also thorough. The fact that no single person will be responsible for taking notes ensures that everyone will feel confident. But at the same time, it might also be difficult for some members of the same team to follow ideas being produced. A lack of an immediate discussion may also trigger disputes among group members. It might help to hold a discussion of the ideas after the brain-writing process is finished so all parties can get a closer idea of what everyone is thinking about and what can be done to resolve certain issues in the future.

B. Constrained Brain-Writing

While the basic brain-writing process focuses on coming up with various ideas as desired, the constrained process focuses on limitations. This includes working with specific situations and plans based on what might be suitable and useful. The brain-writing process can be as detailed and controlled as necessary. This may work in cases where a strict focus is required.

The constrained brain-writing process works with the following steps:

1. Produce a series of starter ideas. These may be based on certain actions in the workplace.

2. Allow each member in a group to write down ideas.

3. Each person takes a sheet a paper with some ideas on it and adds unique ideas. People do not have to openly declare that they are writing specific things.

4. People exchange papers. One possible way to do this is to put them in the center of the table for others to modify. This is for cases where a person working on something hasn't come up with something useful enough.

5. The process should be repeated until all ideas have been utilized.

The goal of the constrained process is to allow people to come up with ideas without having to go through any extra discussions. People are allowed to produce many ideas as they see fit. The key is to ensure the ideas are managed right and work within specific parameters.

Assumption Busting

Assumption busting is a practice where you review the current problems surrounding performance in the workplace. You will consider the assumptions that people have regarding the work environment or the practice. The improvement process helps to fix issues by getting people to focus on different concepts as they arise.

For instance, a fruit cannery might deal with an issue where not all cans are being filled with the right amounts of sliced fruit every time. An assumption might be that the fruits are all sliced differently and that there will always be some variance. But the underlying issue might actually be that the people at the workplace aren't measuring each can correctly based on the mass of the foods involved and how items are filled with fruit slices versus the water used to preserve everything in a can. By defeating the assumption that people are cutting fruit differently, it becomes easier for people to identify what should be done for managing content in any situation.

You can bust some assumptions by using a few standards:

1. Review the problem. In the example above, the fruit cannery notices that the cans of fruit are not filled all the way.

2. Review the rules responsible for the issue. The rule for the cannery is that each can of fruit must weigh a certain total when filled, sealed and labeled.

3. Look at the rule and review the assumption that was used when creating it. The cannery employees might assume that fruit cans will vary in quality based on how the fruits are cut and prepared.

4. Prepare a test to test the assumption. This includes seeing if the assumption is true and, if so, whether the issue can be made untrue.

Let's go into a little more detail with the cannery. The testing process may include a review of how the fruits are cut by machines at the cannery plant. The fruits may be analyzed based on the sizes of those fruit pieces, their textures, weights and any irregularities. You might find that the fruits are being cut in the same shape every time. Therefore, you should have the employees focus more on practices for measuring cans and seeing how well machines are calibrated to ensure they produce the right amounts every time. For cases where the assumption is true, the cannery may review the practice and determine what can be done to get the fruit pieces to be sliced as uniformly as possible.

Assumption busting is all about finding ways to confirm that certain assumptions are wrong. In other cases, this will involve eliminating existing assumptions. The process might be a challenge, but keeping assumptions out of the workplace is important for helping a place to run right while giving people a sense of control over their tasks.

These are all useful ideas to consider when finding the best possible solution in your Six Sigma effort. You can also consider brainstorming and benchmarking as additional solutions for helping you to move forward with your work. The next few chapters will focus on understanding what can be done to highlight your work based on these two points. The life of your business may depend on how well you can adapt to changes and actions in your work environment.

Chapter 41 – Calculating the RTY

It is important to think about how well your products can move through a setup while remain free of defects. The RTY, or Rolled Throughput Yield, can be analyzed to identify what goes into a process versus what is coming out of it. The RTY is the product of yields that comes through each step within the Six Sigma routine. You can obtain this to confirm that whatever you are working with doesn't have any problems or need to be reworked.

The yield produced deserves to be noted, but it is also vital to see how the traditional yield measurement process might not work. Normally, you calculate the manufacturing yield of something by using a review of items passing through a process while scrapping anything that is not good enough. A full review of what is discarded versus what is accepted might help with a traditional analysis. But that process might not always work. Any parts that are produced in the beginning might be inaccurate. The hidden factory concept might not be noticeable at the start.

The RTY works by reviewing many processes and assessing the yields that are produced on average. Every process is explored with the intention of finding other processes where items might still have defects.

The process for calculating the RTY entails the following steps:

1. Review the process steps involved in the routine.

Let's look at how a vacuum cleaner company can handle processes involving the production of many parts or materials. You might have three steps dedicated to specific kinds of materials you want to use in the appliance. Each step will have its own dedicated steps, but they will all link up together. You can produce a close analysis or your work by analyzing each of the overarching three steps.

2. Analyze the yield of each of the process steps.

The first step for the vacuum cleaner company might produce a yield of 50 with five items being defective. The second step will have a yield of 75 with six items being defective. The third has a yield of 60 and only three defective units. You divide the number of units that passed by the yield totals in each segment to produce a yield percentage for each process. The results are 0.9, 0.92 and 0.95.

3. Multiply the ratios you gathered by one another.

Multiply the three totals with each other in the sample to get an RTY of 0.7866. What this means is that about 78.66 percent of the items being produced are actually going through. The RTY gives you a more realistic idea of what has gone through. You can use this to figure out what parts of the process have to be resolved first.

You also have the option to produce a rolled throughput yield loss. This is the inverse of the RTY. The RTY loss for the example above is 0.2134. This means that about 21.34 percent of the materials being produced have been lost. Your goal when going lean is to keep that number down while figuring out a plan to ensure procedures to that end that are easy to follow.

Chapter 42 – The Failure Mode Effect Analysis

Even with all the things you are doing with your Six Sigma routine, there is always the chance that your work might fail. You might come across a problem with your Six Sigma process, including an issue where the effort is going off the rails. There is a chance that there is a failure in your design. This will require you to work with a Failure Mode Effect Analysis (FMEA). The review will help you identify the things that can go wrong in your work.

Three considerations are used in the FMEA:

1. How severe is the possible failure event?

2. How often or likely is the failure to occur?

3. Is there a good way the failure can be detected and monitored?

Let's take a closer look at how the FMEA works.

Two Definitions

Failure mode refers to the ways something can fail. Failures are defects or errors that may develop and which may be dangerous or harmful. Going back to the fruit cannery example, you might find that a machine responsible for slicing fruits is not working as it should. The machine may not slice the fruits the right way, thus causing the fruits to take up too much space in each can. This may make it harder for the fruit to be canned correctly.

Effects analysis refers to how you study the issues that arise. You need to review how the failures in the workplace may develop based on many factors such as your business being incapable of processing its data right. Getting as much of an analysis over these events as possible is vital to helping you recognize what is working in your field and what to expect out of your effort.

How the FMEA Works

1. Identify the function that you are measuring.

The function can be anything you want it to be. For this case, let's look at how a plant that manufactures batteries for electric hybrid vehicles work. A function to review may be the process of designing a lightweight battery. The function of a machine may be to ensure the battery is light in weight. This is to ensure the vehicle doesn't have lots of drag.

2. Look at the possible failure mode.

For the electric battery, there might be a failure where the battery is too lightweight. This includes the battery not being the proper weight. Failure mode refers to the problem that develops. The issue could be significant in some cases. The FMEA is best for when you're reviewing serious problems.

3. Review the potential effects of the failure.

The failure could produce significant issues that might hurt a business. The car battery company might have problems with a battery that is too lightweight. The battery might be likely to leak or crack easily. Conversely, a battery that is too heavy might produce undue stress on the vehicle that battery will be installed in.

4. What is the severity of the issue? This is measured with an S.

You can rank this on a scale of 1 to 10. You can push low-ranked issues to the side and fix them later on, provided that the issues aren't too expensive. It is best to fix low-rated problems if they are the only things that are present. This is to ensure a sense of security in the workplace.

5. Identify the potential causes of failure.

The car battery might not be heavy enough due to many factors. Perhaps there weren't enough raw materials used to construct the battery. Maybe the connections that were installed are loose. You might also have other problems that you aren't seeing immediately.

6. How likely are these causes of failure to occur? This can be denoted with "O".

List the occurrence likelihood for each item on a scale of 1 to 10. Focus on the high-risk issues. Review details on how often such problems have developed in the past and/or whether the materials you are using are putting you at a greater risk. You can use any numbers for these totals as you wish. The key is to ensure the causes of failure are clearly specified. Always focus on addressing the most likely causes first, as they will pose the greatest threats even if they are small.

For the car battery company, the team might look at the resources being utilized and examine whether there are any problems with those items. An analysis may be used based on historic information or on the current variances.

7. Analyze the current process controls.

You might have some current standards in place for what you can do if there is a problem in the workplace. Review those standards to see what you can do to resolve the problems you have discovered. The current process controls are the tests or processes you use now to identify failures and/or to keep those failures from developing. Some controls may reduce the threats of problems or keep problems from developing. Some may also identify failures as they occur so you can fix them before further damage happens or the issue impacts the customer.

The car battery company in our example might use a process control like a weight that analyzes how heavy each battery coming off an assembly line is. The weights can be monitored to note when irregularities arise. This helps detect problems and keeps improper batteries from going out to the public. This leads into the detection rating review.

8. Review the D or detection rating.

The detection rating is a measure of how well your system can detect a failure before the customer is impacted. This is on a scale of 1 to 10. This is another subjective measure you may decide. Prior data on past failures may be used when determining the D rating. The lower number works when the devices in question can detect the problem and things can be fixed before they can get any worse. But the D should be higher if there are problems with the detection process that make it easier for a problem to fall through the cracks.

9. Calculate the RPN.

The RPN is the Risk Priority Number. Multiply the S, O and D totals together. The total number should give you an idea of the general risk. More importantly, you may also use this as a means of figuring out what problems are the most important. This is a subjective number, although it is recommended that you look at the problems that might be the most significant based on what you find.

10. Look at the critical number (CRIT).

The critical number is another subjective point. This should be a general measure of the problems in the workplace. You can organize this on a scale of 1 to 100 if desired while ensuring everything on your chart adds up to 100 if possible. The critical number is optional, but it can be helpful for organizing some of the most significant concerns you might come across within your work.

11. Determine the recommended actions you wish to carry out.

List information on the recommended things that should be done. This includes a look at who is responsible for fixing the issue and the target completion date for getting the task handled. You can also list information on how well the actions were taken and what happened to get the problems under control. The same measurements from earlier may be used when looking at how well your actions are working and assessing whether they are appropriate for your work.

The car battery company in this example should have noticed whether or not improperly made batteries were coming off the manufacturing belt and being sent to the public. A review must be analyzed to see what was causing the problems not to be detected. By finding out what the failures are, it becomes easier for a business to find a way to improve upon its functions.

The process works well during the improvement stage as it helps you get closer to your ultimate Six Sigma goal. You can review your work as needed and create new plans based on what you feel is appropriate and useful for the project. Finding these failures before they can become worse is especially important for your success.

How to Tell if Something Is a Not a Serious Problem

You should use the FMEA to give yourself an idea of how significant a problem may be. Even the smallest problems should be fixed before they can get worse, but sometimes you might find problems that can be put off for a bit in favor of fixing more significant issues. You can use the FMEA to figure out if a problem should be fixed as soon as possible. There are a few signs that suggest a problem in the FMEA is not all that significant:

1. The problem is not compromising the quality of the product in question.

2. The issue is easy and fast to fix.

3. The occurrence of a failure is remote. This may include one failure arising after every couple of thousand items. Your goal should still be to keep that failure rate as minimal as possible.

4. The design in your setup is capable of identifying the problems you come across.

How to Tell if the Issue Must Be Fixed Now

The FMEA also identifies cases when the problem is far too significant. The FMEA process gives you an idea of what to expect out of the repair or fix process. Here are a few things to notice when an issue has to be fixed right away:

1. The problem keeps on occurring. This includes too many failures arising within an hour or so of operation.

2. The problem occurs without much warning.

3. Your design control is incapable of identifying the problems that are occurring.

When Should You Carry Out the FMEA?

The FMEA is perfect for use during the improvement stage of the Six Sigma process, but there are many other times when the process can also be carried out. The FMEA can be utilized when you're trying to design a Six Sigma plan and you want to see how well the process is working. You can do this at the start of the Six Sigma effort if desired, although it is best to use when looking at how well your task is being run. The FMEA routine helps with identifying changes in your work to assess whether you're experiencing any improvements in your work.

You can also use the FMEA process if you have improvement goals that you wish to meet or are noticing new failures occurring. These include failures that are impacting your goals and making it harder for you to move forward and succeed. Any failures in your work can be risky. But the good news is that the FMEA process will assist you at any time when you've got a new issue.

You can carry out the FMEA as many times as needed, particularly during the control stage of the Six Sigma routine. Remember that regular reviews of your Six Sigma routine are vital to its success.

Chapter 43 – Benchmarking

Every Six Sigma task has a final objective that needs to be met. A benchmark standard may be incorporated to produce a final goal for how something is to be planned. You need to check on how your Six Sigma process is working based on benchmarks associated with how well your business is growing and what you can do to keep the business afloat or moving forward. Benchmarking is a process you can use when producing a better solution. This may work during the improvement process to give your business an added control over how a task may work, although it can also work in the analysis process if you need to review things based on certain parameters.

Benchmarking is a process dedicated to identifying best practices. The process focuses on reviewing the best way a Six Sigma process works and what you should be analyzing when trying to improve upon your effort. This part of the improve phase entails understanding how you're going to reach key benchmarks. Whereas the benchmarks are about what you want to attain, benchmarking is about understanding how to go somewhere.

Five Keys

Benchmarking focuses on producing the standards your business can work with when trying to move forward. This is about identifying how a business can grow and what you can expect in that direction. The goal here is to find a setup or solution that is easy to follow and offers a smarter approach to your work. There are four keys to notice when managing benchmarking. These standards should work as you're trying to create a firm goal for your work:

1. Benchmarking is about following the best practices.

Benchmarking concentrates on looking at what is right for your business. You can work with many ideas for benchmarking depending on the goals you wish to attain. This is different from competitor research in that the other concept focuses on performance measures. Benchmarking is all about identifying the things you can do that are different while also figuring out how to shift from any existing practices you wish to use.

2. Your goal for benchmarking is to produce continuous improvement.

Benchmarking is not about improving your business with a quick fix. Rather, it is about planning a routine that fits in with the goals you have. You can produce a benchmark at any standard you might see fit. For instance, a business in the textile industry might have a benchmark that entails producing 10,000 shirts in a day. A benchmark would involve getting the manufacturing process to work with as few defects as possible. The benchmarking process is about finding a solution for reaching that goal. This includes finding a standard that can be used for producing shirts many times over.

3. You will partner with other people in the benchmarking process.

This part of the improvement stage is all about teamwork. You will share data with other workers. These include managers, hourly employees and vendors. Benchmarking is not considered a form of corporate spying. The practice is more about identifying what should be done to resolve a concern while working as a team.

4. The adaptation process is based on what is right for the business.

You are not necessarily trying to produce a procedure similar to what another competitor uses. A textile company might have different fabrics or machines for making shirts than what someone else might have, for example. The original company must adapt based on what is right for the business and how a plan may work. The business may adapt based on its particular needs and any requirements that its customers have. Benchmarking involves reviewing many standards that go into a business without trying to copy the things that another business might be doing.

The Three Forms of Benchmarking

There are three particular forms of benchmarking that may be utilized in your work:

1. Internal

Internal benchmarking works when a company has an established setup for handling content. A business can use this to identify its functions. This works well in cases where a business does not have any competitors or cannot identify any competition that is far too similar. A textile company might use an internal benchmarking process to review how shirt production processes are supported. A benchmark for how well shirts can be made should be established without any outside reviews involved in the effort.

2. Competitive

A competitive review involves a company identifying its position is in the industry. This may be used to figure out the leadership standards that have to be met within the workplace. A competitive review may work with a plan based on how well a business ranks. A textile company may examine its ranking in production with others and produce benchmarks to match or outdo the other businesses. The benchmarking effort does not involve trying to copy those competitors, but rather finding ways to be as productive or efficient as those other entities.

3. Strategic

Strategic reviews focus on attaining certain objectives. A car maintenance shop might use strategic benchmarking to review how long people have to wait to get their vehicles.

The benchmarking focuses on how to produce a more efficient process that involves getting a car ready in as little time as possible.

Each of these processes can be used as required. For the best results, look at what is happening inside your business first. You might come across some critical issues within your business based on what you feel is working or needs to be changed. Look carefully to see how well efforts are being managed.

A Helpful Series of Steps

Benchmarking is about reviewing methods and processes and implementing them to the best possible features for making a Six Sigma routine work. The following steps should be utilized for giving you extra control over the practice at hand:

1. Review the performance gaps within the workplace.

The gaps should have been found in the measurement and analysis processes. Review how those gaps are sized and how they were formed. You can use this to decide what parts need benchmarking the most.

2. Consult your leadership team. You might need to talk with executives and others who are higher up on the Six Sigma totem pole.

3. Review the objectives of the benchmarking task. This includes the scope of the task.

4. Analyze your process as it is.

Review how focused your process is. The odds are the process might not be as focused as you wish it could be. Look at any data that you found in the measure and analysis processes, including any visual representations of that data. You may compare your process versus the desired results of the benchmark you want to reach. Be realistic about this.

5. Determine the metrics for your benchmarks. Everyone in the Six Sigma team should agree to the process.

The metrics should be chosen based on the gap between the current performance and that which you wish to attain. Benchmarking measurements can be reviewed based on how well the business improves and how it changes based on new standards. For the best results, everyone should be performing the same way throughout the process. All measurements should come from existing ideas or concepts.

6. All metrics should be prepared in writing. Review what you are measuring, how everything is classified and included, what should be excluded and how measurements are to be completed.

7. Figure out all the terms that will be agreed upon in the benchmarking process. This includes any gaps in low-performing efforts.

8. Review the data collection effort. The process may be similar to what you use during the original measurement process.

9. Find where you will gather data from and what resources may be used. The resources must be consistent every time.

10. Plan a screening survey.

A survey for measurements can be used based on how reliable the results in a research process are. All people involved should be in consistent communication. You should be able to contact the groups who will screen the content and determine how the work is to be run.

11. Review the surveys that you have done. Identify any sudden changes that have taken place in the work.

12. Perform site visits to confirm that the benchmarking process is working well.

13. Identify what you learned in the analysis process about the performance gaps that were found.

14. Produce a recommended implementation process based on what you feel is suitable for the work at hand.

15. Update processes and change them as needed. The goal is to find ways to get to the benchmarks you have established.

Let's take this process and apply it to the textile company we have been talking about in this chapter. The textile company might notice that its processes in producing shirts are inefficient. The company keeps making errors in how many threads are in the shirts and how some shirts are sized based on specific standards. The measurements and analysis processes for the company will be tested and reviewed. The current manufacturing process should also be documented.

After the current efforts are listed, the textile company can produce a series of metrics devoted to creating a better product more efficiently. The surveys that the company produces will also be planned based on how well the business is growing and what can be expected. This includes a look at who will handle the content being produced. Site visits may be useful.

How Will You Produce Benchmarks?

You can create a benchmark for manufacturing processes, customer interactions, employee efficiency or anything else relevant to your business. The benchmarks will be used for the benchmarking process as the general goals you wish to reach. You may use the following steps for producing benchmarks that work for you:

1. Figure out what you're going to measure.

Going back to the earlier example, the textile company can measure something like how quickly that company's market share or volume is growing. The visitor engagement on a company's website, based on engaged visitors on a site, may be utilized as a benchmark. The reliability of the machines used for producing apparel may also be incorporated. The content must be relevant and easy to measure. The content should also be easy to compare over time based on how well the subject matter is being managed.

2. Review the industry you are in.

The company should look at how other business models in the industry are working and figure out what benchmarks are being used. This does not mean that the company has to directly copy what someone else is doing. That company should instead come up with unique ideas based on its research.

3. Look at your company's size or age. You might have to change your plans based on how new or established your business is.

4. Figure out the average purchase value of anything in your environment. The conversion rate will vary by product, business or industry.

5. Figure out the external or internal benchmarks you wish to use. Figure out the norms within your business or industry.

The textile company can use an external benchmark like working with certain pricing targets that match up with the rest of the industry. An internal benchmark like working with as few resources as possible may also be utilized. This could include a plan for handling money based on how much is being spent within a certain time period.

Everything that occurs in the process should be clearly communicated to your managers, employees, stakeholders and other entities associated with your business. The benchmarks should be reasonable, useful and attainable.

Changing the Benchmarks

You have the right to change the benchmarks in your workplace as you see fit. But when doing so, you need to ensure those benchmarks are planned based on how the business is evolving and moving forward. You can change the benchmarks if you feel certain processes or efforts might work better than those that are currently in place. You may also adjust those benchmarks based on any prior benchmarks you have already met. You can change those benchmarks based on what you have done already and what you feel is the most effective solution for your work needs.

You can change the benchmarks in the workplace by doing the following:

1. Review how your business is progressing with the Six Sigma effort. See how well the efforts are being managed based on what is being found in the testing process.

2. Identify the resources you have. See if they can help you with changing those benchmarks as required.

3. Discuss the changes with your employees and others in the Six Sigma group.

You can change the benchmarks at any time you see fit, although it helps for you to look at how well the content is being managed. The best idea is to stick with a certain benchmark for a few weeks or months to see how things evolve. There's always the chance your business might take some time to achieve your benchmarks. Review your work to see that there are no problems involved with getting your efforts running right.

What About Reviewing the Competition?

As we noted earlier, you have the choice to look at your competitors when thinking about benchmarks. You might conduct thorough research on your competitors to see if there are certain things that they are doing when trying to get ahead. You can get a shareholder or stock report to see what a company is doing. Many companies, particularly ones that are publicly listed, should provide information on their efforts to the public.

But whatever the case may be, you must avoid trying to make your business look too similar to others. Innovating and stealing are two different things.

Chapter 44 – Piloting a Six Sigma Solution

You have a solution for how to improve upon your Six Sigma practice. Maybe you also have something to start the Six Sigma task with. But are you certain that the solution is appropriate? You can assess that by planning a pilot. This is a test to see how well something works.

A pilot is designed as the first run of something you want to handle. You may look at how well the pilot runs based on what you want to do with your task and how far it will go. It can help you find out if your solution works and whether you should implement it in the future. Meanwhile, you might find some issues that need to be changed.

The best way to describe a pilot is to think about the most widely known type of pilot that you might come across, the television pilot. Television studios often order pilots of possible new shows that they might pick up. A pilot is one episode that essentially introduces the characters and plotlines for a show. Sometimes a pilot is accepted, but there may be changes like certain concepts being dropped, characters being removed, added etc. In other cases, the pilot is dropped and consigned to TV history.

You can treat your Six Sigma pilot in the same way a television studio treats its pilots. It could be the start of something huge, but it could also be something that has to go through lots of changes and which might end up having to be scrapped altogether. Either way, the pilot will be your test run.

You'll get more out of your Six Sigma work if you plan a pilot. Here are a few of the reasons why:

1. Confirmation

A pilot helps you to confirm how well a task runs. Whereas a television pilot confirms that the characters for a possible new show will be interesting to an audience, the Six Sigma pilot is about confirming the results and relationships found in a solution. You will identify certain things that work in your task while also finding some natural variations.

Confirmation can go one step further by working with two pilots if desired. The first pilot will test if something is working. The second pilot will confirm the results of that first pilot. That second pilot may be run at a fuller scale. You don't have to run a second pilot, but it might help if you want to get some extra confirmation.

2. Improvement

You can also improve upon your task with a pilot. The pilot lets you look at the ways your tasks are being run and lets you know whether certain changes have to be made. A television pilot is often about improving how a new show works by looking at what characters or situations are not working and why. Your Six Sigma project can include many different changes as you see fit, so long as you look carefully at how the project is running and have an idea of what to expect in your task.

3. Reduce the Risk

You can identify risks and problems in your Six Sigma work if you plan a pilot. You can run an FMEA to see what issues may arise before your product reaches a larger audience. You can also find solutions during the pilot stage to solve those problems.

4. Feedback

You can use a pilot to get feedback from other people in the workplace regarding what you are doing and how you can solve problems in the future. For instance, the managers or others in a Six Sigma task can review what you are doing with your Six Sigma routine and give you ideas on what can be done to fix problems. The feedback can be vital for helping you realize what should be done or how to make your tasks a little easier to manage.

5. Prepare Something for a Small Group

Another idea entails using your pilot to get a product out to a small group of people. You can use this if you want to produce a test market to see what people are thinking about something. Some companies produce items with the intention of releasing them in smaller markets at the start. Those markets act as test groups that review how well certain products or services are received. Tests are often found in markets that are interpreted to be small and diverse. Cities like Albany, Peoria, Provo and Reno are among the most popular test markets in the United States. You can review what the people in those test markets are saying about your work and then adjust your plans based on what feedback you are getting from those people.

When Is It Fine to Pilot?

There is never a bad time for you to plan a work pilot for your Six Sigma efforts. However, there are a few times when a pilot might be most useful.

1. You have a massive project and want to ensure your task will work right.

A television pilot is important in that there is no telling how much money will go into a show, let alone how long the show will run for. The pilot is prepared to see that something of such a massive scope will work right. You can do the same if you've got a huge task to work with. For instance, you might have a big project that entails a new product or service that you want to offer to people. You can use a pilot to identify how well that project will be run based on what you feel is appropriate for marketing purposes.

2. The consequences of something can reach very far.

Going back to the television pilot, there is no telling how that pilot could go. Sometimes a show might become popular to where the stars of the show might be tied up with it for a while. In other cases, the show might have to replace something else on the network's schedule. A pilot helps to confirm what is working so the final project will be suitable and attractive to the public. The same thing can be done when you're working on your Six Sigma effort.

3. The cost involved with getting a design ready or any changes can be high.

Your task might include changes to a product or service. The television pilot will entail a careful review of what is happening to ensure the cost involved will not be too high. The test program helps to review what is happening to see that any costs involved are managed right. Sometimes the pilot might have to be scrapped if the changes are so substantial or expensive that the program needs to be canceled altogether.

4. It will be difficult to reverse any changes.

Sometimes changes in a task might become too hard to manage. In the case of a television pilot, a cast member might have to be replaced. That process is very difficult, especially since it is easy to tell the difference between two people in a show. The pilot is used to look at what should be done.

Piloting is a practice that works for every type of Six Sigma process and will help you with getting more out of your work. Whether it entails a new task or a desire to improve an existing one, you can benefit from getting a pilot project running. Remember that once you start a pilot, you are committing to a possible shift or change in your Six Sigma routine. The pilot might not always result in changes, but the pilots that do produce changes may be to your long-term benefit if handled right.

Who's the Target Audience?

The target audience for the pilot isn't the customers so much as it is the executives and stakeholders in your business. You don't necessarily have to bring the products in your pilot out to the public unless you want to utilize some target demographics or test markets for your work. But the executives and others who make money off your work will be the ones that judge your efforts the most. Those people will analyze your work and see if the task is being managed right or if you need to make changes.

Steps for Managing Your Pilot

Now that you understand what makes a pilot so valuable, it is time to look at how you can make the task work. As an example of a pilot, we will look at a soft drink company. The company wants to work with Six Sigma standards to ensure that the bottling process of its drinks is efficient. This includes ensuring a proper mix of coloring in each bottle and that every bottle is filled to a precise amount. This ensures that people won't come across discolored soda products or cases where a can or bottle is not filled all the way.

1. Assess the situation as it is.

For your Six Sigma task, you will produce a pilot to see what you can do when trying to improve upon your existing line of work. The task should include a full analysis of your current process. A process map can be used at this point. You can gather data and then prepare everything you wish to use for evaluation. A new prospective map for your Six Sigma work can be planned, although that map is designed for basic intentions. Be detailed with the process map so you have a better idea of what has to change in your Six Sigma work.

2. Perform a root cause analysis of the current situation.

Look at the problems that are causing the issue in your Six Sigma work. This might be a continuation of the problem you had at the start, or it may be a review of something else that started midway through your work. You can use the root cause analysis to identify what the focus should be in the Six Sigma pilot task. The soda company may consider looking at a root cause like not enough people reviewing the bottles or cans, or the machines not using the right software for identifying how well the products are being filled. You can add as much information to your root cause analysis as possible so you get a clear answer. That said, the root cause analysis does not have to be overly complicated, provided you get the information you need.

3. Plan the purpose and goals.

What are you looking to do with your pilot? You can look back at your project charter from earlier to see what should be done. The soda company in our example might have a goal to ensure that all bottles and cans are filled with the same amount of soda every time. The company might have planned a Six Sigma task to reduce errors, but some additional concerns have arisen. These include problems that might make it harder for the team to reach the Six Sigma status it wants to attain.

4. Analyze the scope of the pilot.

The scope can be as large as it has to be, but the pilot may help you with looking at the specific things you want to fix in your business. You must look at the size of the project and how you're going to ensure the content in question will be measured and analyzed. You can also look at when and where your pilots are going to be planned out.

5. Look at what you will do with the task.

The pilot task can entail anything you want to do to improve upon an existing process. The soda company might use a new software program to help fill its soda bottles properly. Part of that program may require using specific parameters depending on the type of container being filled. Meanwhile, the same Six Sigma task might entail asking certain people to check the bottles to ensure they are filled correctly.

6. Prepare a timeline of the task.

A timeline may include a review of when you want to complete certain tasks. The time frame should be planned according to your needs, but do not go any faster than necessary. You need the pilot to work as accurately as possible so you can get the best results.

7. Determine the tracking and monitoring efforts.

The tracking and monitoring work identify how well the Six Sigma task is working. Part of this includes an analysis of how well the tracking is managed. For the soda company, it might include using scales with sensors to assess the weights of each soda bottle. This tracking can work alongside people who are manually or visually monitoring things.

8. Identify the team members.

Every Six Sigma process includes team members devoted to specific functions. Ask any employees associated with the Six Sigma routine what they can do to handle work. This includes reviewing measurements. You can use as many team members as desired so long as those members are thoroughly prepared for their tasks.

9. Start running the pilot.

You can run the pilot after you have figured out what you will do with the task. The soda company in this example may work on its pilot for a few weeks or months. This could include a review of the new machines or programming software used to help ensure the bottling processes work well. The pilot will move along while the team monitors how many errors are seen on the conveyer belt.

10. Use different inputs in the pilot if desired.

You can always add some inputs to the pilot if you wish. You can add a new parameter or a slight tweak in the system if you have found certain results or changes in your program.

A good rule of thumb is to add an input at the midway point. You can do this at the sixth week of a 12-week pilot, for instance. You do not have to add an input, but it might be recommended to see if you can improve upon what you are doing or if certain things might be harder to manage than expected. Take a careful look at your work at this juncture to see what is right for the pilot in general.

11. Collect the results of the pilot after you are finished.

Look at the results of the pilot and assess whether or not the project went as well as you wanted it to go. The analysis may help you with figuring out the problems you are seeing and also with determining how effective a setup may be.

The soda company may look at the bottles and compare rate of error before and after the pilot. The team may also look at any possible connection between inputs and changes. The key is to look at what things can be done in the future to improve upon the Six Sigma work and to eventually reach that ultimate Six Sigma status.

12. Communicate the results of the pilot to everyone in the Six Sigma group.

A full analysis of the pilot should be planned at this next point. Your report can be as detailed as necessary. The report can identify special opportunities or other things that can be done to make the work in question effective and organized.

13. See how well you can implement the changes that you found would work in the pilot.

The changes that were used during the pilot session may become permanent changes. But you must also look at whether or not those changes are appropriate for your work. The implementation is all about learning from the pilot.

The soda company may find that there is a better chance at the customers being satisfied when corrective measures are implemented and customers can be assured they'll get the right amount of soda in each can or bottle. But there may also be forces like the cost of producing the soft drinks becoming more expensive. The risk of increasing the price of the sodas due to the added cost of production may also be problematic. The company must review the implications of what it is doing and then see what can be done to address the barriers or other concerns that have been detected. Any feedback from stakeholders should be explored at this point, not to mention an analysis of the project charter.

14. Prepare a root cause analysis of anything that might have gone wrong in the work.

Refer to the earlier report on the root cause analysis and assess how this might make a difference in your work. The root cause analysis will look carefully at the problems in your work and will help you determine what needs to be resolved over time based on what you feel is right.

After all this work, you can eventually arrive at the control stage of the Six Sigma routine after you have improved your routine through a pilot or have an idea of what else you wish to do. Remember that the pilot is not something necessarily easy to carry out, but it is a necessity. If television networks can produce pilots to see if new shows are appealing, you can produce pilots to see if changes to your Six Sigma work are necessary.

Chapter 45 – The Validation of the Measurement System (R&R)

There is always a chance that the measurements you are making are not working as well as they should. In fact, the measurement system itself might be the cause for the error itself. Much of this comes from each person having different ideas of what is good or bad. But a validation process can help you with confirming some of the content in your measurement system.

There are two factors that will be utilized in your measurement system: R&R, or repeatability and reproducibility. You have to produce work that is repeatable, or capable of getting the same reading every time when the same operator uses the same measuring process to analyze the same thing. The content must also be reproducible, or capable of having the same reading every time when different operators use the same measurement standards on the same items.

The R&R standards are measured on a percentage scale. The best way to reach Six Sigma is to have a 100 percent R&R rating to ensure the same results come about every time no matter who runs something. But a 90 percent or higher total is fine provided there is enough work going into the effort. The good news about the process is that you don't have to spend lots of time trying to calculate the results. The measurement system can be analyzed with basic math to give you an idea of what the results or efficiency of something are.

As you validate the results, you will work with what is called the attribute and gage R&R process. You will use a gage R&R routine to identify the general tolerance of something and how well the content is being handled. You can use the gage R&R process to identify the continuous data in your work. The main focus of this is to confirm the accuracy, repeatability and reproducibility of the content.

Calculating Gage R&R

You need to look carefully at the R&R readout when assessing how well your measurement system works. The process for getting the gage R&R total ready is extensive, but it will help you with seeing how effective a setup may work for your needs. You must see what you are getting out of your work in any situation. Later on, we'll discuss what you can do when trying to fix any problems you notice within the gage R&R process.

1. Gather a few test samples.

Get enough test samples to produce a realistic result. Try to get at least 20 samples, although more are always welcome. Be aware of any time restrictions you might have for getting those samples ready. Look for samples that represent a decent variation of circumstances in the process.

For example, let's say you are running a company that makes bowling balls and other pieces of bowling equipment. You can gather a series of samples of different balls that you are trying to produce. You can get 20 to 30 14-pound bowling balls with some of these balls not measuring 14 pounds as planned. You can get a 50-50 mix of perfect 14-pound balls and other balls that have not been weighed as well as they could have been. A 70-30 or 60-40 ratio also works, but you should try to create some kind of mix between what works and what does not.

You can always produce these errors on purpose to have items for testing purposes. You should avoid producing errors that are far too noticeable though; keep those issues as minute as possible. The bowling ball example can entail cases where a ball is a few ounces off the weight standard. Keeping the difference minimal ensures each participant will spend extra time looking at how well something might be working.

2. Have someone appraise the items.

An appraiser at the workplace can review each of the test samples to see if they meet your standards. The appraiser in this example may review those 14-pound bowling balls to see that they are built to the right standards. This includes seeing if those balls are measuring up to that 14-pound standard. The appraiser can create a chart listing whether the items in question are okay or if they are defective. A full listing must be included at this point to show what is working.

3. Have multiple other people test those items.

The master or expert's analysis should be seen as the definite results. That person will have measured each item and reviewed the specific things that should be working for your space. But each operator who reviews the items separately might have different ideas of how something should be measured. In some cases, people might use their measuring materials differently. No matter what happens, you must ensure the people testing your items do not have any idea of what the master or expert's testing results were. As the chart below shows, some of the operators might have different results from what the master says. This can be noticed in test samples 5, 29 and 30 on this listing. But most of the other reviews are accurate.

4. Prepare a new order for each of the test samples. The operators should test the items again.

The new order will involve testing the samples at different times. The first sample in the original test may be the ninth item in the next test, for instance. The operators should review each of these items without any prior knowledge of where they were. You can use a comparison of these items to get an idea of whether or not the measuring process is consistent. Sometimes a person might struggle with errors late in the testing process, for instance.

5. Review the times when the readings from each operator agree with whatever was produced.

Sometimes an operator might get different results for each item he or she is testing. Look at how often this problem comes about in the testing process. The chart below shows examples of how one tester might produce different results for the same item within different testing routines. The example shows that there is a 90 percent chance that the operator will repeat the same results every time when testing something. Although this might seem like a good total, you want to get that total to go up so the testing will be accurate and consistent every time you work with something.

6. Analyze how often the two reviews from the tester agree with each other and with the standards that were produced by the master or expert at the start.

The two reviews must match up well with the tester for the process to be repeatable and consistent while also offering a sense of accuracy. You can do this by reviewing the results of each of the two tests from one person and then comparing them with how well they link to the master's reviews. The tester should have an accuracy rating of at least 95 percent for the test to work well. Anything under that total requires the person to be retrained.

7. Calculate how often the inspectors' results match up with each other.

Review the ways that the inspectors match up and see if they are all siding with each other. A single inspector who has incorrect results might be using the wrong standards. Going back to the bowling ball example, an inspector might not understand how the measurement process works. This includes the inspector using the wrong measurements or scale materials. Maybe a scale being utilized by one inspector is not calibrated correctly, thus producing inaccurate results in the test.

8. Review all of those results from the inspectors and see how they compare with the master or expert's results.

At this point, the individual operators should be analyzed with the master or expert's results. You need a higher percentage based on what people are reviewing and finding in the work process. In the example above, there is clearly a problem with all the operators in that they are operating at less than 85 percent. The team might need to be reeducated or trained altogether to learn more about the specific measurement standards they have to follow. Keeping the numbers close to each other is vital for the success of the measuring process.

What to Do When Fixing the Issue

There comes a time when the measurement system might not work as well as it should. You need to review the general process to figure out what you can do to fix any issues that arise. Let's look at how you can fix gage R&R problems. The process here focuses on the bowling ball example. We'll keep using that sample to help give you an idea of what to expect:

1. Review what you need to measure.

2. Select the material used for measuring the items.

3. Develop a testing method.

4. Produce criteria for determining a passing or failing grade.

For this example, you will measure 14-pound bowling balls to see if they weigh 14 pounds as they are built. You will also use a scale for measuring the balls, and that scale might be a rotary or digital design. The passing grade for the test requires the ball to weigh anything from 13.995 to 14.005 pounds. A failing score will be outside that range.

5. Use a few test samples to test the method and criteria. You can use as many samples as you want, but make sure they are diverse and include a mix of passing or failing items.

6. Confirm the gage R&R to be at or near 100 percent.

7. Write down information on the testing process.

8. Provide the inspectors with details on the testing effort and how they can complete the task. Do not divulge the test results with those people.

9. Test the process and see how accurate the results being produced are.

10. If you have gotten the best results out of the testing effort, allow the test process to become the official standard within the workplace.

For the bowling example, you can develop instructions on how to calibrate a scale. You can even consider using a test or sample item on the scale to help people with the calibration process. After this, people should have a fully accurate scale to work with. You can review future testing results later on, but the key is that everyone can apply the same standards to their work.

The routine you establish can be performed by your employees as often as needed. You can have them review the items based on any changes or controls that you want to use. But the most important part of the process is to ensure the people testing items are aware of what they have to do. Employees must be carefully trained and provided with feedback on what they can do to fix any errors in their work.

Chapter 46 – New Process Mapping

As you read earlier in this guide, the defects per million opportunities, or DPMO, and the Z value of your work can make a difference in your task. You can use these to identify how well your task is working and whether any special changes have to be made. The most important part here for improving upon your effort is to see that the content can build off a new process based on what you have gleaned from a pilot or other process. The DPMO method and Z value can especially help you with identifying things that might help your work run right.

Working with the Opportunities

The new opportunities you wish to plan out can be as thorough or detailed as they need to be. But you must also look at the DPMO method or Z value to get an idea of the problems in your workplace based on the new effort you are implementing. Take a look at the new process you are managing and review how defects may arise. This includes any potential for defects to occur or for any processes to not work as well as they should.

You may be able to eliminate some of the defect issues that arise. Best of all, you might find that the possible DPMO will be reduced when the new process kicks in.

Producing New Targets

The improvements you've come across and anything you've gotten out of the pilot should help you grow and reduce the DPMO in your work. But you must also analyze the new targets that you wish to utilize. You must use a few points for producing the new targets within your Six Sigma effort:

1. Look at the defects that you have eliminated.

You can plan a new target based on the defects that you have noticed and anything you are testing. You can establish a new target based on the defects, but do remember that there is always a potential for those defects to come back, even if they seem to have been eliminated. Keep a careful eye on any sudden aberrations that might develop within your work.

2. Identify how well your pilot went.

You can use the pilot results to dictate where you will go when moving forward. How well did your task improve? Did you remove any waste or eliminate a problem? Study the pilot's result carefully and ensure you have a smart plan for making the most out of your efforts.

3. Analyze a map of the new process.

Whatever you plan on doing, you have to get a clear look at how a process works. A full map may be produced to help you. The map should be explored based on the setup you wish to use and how much content is being produced at a time. You can use as much data as necessary for the map, so long as the content is organized and doesn't have a lot of waste. Keeping waste in check is important, although the new map should probably have less than what you had the first time around. Comparing the old and new process maps is always a good idea for reviewing the parts involved.

4. See how well your company can handle the new process.

The new effort should be a little easier for your business to handle, what with it producing less waste. But you have to see how well the process works and how effectively a process is being managed. You can also review the concepts involved with your work and where the content might move forward.

Special Workflow Plans

The results that you got out of your pilot and the review of your business' ability to handle new efforts should help you. A review can include an analysis of how a project might work. You can use a few things for preparing your workflow while identifying the functions that can make a difference in the work you want to produce. These are all things that should be noticed when planning for well-managed work:

1. Plan an orientation session.

An orientation session should be planned at the start to discuss important tasks and routines. You can let everyone in the workplace know about how the process for producing something works. You'll need to be transparent and direct with your audience and avoid overcomplicating things.

A separate customer orientation may also be planned. The orientation should give the customers an idea of why your service is useful. You can talk about the new things in the workplace relating to what you are providing. Telling the public about the things you want to do with your work is important for your success. The customers should see that whatever is available is attractive and intriguing.

2. Review how items are processed one at a time.

It is fine for you to start out slow when you're trying to get a task running. Reviewing your work incrementally can help you with identifying necessary changes and efforts. Real-time data processing may be a viable solution for your work. The processing effort entails a review of the data being executed within a time period as data comes in. You might notice this in applications like an ATM or a larger computing system. The content being analyzed is reviewed in real time with full reports coming in pertaining to what is working in the new Six Sigma process. You might need to hire extra people to assess how well items are monitored in real time, but the process should be worthwhile.

3. Review the balance flow.

The balance flow in your work is a good gauge of how well your business is handling its Six Sigma functions. You can look at the balance flow based on how extensive a task is and how well new ideas are being incorporated into your work. You have to ensure the balance flow being used is well organized while also identifying many functions relating to how useful and efficient your Six Sigma plans may be. The most important thing is to see that the balance flow is working with many items at a time and not just on one problem.

The balance flow should include a diverse array of variables planned based on what types of materials and equipment are being used. Having only one piece in the balance flow may end up being risky. The single-piece design may make it harder for resources to be used while also producing an unreliable framework that might make it harder for your content to be managed and used as desired.

4. See what you can do about preventing bottlenecks from developing in your work.

A bottleneck is a frustrating issue to encounter in the Six Sigma process, but it is a threat that must be noted. It only takes one component in your work to cause the problem. For instance, a company that makes basketballs might come across a new bottleneck. The basketball company might find issues regarding the supply of rubber materials for the balls. The lack of rubber in a situation might make it harder for the company to produce its materials.

You'll need to look at how a bottleneck in the workplace can be resolved and what you can do to control how such an event might develop. You must notice any changes that come about in your Six Sigma effort based on what is causing errors or what might make routines and efforts in the workplace harder to manage than needed. You can use a full analysis of the Six Sigma effort to get a closer idea of what is going on in the workplace and determine how you're going to resolve the issues you come across.

5. Analyze the parallel processing work that you might put in.

Parallel processing is a routine that entails a process being split into two parts that are executed at the same time. Different functions in the same line will be responsible for handling those individual parts. The best way to describe parallel processing is to look at the way a computer operates by taking separate executable efforts and having them run on different processors within the same computer. The parallel processing work assists in allowing more functions to happen while working with fewer resources. Think of it as a form of conservation that keeps the work being put in under control while not incorporating more complicated details than necessary.

Parallel processing is the opposite of linear or serial processing. The routine involved produces a more appropriate control for content that might be easier to manage than what you might expect elsewhere. The parallel processing effort manages the content accordingly while keeping resources in check. Assess the functions being handled in your manufacturing or service processes. You can use a full review of these functions to identify the problems arising in your work and how effective a setup is or isn't.

6. Keep all hand offs under control.

Handoffs can be frustrating issues to contend with in the Six Sigma process. As discussed earlier, a hand off occurs when a process is sent off to a different party. You might have different people work with certain processes based on what might be appropriate. This may be noticed the most in a call center when a person is constantly being referred to different departments. You'll have to avoid the problems that come with hand offs so your customers will be satisfied and your business retains a sense of control.

Look at the processes in your new routine based on how people are moving data along. Ensure that the content is being efficiently moved based on the subject matter and work that you are putting in. Review any situations where work or responsibilities are being handed off to other people. Remember that hand offs are likely to cause defects and other errors in the Six Sigma routine.

You can plan a great process if you look at how you're going to make it run based on the improvement steps you have utilized. You'll see that the improvements you make are not hard to prepare. The next few chapters will concentrate mainly on how you can manage the control part of the DMAIC or Six Sigma effort.

Chapter 47 – Statistical Process Control

As you get ready to control your Six Sigma task, you have to look at the ways you are reviewing the processes you have devised and what it takes to keep each process under control. One idea to use involves statistical process control or SPC. The concept helps you to monitor and control the Six Sigma task and to regularly optimize the work. You can use this to figure out what changes need to be made and how you are going to go about making them work to your liking.

SPC is a practice that has been used in Six Sigma communities for years. The concept goes back to the 1920s when Walter Shewhart came up with an idea to review how the output parameters in a process work. The general goal of what Shewhart devised was to see how well a business can handle many of its functions while seeing how processes can change over time. The goal is to ensure that the Six Sigma task is running smoothly and that the output parameters being utilized are managed correctly. More importantly, the effort you put in will help you with keeping the risk of waste from being too significant.

The best part of the SPC routine is that you are removing the detection approach. The detection model is often used to identify things that are going wrong in a work environment. As the diagram shows here, the detection model focuses on an inspection of the process to see what issues are arising. This includes a review of the problem that is developing alongside any repairs or reworkings that have to be planned. Not all items will work with the specific shipment that needs to be sent out.

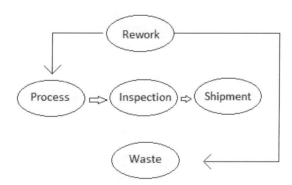

The detection model

The SPC effort moves beyond that traditional review. Instead, it leans towards a prevention model. The model shows everything your business might do to prevent problems from occurring or worsening. You will prevent products that do not meet the Six Sigma standard from moving forward. You will also keep the process from being ineffective. Waste will be reduced, and your company will become more productive.

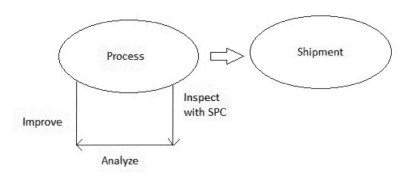

The Prevention Model

With the prevention model, you are focusing on the process. You are looking to carefully analyze and review it while also improving upon the work as needed. This will result in the shipments being sent out being more appropriate and useful for your needs.

How Will You Implement SPC?

It is generally best for you to utilize a histogram at the start of the SPC process. The histogram gives you an idea of the process variation and what might be happening most frequently. The key is to identify what might be occurring in a process in order to assess how your work is moving forward in any situation. The histogram should help you assess your efforts while helping you to carefully plan any updates or changes in your routine.

Meanwhile, a control chart may be incorporated in the SPC process. You can see how the manufacturing or service process changes have worked and assess any aberrations. This includes cases where the data being managed is unstable.

The good news about SPC is that you can use software programs to make the review easier to manage. Histograms and control charts can be automatically created in the workplace based on real-time information. But the programs will only work when you have an idea of how you are controlling errors and keeping them from developing. You can make the most out of your plans for manufacturing if you recognize what you are doing with the subject matter in question.

Chapter 48 – Choosing the Right Kind of Control Chart

You have the choice to work with any control charts you see fit. Any control chart will let you see if the last part of your Six Sigma process is working and whether the status quo you have just created can be maintained. There are many types of control charts to use for the control stage, and each is different based on what's right for you.

The control chart should be chosen based on whether you're measuring variables or attributes. A variable measurement is for where you're measuring averages and how the results in a task vary. The attribute data entails measuring defects or defectives; you have to choose which will be measured before you begin the process. There are seven charts that you can pick from based on what you find suitable for your task.

Note: You can find various software programs that can help you with planning these control charts. Each program gives you the power to enter variable data and calculations. It keeps you from having to work with more complicated data than what you can handle. But you must also look at how well these programs operate in order to ensure your data is organized the way you need it to be.

Charts for Variable Data

I-MR Chart

The I-MR chart is for cases where you are measuring variable data and have a subgroup to work with. The subgroup should have a size of 1. The I-MR chart measures the individual or moving range totals. You can use this in cases where each unit can be measured on its own. This includes cases where automation makes it easier for a task to run. Also, you can use the I-MR chart if you have enough samples to work with during a slow process. The important part is that the I-MR chart is controlled and cautious without risking the data that comes in.

This kind of chart measures individual values. You might notice a particular average and some control limits that need to be followed. Separate observations of individual items being produced can help with confirming the content being utilized and how that work is moving. You can use the chart to confirm when data is moving right while looking at a continuous review. But the process here works best when you can work with one item at a time.

For example, an insurance company may review how many days it takes for claims from their clients to be processed. The I-MR chart will help by reviewing individual cases where claims were filed. Each claim is analyzed based on how many days it took to go through. The chart will reveal trends in how well the task was handled and may also show some trends pertaining to problems that arise. It might help to keep notes on some of the issues so you can confirm whatever problems might evolve.

Xbar and R-Chart

The Xbar and R-chart is used when you're trying to get continuous data, but the subgroup is a little larger in size. The subgroup has a size of two to seven. This means that many items are being gathered at one time, but they are all being measured separately in intervals. You can use the Xbar and R-chart to identify how several items are compared together while assessing how the data is being handled.

You will notice two different charts in this setup. The first entails the Xbar. This is a common type of average used in the research process. The Xbar may include an average of different processes that occur in the workplace. You can use this to gather an average of all the things that have taken place within a spot in a certain time period.

The R chart shows the general variability of the statistical data. You might notice there is a sizeable variance between items within your samples. You can review this to see if there is a trend within the samples. A carefully organized business will have the two parts linked up to be around the same in power, although any issues in change should be documented.

Let's go back to the insurance example. For the Xbar and R-chart, the insurance company will take in five insurance claims each day and assess their averages in each time period. You may plan the average cycle time for these points to produce a better readout all around. You can also see if the timing for each claim is consistent throughout the work. You can use this to see if the two charts match up with each other in order to produce a clearer result.

Xbar and S-Chart

Your next choice for managing a chart is the Xbar and S-chart. This is for when a sample size is very large. For the insurance company example, the company will use the Xbar and S-chart for analyzing massive numbers of claims to see how well they are managed. Thirty or more claims might be reviewed each day. This includes an analysis of how long it took on average for those claims to be processed correctly.

The charts reveal information on the averages and standard deviations produced. You will notice how the quality characteristics change in your work while reviewing how any standard deviations might shift. The intriguing part of the review here is that the Xbar and S-chart can be a little closer to one another based on where their lines go and how the data in question is being measured. You can use the chart to be as thorough and specific with your work as you have to be. But you must also ensure that the standard deviation is kept in check to where the limits remain consistent.

The Xbar review also shows when the data you are collecting might change and when the subject matter might be harder to analyze than expected. You may find that the averages might be inconsistent and that some large amounts of data might shift over time. The sudden changes should be analyzed based on what you find to be appropriate for your analysis. You can also review the sample sizes to help understand if there have been changes between how people complete work tasks in your environment.

Charts for Use When Reviewing Defective Units

NP Chart

The NP chart is useful for when you're trying to review defective units that have to be discarded. The NP chart identifies the number of defective units in a constant sample size. This means you are working with the same number of materials at a time while keeping a careful watch on the samples each time you work on a task. You can use the NP chart to identify as many details in the process as necessary provided that the work is simple enough and can be reviewed to your liking.

The NP is a measure of the process mean. The N is the sample size and must remain the same throughout the whole process. You can use this measurement to figure out the general total of whatever you are handling, thus giving you extra control over your work in question. The measurement process may work in cases where you have certain things to measure within the same total every time. You might want to measure items based on how often you do things within one day, for instance.

P Chart

The P chart is also used for defective units, although this entails sample sizes that are different in quantity. This might include the daily number of applications, claims or other processes being monitored to see what totals are being handled. You might use the P chart to work with anything from 20 to 50 items in a sample. A ratio will be produced based on the defective items that are found versus the problems that develop in the task. You can use the analysis to get a clear idea of how well the task is moving forward.

The P chart works with the assumption that the probability of the items being defective will be the same for every sample. Also, each unit should be independent from the others in the setup. The inspections should also be the same for each sample being generated. In order for the task to work, the data should be managed with as many similar items as possible for the P chart.

There are no particular rules as to how large the sample sizes have to be, let alone their variance. But for the best results, you'll need to review the data with sample sizes that are as equal to one another as possible. This includes data such as being two to five items off the original total you are trying to measure. You can change the P chart sample sizes as you wish provided that the data is managed well.

C Chart

The C chart is designed for defects per unit instead of defective items. You use the C chart when the subgroups or sample sizes you are working with are identical to one another. An insurance firm may use a C chart by looking at the number of claim filings that have incomplete features or lines in them. The firm will gather a sample of a certain size and then review how many of those defects are found in the filings. The process may work with as many samples as needed provided that they are all the same size as the first sample.

The C chart lets you see what specific issues have arisen in certain samples. You might find that some samples are more imperfect than others or that the control process is not as steady as it should be. The C chart may also reveal details on how well the samples are planned based on the content you work with. You may notice some sizeable shifts in what you are working with depending on what might work for you.

The Poisson distribution method should be noticed within the C chart. The distribution layout produces the assumptions that the number of opportunities being handled is large. This includes a potential for many nonconformities to develop. However, the probability of nonconformity may be small according to the method. That probability is also consistent all around. The inspection process should be the same for each item that is being analyzed in the effort.

U Chart

The U chart is the last of the control charts you can use. The chart illustrates the defects that you have within a variable sample size. You can use the U chart to identify average non-conforming functions while working with many samples based on how often they occur in one day. You might come across some days where more errors appear on more units, for instance. You can use the U chart to identify any possible issues in those events based on when certain activities are more commonplace than others. The Poisson distribution feature should also be found on the U chart just as with the C chart.

The greatest part of working with different control charts is that it may be easier for your business to review its functions when the proper chart is used. Review what you plan on measuring in your Six Sigma control process while also assessing any issues that may be revealed in your work. You can use the data you come across to figure out how well the content being managed works, without risks involved. Be as thorough within your charts as possible.

Chapter 49 – Deming's Four Rules for Tampering In SPC

The SPC process can be influenced by tampering. This occurs when the process in control is adjusted to where the variation in the situation increases. The process will cause the entire effort to get out of control while not being all that easy to maintain or organize. The challenge involved might be too complicated. Tampering can be frustrating, although it is vital to notice what makes it happen as you attempt to make the control process of your Six Sigma task functional.

A part of working with SPC is to think about the four rules of tampering according to the funnel experiment produced by W. Edwards Deming. In 1986, Deming produced an experiment known as the Funnel Experiment. People dropped marbles into a funnel that was hung over a target. The funnel is representative of the process in question. The location that the marble drops is the feature that will be produced. The target is the specification that the customer wishes to utilize.

Throughout the test, Deming found that there are four ways people can tamper with the funnel. These can help you understand how tampering works and what can happen when trying to control a process, particularly something involving Six Sigma standards.

1. A person does not make any adjustments to the setup. That is, there is no tampering.

The first rule for tampering entails the best possible situation. The best thing someone can do is to avoid tampering with the funnel or other point for measurement. By keeping the funnel aimed at the target, the process may become stabilized. This means that the only variations that can occur are minimal and may entail changes that are as close to what might happen in the initial or preferred process as possible. But to make this work, the participant needs to gather as much data on the process as necessary.

You can use this concept by getting more data on what you are doing within the Six Sigma process. Review how consistent the process is. Look at what constitutes normal behavior and ensure that your task is working within that frame of normalcy. You might not have to make any adjustments if you notice that there are no problems and everything is moving as normally as possible. A control chart may help you to track all variations. Adjust the process outside of the control standard only when you see any special variations.

2. You may adjust the funnel from the original position.

The second rule is also known as the human nature rule. The funnel might be moved after the initial task. This is in the hopes that the results will be a little more controlled or around a more favorable spot of value. But there might be times when the range will still be the same. Look at the chart above for an example. While something might be changed around in its position or target, the results are still produced with a similar spread. The results just favor a new position.

But what might also be noticed is that, in some cases like in the example above, the variation might increase. Part of this occurs as the movement requires an extra bit of compensation to try and reach a new target. The range might be close, but it may take a while for the new position to obtain a sense of precision or consistency. The variation can increase to the point where the control is hard to manage. Whether or not it can be corrected all the way is unclear, although there is always a chance that positive movements or shifts might develop depending on what develops.

The change in the target in the Six Sigma routine may arise as someone tries to shift a standard measurement. The measurement plan might be hard to manage at times. The new shift will be intended to get closer to the Six Sigma standard, but it might not always be suitable. The work needed is all about producing a more accurate result.

3. An adjustment may be made from the target.

The changes to the target might be interesting to note. The target might be moved around to try and produce a more distinct result based on what might work the best. For instance, there might be times when a measurement is a few units above the target. The funnel should be repositioned to that new spot near where the results are going. The goal is to allow the target to be reached more often.

The risk of this process is that the routine creates an issue pertaining to how well the shift might arise. The change could be hard to handle due to the added oscillations being produced as the process tries to reach a new goal that it is not used to managing. The effort might be inconsistent depending on what is being handled or how well the process works. But you can make this work if you review how well your effort runs and maintain enough control.

4. An adjustment is made from the last drop.

This last form of tampering involves the funnel being moved to another point where the previous drop took place. This is done instead of working with a change in the target spot. What happens here is that the funnel is shifted from one drop site to a new one in a different location. The results produced are further from where the original target was situated.

This process is used mainly for helping to produce a more consistent analysis over what might arise in the work process and how something might change based on reviews and basic forms of analysis. The work that goes into the effort can be extensive, but it is often best to review the new results based on whether any objectives are to be shifted around.

Chapter 50 – The Central Limit Theorem

The central limit theorem is a part of data interpretation that deserves to be noted. The theorem states that sample averages are normally distributed. As you work with your Six Sigma effort, you might notice different things surrounding your content and how its average totals might change. You might observe that there are a certain number of products being produced within the Six Sigma effort. In other cases, there is a change where the number of errors might move up or down depending on any variations or sudden shifts in your work. The central limit theorem helps you to identify a proper space where you can retain a sense of control.

The central limit theorem suggests there is a shift where the results are going to be more consistent in certain fields. The important part is that, for you to get a clearer idea of where the central limit might be, the number of items in your sample size should increase. You can develop conclusions about certain populations in your work depending on the sample size that you utilize.

The central limit theorem particularly shows that the shape is symmetrical and that the mean or average is easy to notice. The specific limit total should be distinguishable when you have more items in your sample size to work with. The general analysis produced here should help you with developing a better plan for your work.

You must keep in mind a few important things when figuring out an effective statistical process:

1. The symmetrical shape should include the totals moving evenly from the mean on both sides.

2. The mean, mode and median need to be about the same value.

3. A bell shape should be noticed in the curve.

4. All the values must be heavily concentrated around the mean. This will provide a better idea of what measurements are likely to occur, particularly things that work with the closest standard deviation you produce.

5. The content should be within three standard deviations of the mean. To attain Six Sigma, if possible, you should get everything within six deviations.

The interesting part of the central limit theorem is that it focuses on how well the data you measure is aligned to move as evenly as possible. Assessing how well the content is reviewed and measured can be vital to helping you manage control in your Six Sigma work.

Chapter 51 – The Control Chart and Control Limits

The process control should be managed based on the performances that come about within the Six Sigma work. You have to look at how the ongoing process works so you can figure out what should be done to keep issues in check. A control system will help you to document how well the process operates and what might occur within the task. Appropriate process metrics and routines should be explored at this point. Any defined metrics that you want to utilize should be explored as well. These metrics can change in many forms, although you have to see that the process works with all of these points in mind.

Limits are useful for the control process. You can use different limits based on what you feel is right for your task.

Working with a Control Chart

You'll need to utilize a control chart to help you see how well limits are running. The control chart is a graph that illustrates how a process changes after a while. The chart shows how the attributes in a task might change based on time. You might notice a control chart that shows how things change based on sample sizes or on how much time has elapsed. The main goal is to see how the defects or other issues in a task are developing after a Six Sigma process is put in place. You can also use your chart to illustrate how well certain parameters might be developing.

The X variable is the time frame or sample number involved. You can look at the timing of your task or how well you are preparing many samples ready in a test. The goal is to keep your work as consistent as possible. This means the Y value is not going to change all that much. Part of this includes staying within the control limits introduced in the process. Such limits are vital for recognizing the things that might occur in a task.

Control Limits

A control limit is based on how well a process performs. The limit entails a certain range that has to be maintained throughout the process. You may notice this through a control chart that shows how well a routine is moving. The three parts in the control limit entail a center line that shows the optimal measure of your process, an upper line to see how high up a process might work and a lower line to see how low that process might work. You can use this to identify how many defects are in a process while ensuring that you're working consistently within your new standards for operation based on your Six Sigma task.

Control limits are set to three standard deviations or Sigmas. The limits are based on the data on the chart and information on when action is taking place. The three Sigmas produce a careful layout of how data works and how you can handle the content in question. You can use the knowledge to your benefit if you manage the data right. The best part of this is that the work may entail a flexible series of limits, different from specification limits where you have to stick with extremely specific standards pertaining to what a process or product should be.

The control levels should be planned based on what your business can handle based on the average Y value within your work. The Y value should be reviewed based on many measurements from several samples or different analytical points. The averages can help you with figuring out the limits to use based on three standard deviations or Sigmas. Remember that the data should not be based on the specification limits that you wish to utilize.

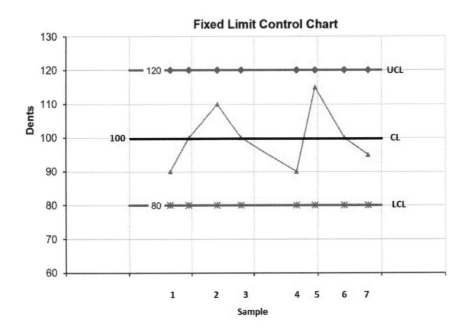

This example shows how the control limits work. The top total is the upper control level that is the highest number of faults you might accept. The lower control level is on the bottom and shows the minimum total that might be fine. Although you might want to get down to that lower level to produce fewer defects, you should still see that you're working with a consistent, predictable process. You can plan out that middle control level based on the average number of faults that you're trying to attain.

You can also move the control limit around if the process improves. This includes cutting the control chart down to be as low as needed. The control limit should be reasonable and yet realistic enough to where you can sensibly plan the work as desired. You have to keep the control limit down to where you can have as few defects as possible, but you should still be reasonable.

The control limits should also be reviewed based on common and special causes that come along. As discussed before, common causes that occur in between the control limits and relate to things that are always present and have small effects that are easy to tolerate. Some random variations may also develop when these control limits are produced. But the variations that are generated should be easy to follow without risking how well the content being managed works. The layout ensures the control being produced is easy to follow.

Special causes should be observed if the control chart shows a strong aberration going outside of the control limits. These special causes are not always present. They might come from outside influences. The effects are significantly larger than what you'd get out of common causes. All of these causes should be analyzed based on how intense they are and where the content is moving.

What Does It Mean to Be in Control?

The goal of the control chart is to show that your Six Sigma process is in control and has consistent results. You will have to change things around if you notice any substantial issues arising. But you must also notice how the concept of being in control can work for you when aiming to make the most out of your work. To start, an in-control process can be estimated before you try to make changes. You'll know, prior to production or continuing an operation, that you'll come across some specific results in your work. Any machine settings may also be adjusted based on what you have found in your research, thus improving upon your chances for keeping the task in check.

Engineers can add statistical tolerance into their plans as well. The control limits that something is managed within will be utilized in the design process to create a clear vision of how well the project in question is organized. Any designs may be produced to fit the required performance yields. The key is to produce a better layout in time for when a new prototype is drafted and ready for use.

But even when something is in control, you must still look at how well the product generation process works. While you might notice a function in control, that effort might still be organized outside of the specifications you want to meet. You must review if the results being produced are appropriate and whether you are getting the work to run right. Remember that the results may be consistent even if you are working with the wrong things in the efforts being planned.

Out of Control Issues

There may be times when your work is out of control and the process is not moving along right. The values on the Y chart change consistently when something is out of control. The problem can develop even if you are within the control levels. The greatest threat is that you might not be able to predict when something is working right. Here are a few of the most prominent things to notice when assessing whether something is out of control:

1. Any data points in your control chart are falling outside the control limits.

2. At least eight consecutive points are found on one side of the central line.

3. Seven or more consecutive points are progressively declining or increasing. This includes moving from one control limit to another without any resistance.

4. At least 14 consecutive points are moving up and down in an alternating pattern.

5. A few consecutive points are in the bottom or top parts of the chart. They are not going around the average as much as you hoped they would be.

6. At least 15 consecutive points are found in the middle part of the chart. This includes areas around the average. This might suggest that the process being handled is too simple and is not making any sizeable improvements or changes.

When identifying when a subject matter is out of control, you can consider a few zones. These zones may be produced within the standard deviations that you are trying to operate within. In this case, the zones will be distinguished by letters. Your goal is to keep too many points from being in the same zone area at once. Here's a look at how this might work in your routine:

Zone C is the spot you want to target, given that you want to be within the proper standard variations. But you should also see that the variance is natural enough to where it works within the proper standard deviations of value. Anything that is stuck in

Zone A for far too long might also be risky, what with the content not changing or shifting all that much.

You might have to conduct new experiments on your Six Sigma process while using a new pilot pertaining to what you have been producing. A calibration effort might have to be reviewed as well. A re-analysis of your historic database may also be utilized to help you identify the things that are arising in the effort. You can try these ideas to keep the process on target or to at least reduce the variability. But whatever the case, you should see that the process is stable enough to help you control the setup without shifting or otherwise being too hard to follow and use.

Common Types of Trends in Maps to Notice

You may notice a few trends in your control analysis depending on how your changes and details develop. You should look at the mean and variation alike to identify any significant changes that might arise in your work. These trends will change over time. Four types may be noticed:

1. Predictable

First, your map may be predictable in nature. The general average is around the same for the most part, while the range or variation does not change much. The chart below gives a good example of how a control chart may be predictable. The layout shows that the chart is not moving out from a certain standard deviation too often, thus producing a more effective readout. It may be easier here to figure out the timing or changes arising in the work.

2. Unpredictable Mean with a Predictable Variation

You might struggle with figuring out the mean or average of your readouts, but the variation will be minimal. You might be stuck near one of the control limits at this point. The limitations produce a difficult design that adds a bit of extra coverage, although the variation can stick around the same value. This could be a sign that there are changes in a process that are using the mean that are different every time something is handled, although the sudden changes in this case might be significant depending on where something might be going.

3. Predictable Mean and Unpredictable Variation

The mean may be around the same, but there is a chance your work will go all over the place between standard deviations. This includes times when the values go beyond the control limits. Those breaks will still be temporary. But they might show a series of extremes surrounding the variation. You'll have to review the variation based on what is working in your space and how you are changing the work being put into the process.

4. Chaos

Chaos is the one situation that you want to avoid. At that point, you cannot predict the mean or variation. It could arise from malfunctions in your equipment, an inability of people to work together or a substantial turnover. But in most cases, outside forces may be the cause for the issue. You'll have to review the chaos to see how the subject matter being managed is handled and ensure that you have a plan in mind to counter the chaos before it gets worse. In most cases, that plan may require a new pilot to produce a different result.

Your effort in managing your work should be based on what you are finding when your control chart works. Be prepared to assess what changes have to be made based on any problems found in your chart.

Chapter 52 – Specification Limits

While a control limit is about keeping the process in the Six Sigma routine within a certain range, a specification limit works a little differently. The specification limit is the exact boundary for how something can perform. Anything that goes outside the specification limits might not be acceptable. Anything that is outside of the specification will be defective due to something having so many defects that the process or item aren't working well.

A specification limit is different from the control limit in that the specification point relates to how well a task runs. Anything outside the control limit is a sign that something is changing. A specification limit involves the rules that may be handled with the intention of sticking within a certain point. You are trying your hardest to keep the specifications in check without these becoming frustrating or otherwise hard to manage.

The specification limits are established by customer demands. You have to produce your work within those limits to ensure the setup is managed right. For instance, you might be responsible for producing cans of diced fruit that are sent out to supermarkets. You might have rules pertaining to how much or how little fruit is added into each can. The specification limits can be minute points stating how much will be added so the customer is satisfied. For instance, you might produce 12-ounce cans of pineapples with the upper specification limit or USL being 12.005 ounces and the lower specification limit or LSL being 11.995 ounces. Anything that goes outside those limits will be unnecessary.

You should use specification limits in cases where you know you can get within a certain total based on what is right. The goal is to see if your process can handle the specific standards that your customers have. This is different from the control limits that focus on how well your Six Sigma process works.

Using One Limit

There might be times when you need only one specification limit. For instance, you might just need the one limit on the left, the LSL. This might include cases where the products being produced have to be above a certain limit. For instance, the fruit canning company in our example might have a standard where at least 95 percent of the seeds in a pineapple are removed before they can be canned. The LSL would be 95. You have to keep the curve with a vast majority of entries over 95 percent, thus ensuring the customers see that you're appropriately removing the seeds.

You can also use the USL as the only limit. This is when there's a limit to how much can be handled. The fruit cannery might have a customer service department that takes phone calls from people who have concerns or questions about products. The call center might have a rule stating that all calls must be answered within 30 seconds. Therefore, a measurement with a USL of 30 can be produced. The key is to have the majority of items on the curve under 30.

You can plan the statistical limits in any way you see fit so long as you look at the things that the customers want. Be aware of the VoC in your work so you'll recognize what makes your statistical efforts useful while being easier to follow. You can plan this as well as desired for keeping your Six Sigma work under control, but you must always notice what the customers want. Anything that goes outside those limits will be useless. Your control plan has to be cared for to where the process is more attractive and functional without problems.

Chapter 53 – Leading and Lagging Indicators (KPIs)

After a while, you might notice some sizeable changes in the Six Sigma charts you use. These changes may include points that occur before and after a defect. These points are known as indicators. You can use these indicators to get an idea of how well the content you are working with is managed. These indicators may also be called key performance indicators or KPIs.

A KPI identifies how well a task works based on the objectives a company has. The indicators should be capable of providing details on what is making a task or routine so useful. You can use one of many indicators in the process, including ones that show how predictable a task may be or how costs are being managed in the work process. If you understand how they work, your indicators will predict the future or show what might have happened in the past.

Leading Indicators

A leading indicator is a point that reveals a trend in the Six Sigma process before your defect occurs. You might notice at least five downward points on a chart, for instance. This is a sign that a leading indicator is developing. The downward trend will eventually lead to the value going outside the control limit, particularly the lower one. You may use the indicator to figure out if there is a sizeable change in what is happening in your business efforts.

Your indicator may be used to figure out if there are any positive developments happening in your work. For instance, an accounting firm might have a Six Sigma plan in mind for handling client queries pertaining to their tax returns. The leading indicators in a review of how effective the team is can quickly show how well the effort is managed. You can use indicators to see how your team is planning different tasks while also reviewing the work in question.

The leading indicator helps you see when you are moving upward in your task or are dropping in value. You might discover that some errors are changing your task and that the work within a group is not all that strong. In the case of the call center, the team might not be doing enough hours of work. The team might be coming across new problems or a lack of an ability to handle an influx of calls. There may also be concerns about fatigue among some employees. You can use the declining totals in your work to figure out what defects are emerging.

There are a few things to notice if you're going to find a leading indicator:

1. What is the backlog?

The backlog might become very large to where a team might not have the people necessary to manage it. The added stress might be harder to manage than expected. This makes it tough for the team to keep working.

2. How much of the team is available?

There can also be instances when you come across problems where the team you are hiring cannot arrive on time to fix certain problems. That lack of availability may hurt the business. The lack of training and knowledge among some members may also be a threat.

3. What types of blockers are in the way?

Blockers are issues in the work process that involve data not being handled well. This includes cases where people cannot get access to the resources or materials that the team requires. Blockers could trigger the drawdown in power and eventually move people back after a while. The blockers involved can be a threat in many cases, although they can be identified if you are careful enough and complete your research over how they might work in your environment.

4. What types of outstanding bugs are in the way?

The bugs in your system can vary based on the functions you plan and any other problems that may be a threat to your work. The outstanding bugs can be frustrating, but they are natural issues that will change over time. Review any known bugs you have. Do not use these bugs as an excuse though. Look instead at how well the content or subject matter might be utilized.

Lagging Indicators

A lagging indicator focuses mainly on your output. The indicator comes about after a defect or other event. You will notice after something happens that the values are going down. This includes you not producing enough materials or having more defects than needed. The lagging indicator will influence the process for managing the content in question. You can also confirm any errors that are occurring, thus letting you resolve the problem sooner.

The lagging indicator is easy to follow and use. The process focuses mainly on ensuring the content works smoothly. More importantly, you can figure out what can be done to prevent the problem from developing again. But this all works best when you've got an idea of where your indicator is coming from beforehand. Having enough control over where the indicator is found helps your success and work routine.

You can measure these two indicators every day as needed. You can look at what signs might cause these indicators to arise and then find ways to resolve them. Your goal should be to produce indicators that move upward instead of ones that come about due to any faults or defects. Getting those defects controlled should move the Six Sigma work back to its normal form. But the indicators should also be identified based on what's happening in your workplace, thus restoring a sense of control over your work.

Chapter 54 – Managing All Risks

The greatest problem with Six Sigma routines and all lean efforts is that there are always going to be chances that problems might arise. When Edward Murphy tried to utilize different measuring devices and standards for aerodynamics tests, many of his attempts failed. This eventually led to the creation of Murphy's Law, a general statement suggesting that anything wrong that can go wrong will go wrong.

There will be risks that arise in the Six Sigma work, especially in the control scheme. Such problems may keep an operation from working to its fullest potential, especially when you're trying to resolve data and keep it consistent. You should look at the risks that might develop in your workplace to see that you keep the problems in your setup from being a threat. But while you might think that you can stop a manufacturing process or other effort to keep the issues in check, you have to look at something of use before any problems develop. This chapter is about studying various risks to ensure you're making the most out of your work.

Analyze the Operational and Reporting Goals

Sometimes the risk to a Six Sigma routine will be greater if the operational and reporting goals are different from one another. The two kinds of goals are different, but they are both about making sure a business works well while also having enough data on its functions recorded as needed. There will be a relationship between many factors.

Operational objectives refer to how efficient and helpful an enterprise is. You may review these objectives based on their supplies, the process inputs involved, the business processes and the job's requirements. The organization should monitor what it is doing for work and figure out solutions for how its goals are to be met. Outcome measures should also be noted.

Reporting objectives are different in that they relate to the strategies that might be utilized. The objectives can be noticed based on growth opportunities or an ability to gain a better advantage. There is also a need to build loyalty or to maintain consistent core customers among other things. You can use these goals to review what a business wishes to complete when trying to succeed. But the reporting objectives should be reviewed versus the operational points.

The goals you incorporate in the mix should be noted based on any changes or efforts that might develop in the work environment. The goals have to be carefully organized while remaining consistent all around.

Talk with Current Members

There are often times when you need to talk with the current members in your work environment about any of the Six Sigma plans you wish to follow. You have to look at whether the current functions are effective without being frustrating. You can review your current environment based on what might be useful. You can talk with the people about whatever might be valuable or controlled. The current risks analysis should be explored with your employees to see what they feel is right for the task.

The Poka Yoke Process

Poka Yoke is an intriguing process for Six Sigma that keeps issues in the workplace from becoming problematic. It comes from a Japanese term relating to preventing mistakes. The concept was developed in the 1960s in Japan to help correct potential defects and to review inspection processes so such defects might be prevented in the future. This is a detective process in a lean routine that is easy to utilize.

Poka Yoke can be noticed in many applications throughout your life. Electric sockets are designed with Poka Yoke standards to ensure that children cannot play with those sockets and be at risk of harm. Meanwhile, a washing machine is designed to where the unit will not start operating unless its door is closed, thus preventing the machine from producing more water when the cover is open. That keeps the machine from flooding a room.

With Poka Yoke, you are spending less time trying to train your workers to manage defects. Some quality control operations may be reduced in intensity or even eliminated altogether. Operators will not have to do the same repetitive tasks either, thus facilitating a simple approach for work. Also, you can resolve problems that develop in the workplace before they can become any more significant than they already are.

The Poka Yoke task ensures items are right the first time around. It becomes harder for mistakes to be made when the Poka Yoke process is managed. The routine can be easy to implement and should not be too costly either; if anything, Poka Yoke helps you to save money when implemented correctly.

Three Types

With Poka Yoke you can work with one of three methods in mind. These each involve the same process steps, but focus on specific things of value within your work. You can use the Poka Yoke effort for all of these processes or routines as you see fit.

1. Contact Method

The first option is the contact method. You will determine the parts of a process that are causing the errors. These include parts that might be very complicated or hard to manage on their own. The contact method analyzes how well the data you are working with is running while also helping you to resolve errors. The process may be described as a direct analysis of the concerns you have. The Gemba walk, which is discussed in detail in Chapter 56, can be used at this point to review the problems involved.

2. Motion-Step Method

You can also identify any motions in the process and see if they are working right. With the motion-step method you can check how well your Six Sigma routine is working based on the rules and whether the process is working right. Depending on your Six Sigma process, you might come across some sizeable problems within your work involving many types of steps that are not proceeding as planned. These problems might trigger difficult results involving more people than necessary to resolve matters. You might have to identify individual steps and then develop a way to keep those steps from malfunctioning.

3. Fixed-Value Method

The operator should be noted in this if a particular series of movements do not take place. This includes some steps that don't begin at all. While the motion-step method involves steps proceeding improperly, the fixed-value is about things that do or don't work as needed. You can use the fixed-value method to analyze how well processes are running.

The Process

You can use Poka Yoke to control various processing errors, missing part issues and cases where the operations process is not managed as well as it should be. The best part of the process is that Poka Yoke is a universal solution that is easy to manage in many forms. The rational design of Poka Yoke ensures that the task you want to put into place is easy to follow and utilize. Here are a few steps to utilize:

1. Review the process or operation that needs handling.

2. Use a Five Whys process to analyze the issues at hand. This includes a focus on the ways something might fail.

3. Review the approach you need to utilize.

You can use a shutout strategy to prevent the error from ever happening. You can also use an attention strategy to identify the defect as it is taking place. A comprehensive approach that follows all of the things that might take place may also be utilized in your work. The approaches involved may help with managing the reviews you want to use while figuring out what might be more appropriate for your task.

4. Determine whether the strategy you want to use is appropriate for the situation.

A contact may be used in the process. The contact is a review of physical attributes that might occur in a task. The analysis helps you to detect errors and to find certain constants that might also change. You can see what steps are being performed in the process so you can confirm whatever it is you wish to do.

A constant number should also work to review an error that can be triggered when certain actions are not performed. A sequencing method relating to the steps being handled and how they are planned in order may also work. The solutions identify the ways certain tasks move about.

5. Test the method with a brief trial. Only one item is needed here.

6. Review how well the method you are using works. Test the routine to see if it works and if you should educate the others in the workplace about how the process works.

The Poka Yoke process should be taught to others in the lean process if possible. Everyone should be aware of how the routine works. The process works for all kinds of risks. As such, you can use it to manage any issue provided that you understand how the process works.

Chapter 55 – Getting a Control Plan Ready

When you feel ready, you can start working with a control plan for your Six Sigma needs. The control plan should be easy to follow and prepare for your use. There are four options for your control plan.

1. Standardization

The first choice for your control plan entails standardization. This is where you produce a standardized plan that entails a series of clear-cut rules for executing your routine to ensure the lean process remains steady. The data should be shared with all people in the workplace in order for them to understand what is happening with your work. The standardization process must have specific rules while also being organized in a series of convenient steps. You can include details on who does what within these steps and when those actions will take place. Don't forget to discuss with people how they can use more complicated or detailed work instructions for the process.

2. Documentation

Documentation refers to a series of rules that can be followed in the work process. You can use these rules to prepare a series of points surrounding the content you wish to utilize and how the effort works to your liking. Think of the documentation process as something similar to what you would see with a large manual that comes with a machine or other item. The document will include specific technical details that have to be noted so everyone in the process can fully recognize what you want to do.

Each documentation process should include a general look at the procedure that you want to lay out for everyone in the workplace to use. The procedure should include an extremely specific series of steps pertaining to your work. The overall layout should add a sense of understanding for everything you want to plan in your task. The documentation should be thorough but also simple enough to use in many situations. The most important part here is to help people recognize what they can do for success even under difficult circumstances.

3. Monitoring

You can use monitoring to regularly review the many things that go into a process. A monitoring task can work with a full analysis of everything that makes your content work without being hard to follow. The work can include an analysis of the process and any output measures. You can educate people to review the results that come along in real time and then change things around in the process depending on what is found. The effort may work well with calculating issues and resolving them before they get worse or people go in the wrong direction.

Your monitoring plan may include details on when data is going to be collected. This can include a look at the process for gathering and recording data and for when you're reporting data on the things you are trying to analyze. The monitoring helps the process to stay intact without risking anything being lost or worn in the routine. The goal should be to meet the needs of the customers over time without isolating anyone or otherwise creating any concerns that might keep the customers from feeling confident about what is being offered by your business.

4. Response

You might need to make some changes within your control setup. You can produce a response plan that entails a review of what will happen if you ever come across anything that has to be changed in the process. You can look at what actions will take place when out-of-control events or problems arise in the work environment. Any data that needs to be abruptly calculated should also be explored. Information on how people can find troubleshooting assistance should be included as well.

What To Get In Your Control Plan

The four options you have for your control plan are all helpful in many forms, but you also have to look at how you're going to plan out your work. There are a few things that you can include in your control plan with an emphasis on helping your employees. These plans should work well for giving your business the extra control and support it requires. To start, you have to produce a clear set of objectives while also including enough learning resources for all your employees. But there are some extra things that have to be noticed:

1. Look at the milestones you wish to produce. These may help people with finding the right goals for the task.

2. Assess what your needs for resources may be within the task.

3. Identify the budget you have for your work task. The budget can be as controlled as it has to be.

4. List points on the documentation you wish to utilize. This includes the documentation based on any specifics involved with the work.

Every process you include in your control plan can be utilized to your advantage as you require it. The most noteworthy part of the plan is that it creates a sense of control in your work. The added help may provide you with a good review of what might make your work stand out.

Chapter 56 – The Gemba Walk

The concept of Gemba, which we briefly discussed early in this guide, is a Japanese term for the actual place where something happens. For instance, you might come across a television report in Japan where the reporter is "from Gemba," which means that person is where something actually took place. The Gemba concept should be explored so you'll do more with your Six Sigma effort. As such, it's important for you to understand how the Gemba walk works.

You need the Gemba walk to help you with moving outward and to ensure you understand the things that are taking place in the Six Sigma environment. You will see what is happening in the workplace while also noticing any wasteful activities. That will lead to you asking why certain things you are coming across are happening. More importantly, you will focus on the Gemba effort with collaboration and control in mind. The weak points in the process are important to notice, not the individuals who are not doing much.

You can plan the Gemba walk with a few steps in mind:

1. Review the theme.

The theme should be chosen based on factors like efficiency, safety and other special points. You should look at the themes involved based on the goals you have and what might need to be done in the workplace. You can plan the theme to review the content in question while being precise and under control. You can also use the theme to prepare the questions that you plan on handling.

2. Plan the team who will help you.

A team can be planned based on things that may happen. Workers will feel more likely to collaborate and work together without problems if content is managed well. The people who will work with you will have to analyze many things relating to the Gemba walk and the process in question. Thus, the team should be supportive in many ways.

3. Review the process.

The process should be explored during the work environment for helping you make the most out of your content. You cannot concentrate much on the people who are working on the task. You have to look at the processes those people are getting into so they will know what's right for any intention. The process should be to simply observe and review the process. Focusing on the people might cause resistance or resentment. The focus should not be on individual people, or else they will feel pressured and may not work as well as they normally would.

4. See where the value stream is.

The value stream should be explored based on many points. You should look at how well the stream runs and whether there are any forms of waste involved. You might notice a situation where it takes extra time to complete a task or to manage certain actions. You must notice the work over how the routine is planned out. The general goal should be to keep the stream intact.

5. Record what you see, but do not observe people directly during the walk.

It is important to keep notes on all the things you see in the walk, although you should avoid being direct with others while on the walk. You do not want to suddenly adjust the process by calling people out. Also, you should avoid trying to produce an immediate solution. You might have an idea, but you need to test that with a pilot first to see if there are any problems with what you're getting into.

Review what you are working on in the task. See if there's a set process that you wish to utilize. You might also look at the problems that come with your work while figuring out how they can be fixed. You can keep that data on hand for when you're planning your pilot. The root cause should be explored cautiously. You can look at who you should speak to when there is a problem.

6. Have another person from your business work with you on the walk. This includes someone from a different department outside of where you normally work.

You can work with someone from a different field that has certain responsibilities. You can learn a new viewpoint from such a person. The questions you ask him or her should be ones that you might not originally have considered asking prior to the test at hand. You might get more out of the work if you plan your questions carefully.

7. Produce a follow-up after the walk.

Share the things you found on your Gemba walk with others in the process. Ask about what they are doing while seeing how your tasks are being run. Let the team know about any changes that you want to produce in the Six Sigma work based on the Gemba run. Also, look at the responses those people might give to your efforts. People might try to resist some of the things that you want to do, so you need to analyze this well enough.

You can get the Gemba walk to help you with obtaining a firsthand review of what you're getting out of the Six Sigma routine. You can use this after the Six Sigma process is planned while also looking at the changes that might develop in your work depending on what you find to be appropriate for your plans or routines.

Chapter 57 – Kanban

Kanban is an intriguing point to note for your Six Sigma work, especially when aiming to manage your control stage. Kanban is a scheduling system that identifies how well your tasks are run and helps you to plan a process that moves smoothly and should not be hard to maintain on its own. The best way to describe Kanban is that it is about ensuring the workflow is handled smoothly. Part of this includes figuring out the timing for tasks. The goal is to produce more work in less time.

Kanban has been a trusted solution for lean management needs since it was first introduced in the 1940s. Toyota engineers noticed that grocery stores restocked their items based on their inventories and not on what supplies their vendors had. Clerks would only order more of a product when they were close to selling out. The Kanban system was devised as a result to ensure that inventory matched up with demand and that the quality levels being handled would be improved or enhanced. The system was named for the Japanese term for a signboard, or a material used to signal messages to people.

The inventory links up to whatever people consume. A signal is generated to tell a company to produce something that comes out to a sales floor or other space. A signal may also be sent to a vendor for cases where something has to come out sooner. The routine schedules the replenishment process and ensures all the content is available. The process is efficient and takes only a few moments to process. However, the Kanban effort has to be used with extremely strict considerations to make it work.

The Kanban routine may still be used for basic tasks that go along with orders or movements. You can use it with different routines such as an ability to handle work based on the things you wish to do. You can produce steps relating to when ideas arise and how far you are moving with the work. You can use it when ordering items at a business or when planning other inventory routines.

The Six Rules of Kanban

There are six rules that must be followed when getting the Kanban process to work for you. These are based on what Toyota uses:

1. Every process will produce requests to suppliers as those supplies are consumed.

2. Every process moves based on the quantity of what is available and how well incoming requests are managed.

3. Nothing can be transported or moved unless a request is made.

4. All requests linked to an item must be attached to the said item.

5. Defective items must not be sent out to any party. All items have to be confirmed as defect-free before movements take place.

6. A limit on pending requests may be utilized.

The last of the six rules is the most revealing. The limit on Kanban requests ensures that the standards used are kept in control. All requests or orders will be maintained well. Also, the limit can reveal any inefficiencies that have to be resolved sooner. You can use these Kanban requests to prevent future problems from developing in any situation or to fix those problems relating to how your work is being handled.

Four Added Principles

Those six rules of Kanban are important, but there are four other rules to note:

1. Kanban helps you visualize your work.

You can use Kanban to review how well items move between parties. This may work for when you need to locate bottlenecks and inefficiencies. The visualization may work with as many transmission channels as needed. You can quickly prepare these channels and produce a clear plan for ordering items.

2. You can limit the work involved in the process.

The limits in your Kanban routine will focus on only a few movements at a time. You can cut down on the time it takes for items to move through the Kanban system through this process. You can also use this to keep from switching between tasks in the Kanban effort. There is also the benefit of not having to go between items. The added focus keeps errors from being likely to occur.

3. The flow of your work will be easier to manage.

You can use a review of the flow to ensure the processes involved aren't too hard to follow. Metrics may be noticed in the flow. You may identify how long it takes certain things to come through. You can use this to plan out any lean tasks with your items or inventory. This is to create a more sensible approach to your work.

4. You will continuously improve within your work as the process goes forward.

There are no limits to how much you can improve upon the tasks you are entering with Six Sigma. Kanban lets you see how the flow moves, how long it takes for orders to go through and so forth. You have the option to control your work or to improve upon any faltering issues that develop within the task.

The Steps for Kanban

There are five important steps for you to utilize when getting Kanban ready for your use:

1. Visualize the workflow.

The workflow should be reviewed with a few columns in mind. The columns will illustrate many values like the things you need to do, what you are planning, how certain tasks are to be completed and so forth. The columns you will use will vary based on your business layout and the demands you have for the work. The columns are steps that include everything that needs to be done where you are, although you can also add buffer steps that go in between certain ones. The buffer steps are optional, but they assist with some of the things that might come through.

The workflow is not intended to be fully permanent. You can change some things around within your workflow as you see fit. This includes changes to the steps you wish to use. You can produce new steps that may be added over time to change the functions you'll need to handle. Also, you can use as many steps as you wish. That said, it is best to keep the number of steps involved down if possible.

2. Add constraints.

Produce some rules that limit what might happen. You might keep only a certain number of items in each Kanban column. You can ask for four items in each column, like in the image below. The limitation ensures you won't adjust your focus all the time or have too much to work with. More importantly, this helps you reveal any inconsistencies involved with your work, thus fixing any problems you might come across. But to make this work, you have to convince the others in the lean process that less is always more; a person who tries to handle many tasks and duties at once is not necessarily going to be more productive or effective.

3. Explain all policies directly and carefully.

Each of the policies you plan on using in your work should be arranged right. This includes looking at the rules pertaining to the items that can be handled. A good rule of thumb is to organize the items being handled based on service classes. One item may be a standard option, while another entails something that has to be expedited or run faster. Fixed-date rules may also be used to help you with planning out certain points depending on what is time-sensitive and has to be resolved sooner. The image above shows items with different colors for each item; you can use individual colors on your Kanban board to distinguish between what is the most important to do now versus what should not be handled too soon or fast.

The best thing to do here is to keep a bit of space on your board for any time-sensitive materials. You can leave one slot open for urgent tasks. This allows you to manage any emergency work. Also, the standard items will continue to use the same flow all around. The risk of items being interrupted within the process should be minimal.

4. Measure your flow on occasion.

Review how all items in the Kanban process are flowing. Make sure the flow works quickly while being easy to use. The flow may include a look at the cycle time. You can time how long it takes for you to move through all steps in the Kanban process. The cycle time should be measured by reviewing how long each process lasts while using an average of all the processes. The measurement gives you a throughput of the units that move through during a time period.

A cumulative flow diagram (CFD) should be used in this process. The CFD reviews how well a task is handled for your use. The layout visualizes the ways you go through each part of the Kanban process. You may notice how long it takes for items to move through based on the steps involved. The diagram takes a bit of time, but you can use it to calculate where you are in certain tasks in your process versus the things that are already done. You can use it to figure out if there are certain stages in the process where it might be difficult for you to get some tasks or routines finished right.

5. Use the scientific method to figure out the optimal setting for the Kanban plan.

The scientific method is vital for your success with the Kanban routine. The method illustrates what you are doing and analyzes the effort by assessing what types of outcomes may be produced in your work. A hypothesis can be used to figure out what Kanban routine is right. You can measure your results over a few weeks or months to see if the hypothesis is correct. The goal is to find a routine that ensures the work you put in is managed right and that you have an idea of where you wish to go with your work or content.

The best part of working with the Kanban effort is that you're using it to keep the delivery process or other work routine running as efficiently as possible. You can keep items moving and flowing at the right delivery times as you see fit. The Kanban routine can be used with any particular type of task that you see fit. Don't forget that the process can work consistently with various types of charts that fit in well with your effort based on what you are using.

Additional Chart Formats

1. Portfolio Board

You have the option to work with many types of charts when getting the most out of your Kanban work. The following examples include many choices that suit all your specific needs. The first of these choices is the portfolio board seen below. This includes tasks based on what has to be done now and, in the future, what people are working on and in what priority the tasks are to be handled in. The Important and Good to Have segments are useful as you can use them to identify what's critical to your business. The future road map listing also shows people what they have to do so they know what to expect out of the task in the future.

2. Development

You can also use another chart for the development of a product. The chart lists features you want to work with and also that are works in progress. You can include steps relating to the tests and tasks you want to use and when you're going to complete a task. Details on anything that has been done should be listed at the end. Again, you can include separate rows for things that have to be done versus things that are optional but which still deserve to be noted.

3. Large-Scale Project

A larger project can benefit from the use of a Kanban board as well. The board may include rows devoted to certain departments or tasks in a process. The layout lets you keep tabs on many teams at a time. The process also assists you with noting how well certain teams are working while seeing if there are any groups that are struggling. You can plan the layout of your Kanban board based on the things that your team members are capable of managing within a certain amount of time.

What About the Gantt Chart?

The Gantt chart is an option related to the Kanban chart that works with some of the same principles. However, the Gantt chart might not necessarily be the best choice. It is true that you can look at details on the things that you are finishing at certain times while reviewing the next things that have to be resolved as soon as possible. The problem, though, is that you are putting limits on when tasks are to be completed.

The Gantt chart lets you review the tasks involved with a project and who will be responsible for the task. Time frames for a task may be noted as well. This includes a focus on specific times for starting and ending the task. Other things may be adjusted on the fly, but the times are still going to be fixed. Therefore, any cases where you are not working with those in mind could prove to be risky.

The Kanban process works better than the Gantt chart in that Kanban does not necessarily put in start and end dates for tasks. While there are some tasks that need to be completed within certain times or might be time-sensitive, those may be in the minority. You will have more freedom to produce tasks to your liking when the Kanban routine works rather than the Gantt chart. The Kanban routine works to help you keep from needing to rush or cut corners to try and finish a task by a specific time.

Chapter 58 – Signing Off of the Six Sigma Task

The Six Sigma project is not going to last forever. The work will end after you have managed to create a consistent approach to work while ensuring the results are better than what they used to be. More importantly, the project will end when the task is confirmed to be fully complete and everything is moving along swimmingly. But even after you have signed off a Sigma Six task, you will have the opportunity to go back to it if necessary.

You will sign off on the project after you have noticed a dramatic reduction in defects or an improvement in customer service over time. The end of the project will entail a full analysis of what has happened within the work in question. This should include a look at how well you were able to manage your efforts and whether the task has been fully confirmed as having worked. A Black Belt or Master Black Belt must agree to allow you to sign off the Six Sigma work.

The time it takes for you to finish the Six Sigma task will vary, although it can be relatively short if you were proficient enough with your work on the task. The Six Sigma work can end in a few weeks or months after you start. The task length will be longer if the process is complex and the corrections involved are extensive. The Black Belt or Master Black Belt should help you with finding a suitable time frame for your task.

A final confirmation run can be conducted before signing off. The review requires a test of a few processes or samples to see that the results are improved and the work situation is now easier to manage. The project can then be shut down as the business has been bettered through the effort. All information pertaining to the project can be recorded. The results should be listed prominently to show that the work in question has been efficient enough for your liking.

The leaders in the task should agree with you on the results that have come about in the effort. You can get your finance manager, process manager and any other important parties to produce a final scorecard of how well the routine has gone. You can also add the benefits of the task. Everyone has to agree to the results produced to ensure the task has worked out as well as it should. Your business should get back to its normal processes after this, but the team will have improved substantially thanks to the work you put in.

Be advised, though, that this is not necessarily a final farewell to the task. You might come across a situation where you have to get the task back up again. In this case, you will have to analyze any problems, reopen the work and use the old documentation that you utilized in the task. You must use a confirmation run to see if the process is working right and then figure out what new problems have arisen. Some revisions to the Six

Sigma task may be produced, although the specifics you go through can vary based on how elaborate the task is.

You can do one last test after you are finished with reviewing the overall layout of the task. The full review will help you identify any significant problems that have come up in the work.

Chapter 59 – Planning a Six Sigma Presentation

A Black Belt or Master Black Belt can plan many aspects of the Six Sigma task and introduce unique concepts, but most of the development may go to a Green Belt. You have to analyze how well the Six Sigma work is being managed so you'll know what to expect out of your efforts. This chapter will focus on what you can do to produce a Six Sigma presentation.

The Six Sigma presentation works to help you illustrate to your higher-ups what you want to do with your Six Sigma work. You can show the others in your project what you wish to do with your plans while letting all White and Yellow Belts understand your efforts in general. You must produce a helpful presentation to add credibility to your Six Sigma work. More importantly, people will trust you and your Six Sigma project if you have an excellent presentation.

1. Keep the presentation within a certain time frame.

Everything you have learned in this guide should help you to design a Six Sigma plan that entails everything from the problem you are addressing, the design of the plan, how you will monitor and analyze it and what you can do to improve the task. You need to describe all that in the presentation and still be brief. Keep your presentation within about 40 minutes if possible. Failing to keep your presentation under 40 minutes might cause audience members to be less interested in your work and likely to tune out after a while.

2. Plan a question and answer (Q&A) session after the presentation.

After your presentation, you should answer questions that people have about your Six Sigma work. Keep the Q&A session to around 20 minutes or less (approximately half the time of your presentation). A 30-minute presentation can provide room for a 15-minute Q&A point. Again, people will check out if your session lasts too long.

3. Plan a slideshow, but keep it short.

You can produce a slideshow with one of many software programs. Microsoft PowerPoint is the most popular choice, although OpenOffice Impress has recently become a popular open source choice. Keep the presentation to 20 slides or less in length. Anything that has too many slides will go beyond the 40-minute length standard you should be following. Take about two minutes on each slide. People can use those two minutes to take notes on whatever you wish to discuss with your audience.

A good plan for your slideshow is to plan your slides based on the information you wish to convey and what you feel is appropriate for your work. Review the slideshow based on the content you want to highlight and how proficient or effective your content might be.

Don't forget to use visuals to make your work a little easier to read. This is where the next point comes in handy.

4. Offer enough visual representations of your data.

Your Six Sigma project will be easier for people to analyze and review if they have enough visual points. A presentation can include several pictures and data charts to help people understand what you wish to do. This includes a look at all the things that come with your task and how efficient the solutions might be. Graphs and other visual points make the data easier for people to recall. You may also use this to simplify what you wish to say in your presentation, thus allowing the process to flow well.

The best part of these data points is that they can tell good stories to your audience. You can explain in your pictures how the data you are working with will impact the business, the employees and the customers alike. Also, you can focus on your visual data points instead of on yourself, to show that everyone has a role of sorts in the Six Sigma work, thus reemphasizing the need for teamwork.

Like with what you do when planning the charts and tables in your Six Sigma task, you must also look at how you're planning the visual representations of your data. Be sure the content is arranged right and is not hard to follow or utilize.

5. Practice your presentation regularly before the big day.

Talk with others about what you want to do. Notice how well the steps of the Six Sigma process are organized. You might have to edit some of the details of your task if needed. You can rehearse your work as often as needed until you feel confident with your presentation.

6. Review how well your equipment is working.

When preparing for a presentation, you must check how your equipment is working. For instance, a computer should be fully functional so it can load your project. Also, the presentation should be laid out to where every part is easy to view. You should ensure any online connections are fully functional. Any cases where your equipment does not work could be a sign that your project isn't professional. Even worse, people might not see you as a fully authoritative figure.

The key for working on your Six Sigma presentation is to produce a project that is easy to follow and offers sensible points that all people can benefit from using. Remember that everything you have read about in this guide will go into your presentation as you aim to make it attractive.

Chapter 60 – Managing Conflicts In the Task

There are always going to be times when people in the Six Sigma group have particular conflicts pertaining to what they do and do not support. You might come across issues where the task is not all that easy for the team to work with. Conflicts may arise regarding the attitudes individual team members have. This happens as people try to do things their own ways within the Six Sigma process. The arguments and frustrations involved can be substantial, but that does not mean you have to struggle with conflicts in the Six Sigma effort for too long. You can use a few strategies to help you with managing conflicts the right way.

1. Accommodation

The first option you have for managing Six Sigma conflicts is to use accommodating tactics. Accommodation refers to your ability to help people share their ideas and thoughts with you. You can get those people to talk with you about what they want to do in the task and how far their work will go. Part of this includes allowing other ideas to be mixed into the process to create a more consistent approach for work. This may work if your business is a little more flexible in what it wants to do and you have a good plan in mind for how you're going to carry out your business' efforts or routines.

2. Collaboration

It may be best to look at how you're going to collaborate with other people at any time. The collaborative effort in question may include a review of how well you are capable of working with others based on certain ideas. You can find ways to allow different ideas in Six Sigma thinking to be merged with one another. The additional support for different concepts or values may help you with getting a bit of extra control over how well the task may work. Best of all, you can keep any problems in the workplace from being exacerbated. You can stop the frustration or anger that comes with trying to handle a task, but only if you have a good plan in hand.

3. Competition

This third choice for managing conflicts is best for groups whose workforces are a little stronger and can handle enough stress. The competition option entails producing different tasks in the Six Sigma process. One group can create a method, and a second group will do something different. The competition allows the business to challenge itself and review what solutions might be best when trying to contend with one another. You can plan many competitive actions in the workplace as you see fit, but these should be organized based on what you find to be appropriate for when you're trying to get the workplace to run well enough.

You should see that the challenge is not too hard and that you have an idea of where the groups will go in the task. This includes letting everyone in the process know what they can do to succeed and thrive. Remember that this task works best when you're trying to create a better group and participants are capable of lasting through the competition.

4. Avoidance

The last option works best in cases where the group and the Six Sigma project are fragile. With the avoidance strategy, you focus on thinking about what can be done to avoid conflicts. This includes finding easier-to-follow tasks and a less risky process for the Six Sigma task. While you might make some sacrifices, you will at least produce a project that is a little easier to run and might not be as stressful as it could be. But this will only work if your group is fragile and you are uncertain over how you're going to make a task work.

Each of these four options for managing conflicts within the Six Sigma process should work well for your business needs. You may find that it is not too hard to get the most out of your work if you review the ways how you're going to manage conflicts within the Six Sigma task.

Chapter 61 – Agile Project Management

The world of Six Sigma is extensive and distinct, as you have read throughout this guide. But there also comes a time when you need to work with very specific standards or routines for getting a Six Sigma routine to work to your liking. This includes working to correct any problems in the Six Sigma effort that may arise before they can worsen. One of the best solutions you can utilize when managing your Six Sigma work is agile project management or Agile for short. The concept of Agile is relatively new in the Six Sigma world, but it can make a world of difference if planned out right. Part of this comes from the use of many techniques that can be managed within the Agile process, the most noteworthy being Scrum.

Agile project management is a task that entails the use of sprints, or brief development cycles, to get a product or service to develop. The goal is to produce a continuous sense of improvement and progress in the task. The concept has become very popular since the 1970s adaptive development processes became prominent in the software industry. But it was not until 2001, when the Manifesto for Agile Software Development was introduced, that the concept of Agile became more popular. Today, Agile works for many industries well beyond the tech field. Manufacturing teams and other entities can work with Agile strategies and plans to get the most out of the work they are putting into their efforts.

Small sections, called iterations, are used within the sprints being planned. The iterations are analyzed in sprints to review how a project develops. The plans involved can assist anyone with making the most out of the content being handled and with responding to any sudden changes that might develop.

The Basic Concepts of Agile

Agile Project Management is a practice that breaks down a larger Six Sigma task into a series of pieces called iterations. The iterations can entail anything in a Six Sigma task from the basic testing process to the design work. Everything handled in the Agile process is done quickly in sprints. In some cases, a sprint can last less than two weeks. But you might also spend four to six weeks completing a sprint. Agile can be interpreted as Six Sigma that works faster.

A continuous approach is utilized when handling Agile. Teams can release their data on the Agile process within a schedule planned based on when tasks are finished. The continuous nature ensures the entire Six Sigma routine can move forward while also reducing the risk of failures in the project. Agile allows for improvements in the work to move along throughout the lifespan of the work without significant delays or other risks.

One vital concept of Agile is that there are no particular managers involved with an Agile iteration. The role of the manager is divided among many team members. While the head of the task issues project goals, the people on the Agile team work together to complete many smaller routines based on the task goals. The manager does have the option to participate in the Agile iteration to allow for more control over the work. But that is fully optional.

The Keys of the Agile Manifesto

The concept of Agile Project Management was developed as a response of sorts to the waterfall model of project management. The waterfall had been utilized as a solution for processes that move in one direction. The process was thorough and entailed tasks relating to designing, testing, deploying and maintaining tasks. But the waterfall process became somewhat obsolete as people found the restrictive nature of the routine to be lacking in quality. This led to the development of Agile as a solution for managing tasks.

The Manifesto for Agile Software Development was produced in 2001 as a series of rules for how Agile works. While it was developed mainly with software in mind, the process has been adapted over the years to work for every field of work, including customer service and manufacturing fields. The keys of the manifesto include four critical values and 12 principles for the development of a task. Every business that works in the Agile field can use these points in the manifesto for its success. These can also be used as rules to guide the process if there are ever doubts or concerns as to how well a task runs.

The Four Key Values

1. Individuals and interactions are more important than the processes or tools utilized.

2. The entity being handled should be working for all. The ability of a process to work is more important than how technical or detailed the documentation is. (This relates to the Six Sigma standard of keeping waste down.)

3. Workers should collaborate with customers rather than negotiate contracts or strict rules.

4. Any changes that come about in a plan should be responded to appropriately.

The key here is that the people in the Agile process must be capable of working together well while also ensuring that they know what they are doing within their tasks. Strong relationships are required between the employees and other parties in the field. Also, flexibility is important in the task. The Six Sigma process can benefit from Agile's allowing for an extra sense of flexibility in managing the work being handled.

The 12 Key Principles

1. Customers should be satisfied by the delivery of services or processes that are consistent and come in early.

2. It is fine for requirements to change even if they come about late in the game.

3. Working processes should be delivered quickly. It should take weeks for the Agile task to be finished, not months.

4. All parties must collaborate with one another. These entities must talk with each other every day.

5. All projects are to be built around the individual. Each person should be trusted.

6. Direct face-to-face communication is best for when people need to talk with each other during the task.

7. The functionality of a product or service is the main measure of success.

8. The development should be sustainable and capable of producing a consistent flow of work.

9. The technical functionality of the work should be the focus over the design. The design can still be managed well, but it is important to avoid anything that might be too hard to follow or figure out.

10. The simplicity of the work is vital to success.

11. Every team can organize itself.

12. The team must regularly review the things that can be done while managing the subject matter being handled.

Your business group can use the 12 principles in your Agile task to figure out what should be done when handling the content in question.

The Positives of Agile

Agile Project Management is useful for many reasons. First, Agile is easy to deploy as quickly as possible. This includes working with the right people for a task without further complicating issues. The resources that you will utilize are a little easier to work with as well. You can change the resources around and work in any order you see fit.

Also, it is easier for team members to get in touch with each other in the work process. The Agile effort allows more people to determine what they can do to make a task work. You can get as many people in the Agile process to work on a task as needed without one person necessarily having more power than everyone else. There is an added sense of comfort and control over the task when everyone feels confident and relaxed over what can be managed at a time. You do have the option to assign an unofficial leader to the Agile iteration if you wish, although you don't have to go that far in the work.

Any Issues?

As useful as Agile can be, you need to look at what issues might develop. There is a chance that a task might go off track if people are not fully aware of what they are doing. A project that does not have any focus might be harder to handle.

The lack of documentation may also be risky to the project. The task is all about getting the process to work well without having lots of papers or other documents to work with. That does not mean that every person in the process is going to have an idea of what to do. There is also the concern that by not having enough documentation in the process, the results of the task might be unpredictable. But these problems are still not deal breakers when it comes to using Agile for a Six Sigma process.

Chapter 62 – Running an Agile Project

The process for running an Agile iteration or sprint must be carefully planned. You have to notice how well the Agile task is run regardless of the type of team you have, the industry you are in or the end result you wish to produce. The process should work with a good program routine and design at the start while moving forward. You'll be intrigued by how well the Agile project works if you plan your work the right way.

For this chapter, we will use the example of an electric car manufacturer. The company has been working hard to produce new electric batteries, but it has come across a new concern. Standards for producing batteries are changing, and the company's batteries are unable to meet those new rules. In particular, the team has to find a way to produce batteries that can handle more power and produce a longer range of operation. That is, the battery has to work for a longer period before the unit has to be recharged. The Agile iteration in this chapter will focus on a team finding ways to produce a better, longer-lasting battery.

Planning a Road Map

The road map you will utilize in an Agile project will include details on how a product evolves over time. This includes initiatives that relate to communication between workers and an analysis of when something should be done. A road map can be planned as you see fit, provided that the road map is managed within the time frame of the sprint in question.

For the electric car company, the team can produce a road map which illustrates the ways a vehicle battery is developed. This includes looking at how to adjust an existing battery based on the weight of the battery and any connections or panels on the inside. Sometimes a review might include an analysis of how well market changes and actions are being managed.

The road map should be designed based on the value of the team's output. Review how well the team in your iteration will work and have a smart plan in mind. Also, the development team should be explored based on its capacity and how well the process might work. The map has to be realistic based on what the team at large can do.

The road map must be planned based on factors like market changes and any limitations pertaining to what can be done. The car company might have to adjust its plan based on how long it might take to produce a new battery. Several initiatives may be produced to create a clear idea for what might work. The initiatives that must be planned should be relevant to the task. The car company can use initiatives like plans for engineering new products or designs for its batteries to produce a more efficient setup.

Each point in the road map should include the following:

1. Look at when each initiative in the map is to be utilized.

The initiatives should be planned based on the dates that you wish to meet. You can produce sprints that are as short as needed, but you can expand them if you have limitations over what you can do at a time. Any dependencies on initiatives should also be explored to give you an idea of what to expect out of your work and planning efforts. The dependencies may include points within the business. You may look at how many teams and other entities might be produced at any time.

2. Analyze any teams you wish to plan in the map based on the initiatives they will handle.

You can get your project to work with as many teams as needed. For instance, a car company might have one team that focuses on analyzing what can be done to get a car battery to become more powerful. Meanwhile, another team will look at the efforts for keeping the weight of the battery down. You can produce as many teams on your road map as you wish, but you should look at how well the process is run to see that there are no problems with the work you are putting in.

3. Review the time frames for those teams.

You can work with as many time frames as you see fit. The car company could use a time frame of a month for one team to produce a new battery layout. Meanwhile, a two-week sprint may work for the team that needs to produce a lighter battery. The time frames should work well together without producing delays in the Agile process. You can start one group's work before or after another group and eventually have many groups working concurrently with one another.

4. Look at how stable the teams are.

Each of the teams you utilize in your work should be stable and capable of working to their best potential. The teams have to be stable enough to where they can handle their duties and tasks. You should also look at any cases where the teams have to be reorganized. You can plan an organizational effort based on what you are expecting to get out of the team members.

Changing the Road Map Around

As important as the road map can be for the task, you might have to change things around for the process to work well. The map may change based on developments in the work and any cases where people enter or drop out of the task. You must look at plans based on when significant things occur and you need to find new solutions for managing your work.

In our example, the car battery company might change its road map around based on things like the developments of new technologies in the battery industry. The map may be shifted by a little bit if there are significant shifts in the manufacturing process. These include shifts that have to be adapted and utilized to their best potential. The team may also change the demands around based on any strategic decisions that must be made.

Review the map every few weeks as necessary. Adjust the map if needed, and review how well you can move people between teams within the map. You can move those people around on your table to produce a more flexible plan for your work if managed right. Communicate your plans with everyone so all the people will understand what you are trying to do with your work. This includes reviewing the ways your content is organized.

Planning Your Agile Requirements

Every task in the Agile process will require a few points to make the most out of the work you are planning. You can get these Agile points to work as well as desired, although you have full control over how each effort is to be laid out. The best thing to do with your requirements is to plan a product requirements document or PRD. The document is responsible for identifying the purpose of the product and the features or functionalities of what you are working with. You can make the PRD as detailed as you wish, so long as it includes:

1. Goals

Illustrate the goals you want to utilize in your Agile work. The objectives of the business and how well the content fits in strategically with other points can help. You can use the goals in your work as you see fit. Going back to the car battery example, the team will have a goal of producing a battery that can meet the newest standards for how such parts are to be made. This includes specifics like producing something that generates a longer range or offers a lighter weight. The goals should be a perfect strategic fit for the work environment.

2. Definition

A definition of the final product should be included. The definition includes details on why the product is being made, the purpose of that product and its features. The overall functionalities and the ways a person is to use the product should be incorporated. You can produce a definition that is as thorough and detailed as it has to be provided you are controlled in your work. The car battery team may produce a definition that includes specifics on what makes the battery a team wants to create worthwhile. The priorities of items, from must-haves to optional, should also be listed if possible.

3. User Stories or Designs

The user stories in the Agile PRD can include points relating to how well the item is to work. This includes seeing how people might use a product and what experiences they will get from it. The stories provide points on how they will interact with parts or items and use them to their advantage.

4. Questions

People might have questions pertaining to whatever is being offered. You can address these questions in your PRD. Talk about the problems that people have and the solutions that may work for correcting those issues. Any clarifications surrounding problems of note may also be included. The overall scope of the task at large can also be explored if necessary.

All stakeholders should be informed of what to expect in the PRD. Everyone can review the content to get a full review of the functions being used at a time. This includes identifying specific requirements based on how efficient a task might be. The best part of the PRD is that everyone will have an idea of what specifics you want to use in your task. You can use these features as desired to give everyone an idea of where you will go with your work.

Ideas for Creating and Changing the Requirements

You have many things that can be done when getting the requirements ready. To start, avoid keeping requirements or rules too rigid. You can allow for an extra bit of leeway in some of your tasks. This is to keep the pressure off some of the people in your groups. You can allow for many results provided that the workplace ends up operating better and any processes work right after the task is finished.

Allow members of your teams to listen to the plans you are putting in for your requirements. You can let those people pay attention to your work based on factors like how much work is to be completed by these people and how often they are going to work on certain tasks. You can get these people to work with as many details in a task as possible so long as everyone has an idea of what to expect out of the work. You can always get real-time feedback on the task so people will know what to expect from your effort. The feedback may help you with changing your Agile task around so people might pursue different routines or objectives.

Next, you should hold regular meetings between the people in your Agile teams. The most important points about these meetings is that you can update people on any of the changes you will use when getting a task ready for your plans. You have to let everyone work with these changes so they can agree upon them. As such, you must allow everyone in your Agile work to sign off on the changes.

The most important thing to do in this situation is to respect the many differences and thoughts that people have pertaining the task. Every team member has a unique perspective. You can ask people for as many viewpoints as needed. You can move through any angle in your work as necessary provided that you recognize what others in your group are feeling about what should be done to fix problems.

The Single-Page Dashboard

As useful as it is to produce a PRD, it may also be easy to produce a single-page dashboard that can be updated regularly throughout the Agile iteration or sprint. You can post the dashboard online as necessary. You can use a software program to list details on your project through your dashboard, and the program can be adjusted to your liking if needed. The following steps should be used when planning your dashboard layout:

1. Look at the specifics of the project.

List data on the participants in the iteration or sprint. Add details on the status of the task. Specify if the work is on target, at risk or experiencing any sizeable delays. You can also include points on the target time when the work is to be finished. This includes when the final result is to be provided to the public. You can include details on specific roles within the group as well. The designer developers you have, QA team members and other important heads can be incorporated in your work.

2. List the objectives of each team.

All goals should be included based on the teams at the time. These goals may be changed based on which teams are working in the Agile task. Be direct in discussing the objectives. Provide information, but keep the content concise and easy to follow. This is to produce a more accurate readout.

3. Include the background of the task.

The background can include how the task meets the business' objectives. Talk about any recent surveys or research surrounding the business that took place. Explain the behaviors of your customers or others in the industry. The background gives the people in your Agile work an understanding of what makes a task the way it is.

4. Add all assumptions to your dashboard.

Assumptions can come from any source. You might have technical assumptions where you believe specific things will happen in the workplace. You may also have business or industry assumptions where you feel tasks should be run in specific forms. Any user assumptions relating to the people responsible for handling your work can be produced in the process. The listing is to help people look at what beliefs they need to challenge and what they feel should be adjusted based on any changes that might develop in the workplace.

5. Include any user stories about the work you are putting in.

Some user stories may be added to give people details on what they might experience within the workplace. These stories can include anything that people are trying to get out of the business as well as certain demands that your customers might have. Add extra notes to each task or routine you plan on working with at this point as well.

6. Include questions about the Agile work.

Every team in the Agile task should be asked questions involving what they are doing. How are their plans for working being run? Are they using the right standards for gathering information and using it to their advantage? These questions should be specific. You can update your dashboard with answers to the questions as people figure them out, or new questions if you wish to ask something else.

7. Specify whatever it is you are not doing.

You have to tell the team members the things you want them to avoid doing in the work environment. These include various things like any routines that can be skipped. Give an explanation for why those things are not to be done. These reasons may include certain things not being relevant or vital to the task. Keeping the specifics under control is critical for the success of a task.

The great thing about using this one-page dashboard point online is that you'll keep all the important things pertaining to your work arranged in one source. Everyone will recognize the things you're talking about while knowing where the task is moving. People will also get enough context for what you are planning and where you want the task to go. Even more importantly, people will want to participate in your work efforts because they know what to expect out of the content and how you're going to make the work task move forward.

Producing the Backlog

When you hear the word "backlog," you might assume the word refers to the specific things that you need to finish. But for an Agile task, the backlog is different. The backlog is a listing of work for everyone in the Agile project. The most essential items in the work situation are listed at the start of the report. The team reviews the specific things that will work in the backlog and how they are to be planned.

Each consideration for the product or service will be included in a list for a separate team. The lists can be divided up among all the people in the workplace. You can create new lists for everyone, from a design team to a marketing group. You can organize these groups in the backlog based on factors like which tasks are of the highest priority or how urgent it is to obtain and review feedback. You can also arrange the items in each backlog based on what is appropriate for the task and what might be easier to work with at a given moment.

Trust Is Critical

All of the things you've read about in this chapter focus on how easy it can be for you to plan an Agile task. But the most important attribute that has to be planned in the effort entails a sense of trust. All people who work on the same Agile task must feel as though they can trust one another with the work being planned. Part of this includes allowing everyone to communicate with each other in real time. You can allow this part of the task to move as smoothly as possible so everyone will feel confident in the work.

Be transparent and open during the iteration or sprint. Let the people working with you see what roles they have to follow and that they can handle those said roles. Teams that allow these roles to function without complications or hardships in the process will be more likely to succeed. More importantly, everyone will be on the same page throughout the work effort.

Chapter 63 – The Use of Epics, Stories and Themes in the Agile Process

One aspect of Agile work for every iteration or sprint involves how you're adding epics, stories and themes into your work. These are concepts that illustrate certain things that help you identify cases where the iteration has to change. Agile is about shifting plans in your work with smaller groups, but you need input to get an idea of when you have to change things. You can use epics, stories and themes to give yourself more control over what should be managed in your work.

The points are first organized with themes being on the top. Themes are focus areas that you will concentrate on throughout the iteration. These are major focus points that you will consider when trying to improve upon functions in your workplace. You can use these themes as desired to produce effective concepts pertaining to specific ideas you want to share.

Initiatives are groups of epics and stories that link to a goal. You may have many initiatives that link to different themes. For instance, a call center might have themes of courtesy, prompt responses and efficiency. You could have one initiative that includes concepts regarding responding to queries on time and being efficient. Another might focus on courtesy and ensuring that responses are managed as fast as possible.

Epics are large groups of work that can be broken down into smaller tasks. An initiative involving courtesy and efficiency in a call center may include epics with stories that are divided up by topic. One epic may focus on the courtesy aspect, while the other point is more about the efficiency you are trying to plan in the workplace and in answering calls. The epics will narrow down the focus, which eventually leads to the stories at the end.

A story is a request from an end user. The story is the feedback that the user provides based on what that person feels is appropriate and suitable for use. Each story will concentrate on a certain thing that you want your business to do. You can combine all the stories together to get a full analysis of what to expect out of your work environment. Each story is unique, so look at all the variables that go into what you wish to review.

All of this data can be gathered through a general research project. You might produce a few objectives for the Agile task and then look for feedback surrounding the work you are incorporating in your efforts. These objectives can be as thorough as needed, but the key is to ensure you have actual results to work with and that people can review the subject matter or content you wish to plan in your efforts. You can also review the evolution of those stories and other data throughout the work to give yourself an idea of what to expect in your work.

The types of data you will work with should be planned based on how long your iteration will work. A shorter sprint can benefit from reviewing many stories. Meanwhile, a longer iteration that lasts for a month or two should review many epics that include all those stories. A larger project that lasts for at least a full quarter can work with a larger initiative or several more epics. In short, the number of materials you will work with in the task will be greater in quantity when you have more things to work with.

Here's an example of how these points can work. Let's say your task is to get the expenses in your manufacturing warehouse cut down by 10 percent in the next three to four months. You can produce epics that focus on some of things that people in the workplace do. You can then use stories in each epic pertaining to the things the employees are doing to keep costs down. You can get these details in your work organized as you see fit. The layout of an epic with some stories may work as follows:

Epic: Cut expenses by 10 percent in three to four months

Story: Keep all machines lubricated; add new lubricant two or three times a week

Story: Reduce the consumption of battery power by all vehicles in the warehouse by 20 percent

Story: Replace all lighting fixtures with LEDs

The stories are all linked up to the epic based on the experiences people have put in or the things they are trying to do to make a task work right. But don't forget that individual teams can come up with their own stories or do their own research to find specific stories relating to their fields. These groups can be as specific as they have to be. Best of all, the work you put in can be as thorough as desired, although you must notice how effective the content is based on the group providing you with data and how that entity works.

Creating an Epic

You can produce any kind of epic in your Agile work, but an epic should be planned by looking at things that managers or executives will want to report on. The subject matter has to be something the managers will work with and measure throughout the effort. You can plan this content based on what you feel works right for your task.

The stories that you produce in your epic should be rolled up into one format that reflects everything you wish to discuss. You can talk about how you arrived at certain conclusions while getting ideas for how well tasks are to be planned. The culture within your workplace can also be analyzed to assess how well the work you are managing is organized. The best part of the epic is that everything conveys your goals and gives you a careful link for how well your content can be used to your liking.

The Use of Stories

The stories that you plan in your Agile task will place a focus on things like what users have to handle or what your business is doing to try and attain a goal. The stories will encourage collaboration among everyone and give the participants in the task an idea of where you want to go with your work and how it will all be planned out. The effort you incorporate into the mix can be essential to giving your work the control and support you deserve. More importantly, the stories will drive creative solutions and help people think about what might be appropriate and suitable for the task work in question.

Also, people in the Agile group can maintain a sense of momentum with each new story that is produced. As you explore how the stories grow and develop, you will see that the work being planned might be specific to your work. But to make those stories work, you have to plan ones that are intriguing and which give your business an idea of what it can do to move forward. Let's look at some of the things you can do when writing stories for your task:

1. Review what you interpret as being "done." This refers to when you feel the task in question has been finished.

2. Review the steps that have to be completed so you can finish your work.

3. Identify the user personas of the people producing the stories. When you plan the right stories, you can get an idea of what makes these people act the way they do.

4. Incorporate the steps you wish to use in the stories. Look at how well the stories are planned out and how well people might move forward with certain efforts.

5. List the feedback for the tasks you are putting in. The data can include anything specific about the work you're handling and how that data might work for you.

6. Timing points can be included, although you should not be too specific.

Chapter 64 – Using Story Points in Agile Work

Time is of the essence when it comes to your Agile task. The sprints and iterations you plan have to be managed quickly and handled to where the data is easy to review. The best way to handle your content is to use story points. This may be used in lieu of measuring the hours or time frames for your work. You can use this to simplify the timing of your work and how you're going to report on the content you want to utilize.

Story points are used with estimation efforts in mind. These are aspects that include everything involved with your task and the approximate rate at which you are getting that content handled. You can produce story points in any way you see fit, although it helps to see what you are getting from the work. In fact, the story points are different from the regular timing efforts you put in as those points will give you extra control over how your data is handled and where you might go with your work.

While a traditional project in Six Sigma might focus on timing based on days or weeks among other points, an Agile team may use story points that focus on certain things you want to utilize. A story point will involve a timing point based on how much progress you have made in your effort. For instance, you might have a story point of 50 when you are midway through the task. The maximum number is 100, which indicates you've finished your work.

The problem with specific dates is that they might not account for many of the specific things that come about in the work environment. You're always going to be sidetracked by assorted things in your work. These include the meetings and interviews you have to complete, emergency tasks and any messages that you might need to handle. Keeping those dates intact might be hard, especially with you having to go through so many changes in your schedule depending on where you are going. The good news is that the story points you use, instead of a fixed time schedule, can help you find something suitable and effective.

Also, specific dates often have emotional attachments to them. People might have specific feelings about dates based on what they want to do in the future and what they have done in the past. Having estimated story points is easier to follow because the emotional links to your work will be eliminated or at least reduced. This gives you more focus on the things that you want to do with your work.

The most important thing about using story points is that they will help people to focus on the task. People need to spend more time on working with a task and less on thinking about future schedules. Story points, used instead of dates, produce a better sense of control.

The main consideration when it comes to using Agile is to help you with developing a better sense of control over your work. You will be impressed with how well the Agile task functions. But to make it all work, you have to plan a sensible series of time points that are based more on how well your task is run and less on how many hours you are working. You can do this to keep the emotional issues and other worries in your task from being too prevalent.

Chapter 65 – How to Incorporate Agile into a Six Sigma Routine

Agile works with a goal similar to Six Sigma based on what a team wants to do when handling content the right way. But it is important for the Agile task to be integrated into your Six Sigma work with ease. In fact, the Agile work can be planned in the middle of any part of your work as you see fit. You can get Agile ready for your Six Sigma routine if you look at a few points for making it work. Remember that while Agile takes less time than Six Sigma, the Agile work will add to the value of the Six Sigma work that you incorporate.

Process Increments

Process increments can be utilized in the Six Sigma effort. This aspect of Agile work entails working with small chunks of a project at a time. While the Six Sigma work will entail a thorough plan based on what you feel is appropriate for your use, the Agile task will focus on breaking down all those points you're working with. These process increments can be as specific or distinct as you want them to be. For instance, you might take one part of the Six Sigma effort that will work for one to two weeks at a time and produce individual groups devoted to that task. Keeping that specific task in check keeps the Six Sigma work organized while also allowing for progress.

This links up to Six Sigma even further by producing a plan for managing content based on the unique things you wish to plan. The process increment should be planned out with a name for the specific task and then the conditions for satisfying the task. An estimate of the task's size should also be considered. The size should be based on an estimate when compared with the other tasks being handled. A process area point will include details on the theme or category of the content you wish to utilize.

Here's an example of how you can get a process increment to work for you. You might have a larger project that entails cutting expenses in a manufacturing warehouse by 20 percent. You can use many steps to get to that goal. Part of those may include looking at how you can reduce fuel usage in the warehouse. An increment can be planned for two to three weeks where new standards or materials for reducing fuel usage will be implemented.

You can produce the process increment with the DMAIC effort in mind. Think about this smaller Agile task as a brief Six Sigma routine that works for a few weeks at a time. The DMAIC steps will be used as usual. You should still plan your Six Sigma routine based on what you feel will work for the task and how the content is to be generated or made ready for your use. You will find it is not hard at all for you to get the results you desire if you plan a Six Sigma process that fits in well and gives you good results all the way through.

Concentrate on the Planning and Not the Design

The design of something might be appealing in any Six Sigma routine, but Agile functions require you to look at the planning or coding for the task. For instance, a software program may be planned out with an extensive code that is easy to analyze. The code may be as thorough and detailed as it has to be. This may work better than the design to create a setup that is easier to follow. The employees and others in the Six Sigma task will have a better time managing the design effort when the planning is appropriately organized.

Skills of the People

The steps in the DMAIC routine are important, but every person in the work environment has unique skills. Agile tasks allow people to use those skills to work well. One employee on a team might be very helpful at contacting customers and educating them about new products or services. That person's skills should be exploited as a means of improving upon the image that the business is trying to convey. That person's individual power is being used while showing off the things that he or she is capable of.

You should assess each person involved with the Six Sigma process to see how they can work with different skills and qualities in mind. You can monitor all of these people based on how efficient and helpful they might be for you. Also, the team members should be given the freedom to do what they can with each of the tasks they are asked to handle while working with the many things that might make their efforts or routines so valuable in the Six Sigma routine.

Accept Change

The best thing anyone can do when incorporating Agile principles into a Six Sigma task is to respect the changes and adjustments that may come about. Every Six Sigma routine will have unique elements. You have to accept that not everything is going to be consistent. The shorter actions that Agile tasks work with are focused on giving you the positive change and control that you demand. You can accept the change in the workplace to help you go forward and keep the DMAIC effort organized to your liking.

Chapter 66 – The Scrum Process

One aspect of Six Sigma and Agile development that deserves your attention is the Scrum process. The scrum is a unique process that entails smaller groups of people who work together to attain a goal. The tasks are planned in shorter time frames to help everyone move forward toward the same end result even with all the people in the group working in unique roles.

The best way to explain the Scrum process is to think about the athletic event that the process is named for, the rugby scrum. A rugby scrum works with many people on each side lining up with their arms connecting each other and their heads down. The two sides push against one another with the goal of trapping the rugby ball in the middle. Each person in the scrum has a role for moving forward and for blocking others from getting the ball. The side that gets the ball will have the advantage because that group has an easier chance at scoring next.

You can do anything with the Scrum process if you look at how well the content you want to plan is managed while thinking about where your coworkers will stand in the effort. Whereas Six Sigma concentrates heavily on a process and the aspects of making it work, Scrum is all about teamwork. If anything, Scrum is closer to the Agile setup than anything else you may come across.

Scrum works with the belief that a task is all about the people who will work together in the same environment. The people in a group all have unique skills. The Scrum layout helps people to use their individual skills while also producing efficient results everyone will benefit from. Also, Scrum focuses on working in short bursts of time with each task working within those brief moments.

It should also be noted that while Scrum was designed mainly for use among teams that are working on software programs, it can also work for any kind of business. The design of Scrum is all about producing an environment for work that is easy for businesses to support. You can get more out of the work you are putting in when you use the Scrum process to your advantage and review how the data you are managing works.

The General Uses of Scrum

Scrum, though ultimately easy to understand and follow, can initially be hard to master. The process is a framework where you are working to improve upon a product or service or process. The team and the environment everything takes place in are all expected to improve and grow.

You can use Scrum with many intentions in mind. First, you can use Scrum to research markets in your field. This includes any special technologies you wish to work with, capabilities that may work well, and any possibilities for improving your products or processes and/or achieving sustainability.

The most important use of Scrum is to produce new ideas and concepts in a controlled environment where the people who are working can handle new ideas with ease. The concepts produced by Scrum team members are created by people who each have their own parts to play in the process. The smaller sizes of Scrum teams ensure that everyone has a sense of control over whatever is being handled.

Three Parts of the Scrum Theory

Scrum theory makes it easier for concepts and ideas to be developed. But to make it work, everyone in the Scrum team has to be clear on how the process works. The three parts of the Scrum theory are designed to produce a more efficient setup for managing content:

1. Transparency

People always have to be in the know when getting a Scrum task to work. This includes being able to identify the things that are changing within a task. Knowing how the process works and where people can go with it is vital to identifying the errors. Part of this can include working with the same standards in mind. Transparency helps to produce a sense of consistency in the work efforts you are planning.

The people responsible for producing a Scrum task must notice any changes coming about in a process or product. Transparency is about noticing the ways a task can work and how effective it is based on what someone wishes to produce or plan. For instance, transparency means everyone in the Scrum team will recognize a language for a process or project. That language can then be used by every person, regardless of role. Meanwhile, the people who are trying to produce work should share a definition on one item to produce a better approach.

The problem with some businesses is that they might not fully understand what they are doing when trying to move forward with a task. They don't recognize some of the things that can be done when working on a project and instead concentrate more on the problems they are noticing. Scrum transparency efforts let people see what they are doing and makes the things they are planning easy to recognize and take advantage of. With the right Scrum work, everyone on a team will see what makes a task effective and ideal.

2. Inspection

The inspection process entails a regular review of everything being handled within a certain task. Any sudden changes or unwanted effects in the process may be noticed.

You'll have to look at how well the subject matter works based on the updates taking place and what might work in any condition. That said, inspections should not be too frequent . The inspections must be spaced out enough to keep the work from getting in the way or being otherwise too hard to follow.

All inspections are designed to review how thoroughly the business operates. The Scrum work lets you see that a team can figure out sudden changes on the fly. You can plan the inspections in your Scrum work to give you the control you need to move forward with your work. Don't forget to establish how many people in the same Scrum group can efficiently inspect one another's work.

3. Adaptation

The process being handled within the Scrum effort should be easy to adapt depending on what has to be done. You can use an adaptive process for managing content as you see fit and for changing the Scrum effort depending on any problems. Future adjustments must be made to produce a consistent project without worrying about sudden deviations that might occur. The adaptation process may entail a review of how sprints are planned out and what you can do when reviewing them. Daily analysis projects may be included with each member of the Scrum communicating his or her efforts to help figure out what changes might need to be made.

The most important part of these three aspects of the Scrum task is that they focus heavily on ensuring that the content planned out is simple and everyone has an idea of what to expect out of a task. More importantly, people in the Scrum work can trust one another and feel confident in what they are working toward achieving as a united team.

An Additional Word on Transparency

The transparency that you will utilize might be the most important part of the Scrum work. It is through transparency that everyone will know what is happening on a project. But there are often times when the work is not as transparent as you might hope it could be. The good news is that you can get transparency to work in many forms within your task.

You can look at each piece in your Scrum task and examine what parameters work with each other. The goal is to keep those efforts both useful and streamlined.

Of course, facilitating communication throughout the Scrum process requires effort. You'll have to do plenty of persuading and convincing around the Scrum task to make the work run right. More importantly, the effort will require people to learn more things about the content that is being handled and how the subject matter might work. Transparency and getting everyone on the same page are important to how well work is managed. The effort that you put into the Scrum process can be immense, but the end result will be worthwhile if you can ultimately see how effective a task is and get everyone on the same page in the process.

Chapter 67 – The Three Roles of the Scrum

A Scrum will include three distinct roles. Some groups include extra roles relating to specific tasks, but the three roles listed here are the only ones that are truly necessary. Each person works with different tasks, but everyone is ultimately working with the same goals and routines in mind.

1. Product Owner

The Product Owner is a fancy word for the customer. Specifically, for Scrum purposes, the Product Owner represents the stakeholders. That person works with the VOC or Voice of the Customer in mind. The Product Owner will analyze what a business wants to do and will define the project with the intention of identifying things that arise throughout the course of a project. The product owner may order the necessary resources to successfully complete the task.

The Product Owner is responsible for handling the product backlog. This is a listing of the features that will be utilized in the Scrum process. The descriptions in the backlog illustrate the things that have to be done in order for a task to work. The backlog can be as detailed as necessary when it comes to both the positive and negative aspects of the work in process.

The Product Owner is accountable for explaining to people what the task will entail and how the content is managed. Though the Product Owner is one individual, one or two other people may be consulted for help with this role if necessary. Also, the Product Owner will be responsible for adapting the backlog as necessary and controlling the content being handled. Everyone else in the Scrum process must be respectful of what the Product Owner wants to do.

But who in the workplace should be the Product Owner? A manager or executive might be the owner in this situation. That person will be the one who acknowledges and reviews all the things that take place at a given time. The product owner will also have an idea of what objectives should be supported within the work environment. Keeping those objectives under control is critical to the success of the work. Having an executive work as a product owner provides a sense of formality and control over a process.

2. Development Team

A development team is vital for the Scrum process. You can get three to nine people to work in your team. The small number ensures that the task is easy to facilitate. Each person will be responsible for carrying out the assorted tasks that are required of the team in the Scrum effort.

The team members, or developers as they are also called, are people responsible for managing several tasks involved with the Scrum effort. This includes the analysis process, managing the design for something, developing a new plan, technical writing aspects and many other points. Each team member or developer will be responsible for a specific function. Since individuals will have specific areas of expertise, each team member will work with different routines and plans in mind. The roles of the people on the team can be discussed prior to the project being started.

The team should be a self-organized unit. The people involved should work together to develop a plan for their task. Multiple people can work on many parts of a task, although the effort should be efficiently managed.

As mentioned earlier, the team is deliberately small in size. A large group may try to handle far too much information at a time while going in too many directions. A small group allows for a tighter focus. The product owner and Scrum Master should not be interpreted as being part of this group unless they are going to participate in some of the backlog activities.

An example of how a development team can be organized is a web development team. The team may include several people in a Scrum that are dedicated to specific routines. These include a project manager, a project architect, user interface and experience designers, web developers and quality assurance and monitoring teams.

3. Scrum Master

The Scrum Master is the person responsible for organizing and running the project. That person will deliver the product goals and will keep at bay any outside influences that might distract the team. The master also works to keep the Scrum framework in place. This includes preparing a schedule for how the Scrum work is to be managed and ensuring that teams are working in an organized fashion.

The Scrum Master will hold meetings to plan work and to follow up on how things are proceeding. The master may also communicate with the stakeholders about what the team is doing and how it is going to carry out certain processes.

a. What the Scrum Master Does for the Product Owner

The Scrum Master will work as an assistant of sorts to the Product Owner. This is ironic when the names of the positions are considered, but the master will ensure that people are handling the task right while the owner updates tasks and maintains them. The master will review the goals and scope of the task that the owner has produced. The master will then convey that information to the rest of the team so everyone will understand the ins and outs of the task being handled.

The master will look at how the backlog is being managed. The project planning effort must also be discussed based on what is happening with the work and how a routine may be planned out. The master may also analyze the agility of the Scrum work with the owner and plan strategies based on what that person finds to be appropriate and useful for your goals.

b. What the Scrum Master Does For the Development Team

The master must educate the team on how its members should be organized. Also, the master will be responsible for identifying how well the task in mind is prepared. Any problems that arise should also be identified. The master must find ways to keep those issues from developing or worsening. The team may also be coached through each new process by the master.

c. How the Scrum Master Serves the Organization

The Scrum Master is responsible for reviewing what the organization in general can handle. The master must discuss the things that a business can do when getting the Scrum adopted. All stakeholders should be consulted pertaining to how the Scrum is formed and what results are expected. Any developments within the Scrum process must be communicated to the employees and other people outside the Scrum. This ensures everyone in the business is on the same page with the work in question.

Chapter 68 – The Project Backlog for Scrum

Every Scrum process needs to utilize a backlog. The backlog is a features list that shows what you might need based on priority and effort. The team will use the backlog at the start to figure out the things that should be done in any situation. This includes figuring out how well the Scrum is planned and whether a task is agile and easy to follow. The backlog includes descriptions about desired outcomes, but also reviews of anything that might go wrong.

The backlog is produced by the Product Owner and will be acted upon by the development team. The owner and the Scrum Master may also work with the process if desired, although this is optional. The effort should be organized based on what your team members feel is appropriate to a task.

The greatest thing about the Scrum backlog is that it is very flexible. There will never be any case where the backlog is complete. Even when the backlog appears to be finished, the Scrum will still have to control the task and see that the work that was completed was handled right.

The Key Features of the Backlog

1. Features

There are many aspects of the project backlog that a Scrum task must follow. The first involves the features of whatever is being developed. Whether it entails new features for a car being built or changes to the way said car is to be produced, the features should be direct and diverse. Every feature should be described based on what it can handle and how it will be to the benefit of everyone involved. Any changes in those features can be included in the process.

2. Bugs and Fixes

There are often times when bugs (unwanted issues) arise in the production or design process. These bugs may include some effects that might develop over time. Potential bugs should be considered ahead of time in order to plan for possible fixes should problems develop.

You can plan a backlog by looking at how fixes may be produced or by setting goals for creating them. The goal is to find concrete solutions for handling the bugs that may come along in your work. Knowing how to resolve these problems before they can become any worse is critical to your success in the Scrum routine.

3. Technical Aspects

The technical aspects of your work should be noticed as well. This part of the backlog can include details on requirements. For instance, a team looking to produce a new engineering process might be told that it has to use specific computer features or software programs.

4. Knowledge Acquisition

Everyone in the Scrum has to build upon what they understand. The knowledge acquisition process involves people in the workplace exploring many aspects of the work they are getting into. You can establish a good knowledge acquisition process to ensure people make the most of their individual work.

Checking the Backlog Throughout the Work

The most interesting part of the backlog is that it will expand by many items throughout your work. The backlog may include a few requirements before the first sprint. Then the second and third sprints will result in some extra requirements. You will get more with each other sprint after that.

The Product Owner will introduce all of these features depending on what you feel is right for your work. He or she must explain all the ins and outs of the requirements in your backlog while creating connections between each one.

Changing the Backlog During the Process

You can make as many revisions to your backlog as necessary for your task. The backlog can work with many concepts ranging from the addition of new ideas to refinements of the work routine. The Product Owner should update the content of the work as necessary. The development team may also be responsible for making some of these changes.

Trade-offs may also be planned within the work. Trade-offs are cases where some things in the backlog are removed and replaced. The trade-offs can be as detailed as they have to be so long as they don't impact the overall project in a negative fashion.

The most important part of the backlog is that this point in the Scrum will help everyone understand the ins and outs of the task in question. Everyone will get a better idea of what to expect out of the work being put in. You can use the data you get for the Scrum to work to your advantage while also keeping it simple for all people in the process.

Planning a Backlog for the Sprint

The sprints that you plan in the Scrum routine are important to its success. These shorter events that utilize smaller goals and efforts should be planned right. Part of this includes working with a unique backlog for each of these events. You can prepare the backlog for the sprints with small individuals goals in mind to maintain control over your work.

The sprint backlogs you produce should include any details about features or changes in the task or necessary fixes. You can use these backlogs to produce detailed layouts on anything you wish to utilize in your work. The best part of planning a backlog is that the work can include the smallest changes throughout the Scrum work. The backlogs for each sprint will identify the things you are doing with your work while giving you a clearer idea of what to expect.

Any new work on the task can also be added to the backlog. This includes any new details based on what might be handled in the sprint. Your development team can review the new events and then produce a cumulative report based on what is found in the backlog.

What Are Increments?

The last things to notice in the backlog are the increments you are working with. These increments are measures of the backlog items being produced throughout your work. This includes anything being planned within each of the distinct segments or sprints being handled. Each increment should be seen as a step towards the final result of your Scrum task. Each new increment should be listed as being finished after every sprint is completed. The sprint should continue if those increments are not being handled as well as desired. At that point, you will have to correct your issues as needed within the time frame of that sprint. You can work with as much data as necessary within these increments, but the Product Owner will have to approve of what you are doing.

Chapter 69 – The Events of a Scrum

You can go through various events within your Scrum process as you see fit. These special events work with several goals and efforts in mind. The events should be planned within a rigid time frame if possible. Scrum is all about working efficiently and producing results as soon as possible. This aspect of Six Sigma work can help you with moving forward with all the improvements you wish to plan in your routine. With all this in mind, it is time to look at the many events that go into a Scrum.

The Scrum focuses on a backlog where individual items are gathered in a sprint. The backlog is then produced with those sprint goals in mind. Those details are shared among everyone in the Scrum with the goal of producing a better task that can be handled with enough increments in mind. The goal here is to allow more of these Scrum events to work towards producing enough increments while also remaining useful for managing the task. The sprints should still be reviewed at the end, although the process should be simple for use. The framework may be utilized for any kind of task, regardless of how large or small the Scrum group is or the scope of the project.

Sprint

The sprint is the basis of the Scrum and needs to be followed every time. The sprint is a process where you complete a project or task with an ultimate expected result. The sprint gets its name for how short it is in length. The longest sprint should last about a month. The product that is produced at the end should be useable and releasable.

For instance, a car company might develop a sprint for a process where new tires are produced for a vehicle. The sprint will be a part of a more extensive task where the company is looking to produce new vehicles that are more unique and efficient while also producing several qualities or features that may spread over to other models. In this example, the team is producing tires that may be used for future models while also working on various cars that a company is already selling. The tires may be designed to reduce wear and to handle more road conditions and surfaces. The company will need to produce the new tires within a month if possible.

For the work to be effective, a sprint has to be fully completed within that established month-long time frame. A new sprint may start after the old one is completed. The sprints will link together to produce a more effective process that is easy to follow. For instance, the sprint for the car company might include work with a new tire, and the second sprint after that will involve planning a new air-conditioning system that can be utilized in various vehicles. The switches between different sprint tasks will help a company to focus on a various of tasks in order to produce a good setup.

A sprint can include the following things:

1. A plan that includes the general goals of the sprint

2. Daily meetings to review how the plan will be managed

3. Developmental work to reach the goals of that plan

4. A full review of how well the plan was managed

5. A retrospective of the plan to review what can be done for future sprints

The task is about looking at how well the goals of the sprint can be handled while also reviewing the positive things that can be managed in the work. You can use the details in the work to your liking provided that the efforts are managed well enough and are documented at every point. The review will also help you identify what changes should be made so the work in question can be revised and adjusted as you see fit.

Remember to ensure that the sprint is planned within a one-month time frame. Anything that runs faster can be too risky due to a task possibly being more complicated than expected. There is also the issue of the sprint costing more than necessary if the work goes for more than a month.

Planning the Sprint

A sprint has to be properly planned for the work to move forward efficiently. The planning process will involve a look at the product backlog that was generated. Anything in the backlog may be analyzed and then moved into a new sprint backlog. The smaller backlog will be devoted to the certain sprint you wish to utilize. The Scrum Master should plan the sprint based on the objectives and needs that the Product Owner has produced. The data from the master will then go to the rest of the team so it can begin the work.

The sprint is planned with the product backlog in mind and the materials that might be utilized for your work. Any increments you have reached surrounding a product in the past may be reviewed. The development team can work with many items in the backlog as well, although the team should be realistic in its objectives. This includes ensuring that the right amount of data is managed. Also, the work should be planned based on what might be easy for people to plan, with individual team members working with each of the key goals that come with such a task. A well-organized team can handle many skills in the sprint.

The development team will look at how the Scrum task is handled and what makes it suitable for use. The best part of the development process is that it can include a thorough plan for how things are done, including in what order. The plan may include a look at what specific things must be handled during the first few days of the task.

Some flexible goals should also be established. Flexibility can entail the team having the right to do as many things as it is able to handle. These can include many routines for handling content in as little time as needed. Sometimes the easiest parts of a task may be planned out first, followed by the more difficult ones. But a team can also go in the other direction and try its luck at some of the harder things at the start. The team can plan any routine it wants, but the work in question should be managed right.

Canceling a Sprint

There are times when a sprint may be canceled before it is finished. This could be for cases where the Scrum was efficient enough that the task was finished within a month. Or, the Scrum may be canceled due to an overall goal no longer being relevant. The Product Owner is the only one who may cancel the Scrum sprint. Any work that was completed within the sprint may be reviewed after the cancellation takes place.

Everyone in the canceled sprint will then move on to a new sprint. The planning process will begin right away. Bear in mind that the cancellation might hurt the morale of the Scrum team. The cancellation will waste resources and may give the impression that the task is not as effective as it should be. Members might not be happy with whatever they are getting out of the work and may feel dissatisfied overall.

What Is the Daily Scrum?

The Daily Scrum is designed to keep the Scrum work organized. You can utilize the daily meeting to let everyone on the team know about the standards and plans you wish to work with. Each member of the team can also use the daily meeting to hammer out details of what has to be done in the workplace to keep the Scrum moving forward.

The Daily Scrum takes about 15 minutes to complete. It ensures that everyone in the group is on the same page. This can be the first task that the team plans every day during a sprint. The group members will get together to explain what they are doing and where they want the task in question to go. A few things should be addressed in the Daily Scrum:

- What has been done within the Scrum so far

- How the sprint is laid out

- What individuals will do within the sprint

- The links to other sprints if needed

- Any contacts that need to be made during the day to allow the sprint to move forward

The things that can be discussed in the Daily Scrum are endless. Let's go back to the car company example. The team might be in the middle of a sprint to produce a better air-conditioning system. One team member might address the testing process and review the methods utilized. Another will get in touch with engineers to determine how parts for the air-conditioning unit can be produced. Each team member will plan some steps in the process, although the work being organized should be planned based on what the team will handle and how its functions may run.

Questions For the Daily Scrum

Every Daily Scrum should have a few talking points. While it is fine to talk about the things that are going on within the sprint and how things are moving forward, it is even more important to talk about some of the more intricate aspects of the sprint and what people can expect out of it. The Daily Scrum should include some helpful questions for your needs. Some of those questions can be:

1. What did the team members do yesterday?

Ask about what the team members did for the sprint yesterday. Talk about the developments in their tasks. Look at how well people are handling their efforts and what can be done to manage different actions. This includes seeing if people had any sizeable improvements in their work. Anything that a team has handled over the course of the task should be explored in detail based on what is being managed.

2. What will the team do today to help the rest of the group meet the sprint goal?

Everyone has to work together to achieve the sprint goal. Ask what the team is doing for the goal and how the task is being organized. You can ask as many things about these sprint goals as you wish provided that the work is planned right and has enough of a sense of focus in what the team wishes to do.

3. How will the team members stick to their specific goals or routines?

Every team member has to work with certain goals or plans based on what needs to be done. A team can ask questions about how each member is planning his or her tasks. The goal is to see that the people involved with the sprint do not veer off their plans. They have to stay focused on what they wish to finish if the sprint is to move forward.

4. Are there any obstacles that might cause the team to be unable to meet its sprint goals?

This question may work for both the daily goals and the month-long period involved for the task. The obstacles should be discussed based on what can be controlled and any problems that might need to be resolved. Any plans for controlling or at least mitigating the obstacles should be discussed at this point. The sprint plans might have to be changed depending on any problems that have arisen.

Can Others Attend the Daily Scrum?

The Daily Scrum should usually only be attended by people responsible for the work. These include all the people in the development team. That said, the Product Owner might allow other people to take part in the work. This is provided that those people do not disrupt the meeting or try to change the setup of the discussion at large. You can allow others to see what is happening in the meeting as a means of letting everyone know what is happening in the work environment. The information in the Daily Scrum should not leave the meeting itself.

Planning a Board

You have the option to create a board that lists details on all the things happening in your Scrum process. These include things that relate to the actions that are working now versus the things that you are waiting to complete and what needs to be done. The design works just like what you would get out of the Kanban board. But you also have to add a few points into the board.

1. Backlog

The backlog reports all the things that have been listed. As mentioned in this chapter, you have to keep the backlog growing for the best results. The log can be reset as you see fit and for when you prepare the next big sprint. You may set a limit on the number of things you add to your backlog, but this is only if you feel the efforts are useful enough. Also, each item should be listed directly to help you determine what might work well in the task. You can also use details on what might be more important depending on where you are going.

2. Team Data

Each of the items on your Scrum board should include details on the teams responsible. The board can include colors on each item reflective of the teams that are working on specific tasks. You have to keep the colors noticeable while also linking everything up to whatever might be incorporated in the process. You can also use these in many rows depending on what is more important versus what does not necessarily have to be handled right away in the process.

3. Sprint Duration

The sprint duration must be specified within the chart. The board should include a time frame based on what you're trying to do. While the Kanban chart does not require much of a time frame for most items, the Scrum board should include plans based on when you're going to start things versus when you will finish them. Your goal is to get things done as fast as possible. However, the time frame should be suitable based on what is best for your work.

Chapter 70 – What Does It Mean to Be Done in the Scrum?

The Scrum process can include a look at the ways how the research and process being handled is organized. You can look at the items handled in the work and then determine if they are "done" or not. But the fact is that "done" entails more than something just being finished. The term is very different in the Scrum process. Everyone needs to agree on what can be handled at any time in the task.

The definition of "done" in Scrum processes entails a review of everything that is going on in the process. This includes an analysis of what is working based on how effective a process might be. You can look at the work that you are planning. You can use an analysis based on factors such as how well a company is saving money on its process or how easily a product or service can be made available to the public. Anything that is thorough or simple for use can be utilized depending on your plans in mind. The problem, though, is that the word "done" can mean anything.

So, what can you get out of the word "done" in the Scrum practice? Well, it can include something like a product or service being made available to the public. You can discuss refining a new feature or shipping to different places. Testing processes can also be discussed. You may also discuss how a task was done based on how much money was spent in the process and whether you were able to cut down on the costs associated with the work at large.

The "done" definition has to be consistent throughout the work. You have to let everyone in the group know what it means to finish something so no one will try to get ahead or possibly fall apart. The most important thing is to find something that is not hard to manage. You can use the definition as you see fit to produce a good layout for your content and work as needed.

You can also use the term for increments as needed. You might create milestones within your work based on what you feel is appropriate for the task. Milestones can involve certain processes having been fully finished and completed, although you can work with any particular plan that you might feel is ideal for your work. The increments should be shared with everyone in the task so all the people in the work process will recognize what it takes to make the effort possible.

One idea to use for planning when things are "done" is to test each increment consecutively to see that the work is well organized. You can test everything to see how each piece of content works together and have an idea of what to expect out of the work at large. Any concerns or issues that might develop in the work can also be analyzed based on what is appropriate. You can work with as many details or increments as you see fit.

The main goal of planning when a task is finished in the Scrum process is to see that the work is easy to analyze and review. You have to ensure that the task being handled works right and that you know what to expect out of the effort.

Chapter 71 – Planning a Review for the Scrum Process

After a while, you'll have to review everything that took place within Scrum. The review after the Scrum is completed will look at the final results involved with your work. You can use the review to improve upon how well the sprint was managed.

The people at the review should include the members of the team plus the Product Owner. Any other stakeholders that the owner wishes to invite can also attend. The owner should talk about the things that were done. The backlog should be discussed in full along with any time frames for the future and budget considerations. Anything that went well in the sprint can be discussed alongside any problems that might have developed. A thorough review will help the team recognize the things that went well versus any issues that have to be resolved later on.

The end result of the review is a new edition of the project backlog. Ideas for the next sprint can be discussed. The backlog should be reviewed based on what has been finished versus any new concepts that might be developed. There is always the chance that new ideas might work for distinct sprints in the future.

Planning a Retrospective

Another part of the Scrum entails working with a retrospective. This is like a review, but is much broader in its scope. You will look at how well the past sprint went while reflecting upon the unique things that went into your work during the sprint.

Going back to the example of how a car is developed, a retrospective might look at the process that was run for improving upon a vehicle. The retrospective might include details on how a task was completed versus the effort required. You might look at how the new air-conditioning unit was managed based on ideas that were incorporated and any specific techniques used. Successful strategies may be carried over to the next part of the task.

During the retrospective, you can always look at how the project backlog has changed over time and assess any trends based on prior sprints. The analysis can help you with figuring out what makes the work you put in valuable to your work routine.

Chapter 72 – Helpful Tips for Six Sigma Efforts

The following tips may helpful ideas to you in making the most out of your Six Sigma routine.

1. Look for possible improvement opportunities that are of value to you.

While there is a dedicated stage for improvement in the Six Sigma process, you should think about how you're going to utilize those improvement chances to your advantage. Think about how well any ideas for improvement will work within your task and adapt them as you see fit.

2. Every analytical process must entail a simple conclusion.

Your conclusions should be simple and clear—one sentence is often enough. The point is to clearly convey the information to your employees and other Six Sigma team members. You want to succinctly summarize your analysis efforts.

3. Maintain a healthy sense of communication with everyone on your team.

Every person in the Six Sigma process must be consistently updated on developments with the task. This keeps everybody in the loop. More importantly, people who understand why certain things are happening will not try to make changes to the Six Sigma process without your permission. Because they're informed, they'll be able to see the bigger picture.

4. Perseverance is important, but you should also know when to back down.

Perseverance is about ensuring you stick to your Six Sigma work and find ways to improve upon your efforts. But you should feel free to walk away from the Six Sigma task if you cannot get it to work all the way after a few changes or adjustments. You can then scrap the task altogether and produce a new Six Sigma plan with different ideas for improving your business.

5. Allow for enough time in your work.

You can take as much time as necessary for most Six Sigma processes. Avoid rushing the tasks you want to complete, or else you may end up making errors. Be sure to also double-check everything in the routine as well. This includes possibly running multiple tests within your work.

Chapter 73 – Handling the Exam

Now that you understand the many aspects that come with the Six Sigma process, you can get started on properly preparing for the exam. Now we'll discuss how to best approach that task.

The Six Sigma exam process is intended to gauge your ability to manage Six Sigma work. This is to ensure that all people who participate in Six Sigma projects are fully certified and ready to handle the task. To be assigned a task, you must complete the appropriate type of exam first. The exams are for White/Yellow, Green and Black Belt participants.

The exam standards for Six Sigma are established by the International Association for Six Sigma Certification (IASSC). The organization, which can be found online at iassc.org, has information on what people can expect to be tested on when aiming to reach Six Sigma certification. This includes all of the things that people should focus on when working on any of the belt options.

You can complete the Six Sigma exams in various forms at one of the many IASSC Accredited Providers that offer tests at many times in the year. You can also look at online test-taking plans through the IASSC Web-Based On-Demand test available through iassc.org.

Yellow Belt

The Yellow Belt test does not have any prerequisites since it is the lowest level of Six Sigma you can participate in. The test has 60 questions and takes up to two hours to complete. The information here is basic and entails the introductory points to Six Sigma that you may use for future tasks.

You must get at least 230 out of a total 300 points to get your Yellow Belt certification. The certification test entails questions with various scores attached to them. The IASSC does not divulge information on what scores are included or how the questions are spread out in the task. You may expect the questions to be posed based on the Body of Knowledge.

The test does not require you to participate in an official training program. You can use a guide, such as this one, to review for the test.

The required voucher to complete the test costs $195. Study carefully for the exam. Since the IASSC does not provide any specifics on how long you must wait before retaking a test, it's best to pass it on the first attempt.

Green Belt

The Green Belt test is more complicated, what with the Body of Knowledge being more thorough than the Yellow Belt standard. It's a higher level, so it's natural that the test is also much larger in size and scope.

The Green Belt test requires you to complete 100 questions in three hours. You must score 385 points out of a total of 500. There is no time frame for when you can take the test after you get your Yellow Belt certification. The Green Belt certification test costs $295.

Black Belt

The Black Belt exam is a challenge since it entails the greatest Body of Knowledge. In other words, everything you have read about in this guide will be included in the test. Therefore, the Black Belt test is the most elaborate and detailed exam. The test is 150 questions in length and takes four hours to complete. The test requires you to score 580 points out of a possible 750. Again, details on how many points each question is worth are not made public. The test vouched costs $395.

What Your Certificate Includes

Once you pass a test, you will be listed on the Official IASSC Certification Register and provided with a certification number. The number confirms your work in the Six Sigma process and identifies you as being capable of handling particular Six Sigma tasks. You can use the official certification on your résumé and anywhere else you list your professional credentials.

What About Recertification?

You will need to complete a recertification exam every three years.

The recertification exams for each belt are smaller in size. The Black Belt test has 75 questions in two hours, the Green Belt has 50 questions in 90 minutes and the Yellow Belt includes 30 questions in one hour. Each example gathers around ten questions for each major part of the Body of Knowledge for each project. You must attain a score of 70 percent or greater to be recertified for another three years. Recertification fees are less than those for regular tests; the Black Belt recertification test costs $235, for example.

You must complete the recertification test within 90 days of when your certification has expired. To get recertified after that 90-day period passes, you will have to take the full test and pay the full cost, as though you were testing for the belt for the first time. You also have the option to complete the test before your current certification ends.

Be advised that you can only complete the recertification test twice. Also, you must wait two weeks or more between attempts. If you don't complete the test, your Six Sigma certification won't be revoked; you just won't be allowed to participate in Six Sigma projects. Your status will be "lapsed," essentially, until you complete the exam.

You might meet more experienced Six Sigma participants who do not have to complete recertification exams. These are people who were grandfathered into the Six Sigma process. IASSC changed its standards for certification on March 1, 2017. Therefore, anyone who wants to receive certification after that date will have to apply for recertification every three years.

Now it's time to look at the individual exams. The sample tests in this guide are laid out in three forms—White/Yellow, Green and Black Belt. These tests include various types of data you will come across within your work.

The questions you will see in the following sample exams are not necessarily ones that you will actually see on the real test. These exams are designed to give you an approximate idea of what you might encounter. The IASSC does not list specifics on the types of questions it asks and each test is made up of random questions. Regardless of whether you complete your test at a certified testing center or online, the questions will be randomly assigned. The IASSC also adds various new test questions and answers throughout the year.

White/Yellow Belt Certification Questions

1. What is the main goal when preparing a Six Sigma task?

    a. Consistency

    b. Repetition

    c. Increase

    d. Decrease

2. The DPMO is a measurement of what?

    a. Defects

    b. Potentials

    c. Profitability

    d. Effort

3. The Six Sigma standard states that you can only have this many deviations in every million opportunities:

    a. 1.7

    b. 3.4

    c. 230

    d. 6,210

4. The hidden factory is a concept relating to the following:

    a. Costs

    b. Processes

    c. Input

    d. Output

5. The main work of a Champion in the Six Sigma routine is to:

    a. Plan the task layout

    b. Organize other members

    c. Review finances

    d. Dictate what a task should be about

6. Which of these is not one of the five voices that must be utilized within the Six Sigma effort?

    a. Customer

    b. Data

    c. Employees

    d. Environment

7. What makes precision different from accuracy?

    a. Frequency

    b. Closeness of results

    c. Range

    d. Detection

8. What voice should be reviewed the most in the Design part of the DMAIC process?

    a. Customer

    b. Data

    c. Business

    d. Employees

9. What is a root cause?

    a. An employment concern

    b. A measurement issue

    c. An in-office routine

    d. A problem causing the workplace to be inefficient

10. What type of chart is suitable for use during the control stage of the Six Sigma task?

    a. Histogram

    b. Pie chart

    c. Control chart

    d. Scatterplot

11. What is the first general step in a Six Sigma routine?

    a. Plan a pilot

    b. Map out a process

    c. Review root causes

    d. Conduct a cause and effect analysis

12. How long should a Six Sigma task last?

    a. One month

    b. Two months

    c. One year

    d. As long as necessary

13. What is the main thing that needs to be eliminated during the Six Sigma task?

    a. Human interaction

    b. Resources

    c. Waste

    d. Budget

14. What makes a defect different from a defective?

    a. The defect cannot be repaired

    b. A defect is not easy to notice

    c. The quality of the product in a defect is not as strong as in a defective

    d. You can use a product that has a defect

15. An internal customer is different from an external one in that the internal customer:

    a. Has a contract with your business

    b. Operates in the same industry as you

    c. Works for the same type of target market

    d. Is directly in the business

16. What goes in between a need and a requirement in a CTQ tree?

    a. Person

    b. Idea

    c. Thought

    d. Driver

17. The business case in the project charter entails all of the following except:

    a. Expansion efforts for a business

    b. How something might be of use to the customers

    c. Why the project is important

    d. What consequences arise from not completing a task

18. Which of these is not a part of the RUMBA standard for the project charter?

    a. Reasonable

    b. Measurable

    c. Believable

    d. Affordable

19. What can be considered a constraint in Six Sigma work?

    a. Not getting enough money for the task

    b. Vendors not shipping things on time

    c. Machines are not working right

    d. Employees do not fully understand the task

20. The inputs in the SIPOC process focus mainly on:

    a. Things that will be influenced

    b. People who supply the content

    c. The customers you are getting in touch with

    d. How the process in general may vary

21. A swimlane map is distinguishable by:

    a. Including details on how long processes last

    b. Having many rows featuring individual persons in the task

    c. Linking to many subprocesses

    d. Helping you to switch between processes and then back again

22. What makes internal error costs different from external costs?

    a. Internal costs occur before items go to customers

    b. Internal costs are always higher in value

    c. External costs cover manufacturing issues

    d. External errors are hard to prevent

23. Internal costs that may be produced by errors include:

    a. Overtime for fixing a problem

    b. Repair costs

    c. Harm to the company's reputation

    d. All of the options

24. A measurement system analysis (MSA) process focuses on:

   a. Reproduction

   b. Accuracy

   c. Control

   d. Confirmation

25. A run chart works to review:

   a. Sudden shifts

   b. Volume totals

   c. Stability

   d. Proportions

26. What works best when reviewing proportions?

   a. Bar chart

   b. Scatterplot

   c. Pie chart

   d. Histogram

27. This person in the Six Sigma task is responsible for making important statistical decisions:

   a. White Belt

   b. Green Belt

   c. Black Belt

   d. Master Black Belt

28. The Champion in the Six Sigma process works best as a/an:

   a. Sponsor

   b. Surveyor

   c. Analyst

   d. Employer

29. The goal of Six Sigma is to:

    a. Use accounting to make a business profitable

    b. Eliminate variation

    c. Review processes

    d. Identify losses

30. A common measure of variation in the Six Sigma process is:

    a. Standard deviation

    b. Variation

    c. Mean

    d. Dispersion

31. A scatterplot shows a series of dots moving from the lower left of the plot to the upper right. This means that the following can be noticed between the variables:

    a. Positive correlation

    b. Negative correlation

    c. No relationship

    d. Higher order

32. The distribution curve appears to be negatively skewed in your work. What does this mean?

    a. The project is running fast

    b. The project is accurate

    c. You might need to scrap the task

    d. The curve is faulty

33. The number of defects in a task might increase while productivity decreases. This means that the following correlation may be found:

    a. Positive

    b. Negative

    c. None

    d. Minor

34. What is the project like if the Cpk is under 1?
    a. Capable
    b. Incapable
    c. Stable
    d. Uncertain

35. Which is not a part of the cost of quality in the Six Sigma process?

    a. Change management

    b. Failure

    c. Prevention

    d. Appraisal

36. Your project currently produces about 20 defects per 100,000 units. You are trying to cut that total down to 10 defects per 100,000 units. What is the best thing to do to reach that point?

    a. Move your mean performance standards

    b. Adjust your specification limits

    c. Scrap the old specification limits and use a new range

    d. Wait and see what happens next

37. The Critical to Quality (CTQ) review in your project is based off:

    a. VoC

    b. Regression

    c. Data dispersion review

    d. Central tendency

38. What is the first thing to review in the FMEA process?

    a. Cause of failure

    b. Function

    c. Failure mode

    d. Process control

39. The S, O and D totals on the FMEA test are respectively 5, 8 and 4. What will the RPN total be?

    a. 17

    b. 44

    c. 60

    d. 160

40. The greatest concern for a problem found in the FMEA process is that it could be:

    a. Something that occurs far too often

    b. Something that cannot be resolved through your current design control setup

    c. An issue that develops without warning

    d. All of the above

41. The first thing to assess in the benchmarking process is:

    a. Objectives

    b. Process review

    c. Performance gaps

    d. Any part of the task

42. How long can a pilot task work for?

    a. 2-4 weeks

    b. 8-12 weeks

    c. 16-20 weeks

    d. As long as necessary

43. The detection model may require you to inspect things many times over. This happens when you:

    a. Need to ship items

    b. Have to repair things

    c. Scrap items

    d. Check labels

44. SPC is designed to:

    a. Prevent items from coming back for a second review

    b. Identify where items are to be shipped out

    c. Analyze the accuracy of the content

    d. None of the above

45. The Xbar in a control chart is a:

    a. Limit

    b. Average

    c. Analysis point

    d. Variant

46. What type of control chart works for reviewing defective units?

    a. NP

    b. S-chart

    c. R-chart

    d. I-MR

47. The distinct part of the U chart for reviewing the control entails the sample size. The size in this case is:

    a. Constant

    b. Variable

    c. Rising

    d. Falling

48. To recognize how a process might work, a parametric distribution can be utilized with this measurement:

    a. Range

    b. Mean

    c. Median

    d. Variance

49. A median is useful for all of these purposes except:

    a. Qualitative review point

    b. Extreme values which will not impact the median all that much

    c. Ease of review

    d. Open-ended concepts

50. A control chart will review of the task to see if it is:

    a. Stable

    b. Relevant

    c. Predictable

    d. Capable

51. What can you utilize to identify a relationship between the X and Y variables?

    a. Pareto chart

    b. Cause and effect review

    c. Control chart

    d. Scatter diagram

52. A predictable control chart shows that the things being reviewed in the process are:

    a. Close to the median

    b. Close to the standard deviation

    c. Moving up and down fast

    d. Sticking with the same value throughout the process

53. A control chart is out of control if the following number of points in a row appear on one side of your average:

    a. 3

    b. 5

    c. 6

    d. 8

54. What does it mean when the control chart is in a state of chaos?

    a. You cannot predict the mean

    b. You cannot predict the variation

    c. You cannot predict the median

    d. A and B

55. The USL can be the only limit in your task if:

    a. You are in the middle of the planning process

    b. You have a limited budget

    c. There is a limit over what you can handle at a time

    d. A and B

56. A lagging indicator concentrates mainly on your:

    a. Input

    b. Volume

    c. Output

    d. Shifting

57. The main goal of Kanban is to:

    a. Identify errors

    b. Find solutions

    c. Visualize the task

    d. Prioritize things

58. The greatest concern with the Gantt chart is:

    a. Keeping things disorganized

    b. Not getting tasks to the right people

    c. Lacking detail

    d. Rushing tasks

59. If the distribution curve in your task is moving in a positive direction, that means the task in question:

    a. Is within the right limits

    b. May need corrective action

    c. Can be observed longer

    d. May be skipped

60. What can you measure against a benchmark?

    a. Outcome of the Y variable

    b. Operational efficiency

    c. Performance

    d. All of the above

61. A box plot will help you to identify:

    a. Outliers

    b. Things that happen before and after changes are made

    c. Ordered data

    d. A and B

62. The Pareto graph identifies the following type of measurement in the Six Sigma process:

    a. Nominal

    b. Ratio

    c. Ordinal

    d. Progressive

63. What has to be done before you can move an item during the Kanban process?

    a. Payment must be sent out

    b. A request must be made

    c. Confirmation should go through

    d. You can get something moved out soon

64. The main goal of the Kanban process is:

    a. Visualization

    b. Planning

    c. Organization

    d. Detail

65. Six Sigma works best for an organization when it is planned based on:

    a. Needs and goals

    b. Balance sheet

    c. Shareholder data

    d. Big data report

66. The C part of the DAMIC process is:

    a. Configuration

    b. Calibration

    c. Control

    d. Commenting

67. A Black Belt is able to train:

    a. Those listed under that person

    b. Only Green Belts

    c. Only Yellow Belts

    d. No one

68. Two items on your review do not appear to have a relationship with each other in the Six Sigma task, and yet they will both influence the output of your task. The two items in question may be interpreted as going through:

    a. Coincidence

    b. Impossibility

    c. Oddity

    d. Interaction

69. The main key for avoiding bias in your work is to use:

    a. Added control

    b. Cautious planning

    c. Independent thought

    d. Outside sources

70. A value chain may be produced in the Six Sigma effort. The chain works to identify inputs and processes based on:

    a. Customer outputs

    b. General economic standards

    c. Internal affairs

    d. Reporting news

71. What can you do with the diagram that reviews the X and Y variables together?

    a. Notice the changes in the workplace

    b. See how much of a relationship has developed

    c. Identify which X variables are the most important

    d. Arrange items by time

72. You can use a fishbone diagram to identify such things as:

    a. Potential results of a task

    b. How much money has gone into the task

    c. Causes for certain things of value

    d. How different variables link to each other

73. An input that impacts a process but is not all that important in value is a/an:

    a. Pest

    b. Irritation

    c. Deviation

    d. Noise

74. Which of these is not a vital part of the Scrum process?

    a. Transparency

    b. Adaptation

    c. Inspection

    d. Retort

75. The Product Owner in the Scrum is another term for the:

    a. Manager

    b. Customer

    c. Task operator

    d. Webmaster

76. The best way to manage bugs that arise in the Scrum task is:

    a. Allocate some extra space for planning out the Scrum task

    b. Analyze the types of bugs that might develop

    c. Study the changes in the task to see what problems have developed

    d. Control certain problems

77. An ordinal set of data being used in a task will involve reviewing the content based on:

    a. An order where everything moves

    b. A select series of options for managing the content

    c. When items might be physically placed in certain areas

    d. Multiple concepts based on many people of value

78. Discrete data entails:

    a. Things happening now

    b. What can happen in the future

    c. Past events

    d. Prospective ideas

79. A multi-vari chart will help you with:

   a. Charting many forms of variation

   b. Plotting data with ease

   c. Reviewing time frames

   d. Identifying more concepts

80. Descriptive statistics are used to explain things based on:

   a. What people say in interviews

   b. Comparisons with other companies

   c. Charts and graphs

   d. All of the above

81. Inferential statistics are used to explain concepts in your work based on:

   a. Shifts in culture

   b. Population reviews

   c. Correlations

   d. None of the above

82. The ANOVA analysis focuses on the:

   a. Mode

   b. Mean

   c. Median

   d. Standard deviation

83. What is not included in a fishbone diagram?

   a. Root causes

   b. Results

   c. Affinities

   d. Changes in procedures

84. One of the best parts of assumption busting is that the process helps you to:

    a. Eliminate challenges

    b. Establish rules

    c. Confirm biases

    d. All of the above

85. The main focus of the cost-benefit analysis is:

    a. Business decisions

    b. Changes in culture

    c. Economic parameters in a work environment

    d. None of the above

86. What is the main concept of the lean principle that much of Six Sigma is based off?

    a. Regular improvement

    b. The elimination of waste

    c. Teamwork

    d. Managing costs

87. Random sampling ensures that:

    a. You can use as many items in a sample as desired

    b. The sample is diverse enough

    c. Every item in a population has an equal chance of being selected

    d. The sample is predictable

88. The following tool is regularly used in the define stage of the lean Six Sigma task:

    a. Control chart

    b. Data collection review

    c. Histogram

    d. FMEA

89. A multi-voting process for brainstorming produced 45 ideas. How many of these should be incorporated into the final task?

 a. 5

 b. 15

 c. 25

 d. 40

90. Delighters in the Kano model are:

 a. Attractive

 b. Necessary

 c. Functional

 d. High-performing

91. What factor can influence the points on the Kano model more than anything else?

 a. Value

 b. Resources

 c. Employee effort

 d. Time

92. A must-have in the Kano model may also be called a:

 a. Basic

 b. Delighter

 c. Power tool

 d. Objective

93. What is a one-dimensional quality?

 a. A predetermined item

 b. Something with only one state

 c. An item that cannot be changed

 d. A material that is incorporated into the process at any time

94. The most important things that appear on the Pareto chart will show up:

    a. On the left end of the X axis

    b. At the top of the Y axis

    c. On the right part of the X axis

    d. In the middle of the chart

95. How many requirements may be produced by a driver?

    a. 2

    b. 3

    c. 5

    d. As many as needed

96. A target value is:

    a. A variable

    b. A brainstorming tool

    c. An analysis point

    d. A goal

97. A potential failure mode may be identified by:

    a. The cause of a problem

    b. Any natural event that takes place

    c. Sudden aberrations

    d. A general problem that develops

98. A CRIT number of 85 means that something is:

    a. Extremely dangerous

    b. Not a problem

    c. Vital to a process

    d. Easy to manage

99. What should be done if an FMEA review finds that a problem keeps arising without warning?

    a. Put the issue to the side

    b. Reorganize your work data

    c. Plan your routines as desired

    d. Find a solution as soon as possible

100. During what stage of the lean task should the FMEA be carried out at?

    a. Design

    b. Analysis

    c. Improve

    d. Control

Answers to White/Yellow Belt Certification Questions

1. a. The results should be consistent so you see an improvement over what you are trying to manage.

2. a. The DPMO is a measure of the Defects Per Million Opportunities.

3. b. The 3.4 standard is key in Six Sigma, although that standard may be adjusted slightly depending on the business' ability to handle the work in question.

4. b. The processes involved in the Six Sigma task can be hidden from plain view depending on how elaborate or complicated the task may be. Such processes might produce unnecessary routines.

5. d. The type of work that a Six Sigma Champion handles focuses heavily on how well the project should work based on the task you wish to pull off.

6. d. Although Six Sigma processes can help with reducing a company's carbon footprint or other form of environmental impact, the processes are not explicitly designed for such purposes.

7. b. While accuracy involves working to get a particular range or result every time, precision is about being extremely close. This may work many times over, but the key is for the correct results to be the same every time.

8. a. Although all parts of the process are important, it is the customers that should be most closely considered.

9. d. A goal of Six Sigma is to review the possible root causes of the issues that have developed in the workplace and to determine how to fix those problems.

10. c. Any of these options may help with measuring things in the Six Sigma task, but the control chart is all about analyzing how well the task is working and whether problems are being fixed. This includes looking at whether the newfound changes or results in the process are consistent and easy to follow.

11. b. Mapping out the problem at the start gives you time to review what is happening in the task.

12. d. There are no rules surrounding how long a Six Sigma task is supposed to last for. The task can work for a while if there is a need to monitor significant changes in the workplace.

13. c. Waste can entail anything, but it is generally the materials in the task that are not relevant to whatever has to be done at a time.

14. d. A defect is a problem found in a material. You can still use a product with a defect, but it will not be of the best quality. A defective item is something that cannot be safely used.

15. d. An internal customer is someone who is directly in the workplace. An external customer is from outside of the group.

16. d. A driver is a point that will be influenced by a need. A driver will move the need forward, which in turn produces a few requirements for getting that driver to work. As all the drivers are produced well, they will all fulfill the same need that you introduced early on.

17. a. The expansion efforts are not a part of the business case, although the things you consider in your task might help you with looking at what can work to fix a problem or to make it easier to manage.

18. d. The A in RUMBA refers to attainable. The U is for understandable.

19. a. While the other problems may be bottlenecks, the first is a constraint in that the problem is keeping you from going far enough in your scope as you plan the Six Sigma work. You might have to adapt the task over time to suit certain needs.

20. a. The inputs will be the points that you plan on changing around. The suppliers provide you with the inputs, which are then configured and changed through the processes involved in the SIPOC work.

21. b. The swimlane map shows the individuals involved with your task alongside details on how much effort will be handled by those people.

22. a. An internal cost entails anything that happens within the business. This can include something that involves manufacturing efforts. An external cost will come about after the customer receives the product or service and notices a recall or warranty coverage problem.

23. d. The internal costs will depend on many problems that might develop in the task. This includes expenses that arise from trying to fix a problem, not to mention expenses from when the company's image has been harmed.

24. a. The MSA concentrates on reproduction and how often things can be repeated. This includes a look at the tolerance for something based on how well a task might be handled.

25. c. The run chart moves in one direction. This works with time in mind.

26. c. The pie chart reviews proportions within a larger sample.

27. d. The Master Black Belt should help with reviewing the key processes.

28. a. By providing the Six Sigma group with the details involved and reviewing everything as it moves along, a Champion may be seen as the sponsor of the task.

29. b. Keeping variation out is the most important part of Six Sigma.

30. a. The standard deviation is important for analyzing how data varies and how certain points may be more acceptable than others in the Six Sigma routine.

31. a. The variables appear to be changing with one another on different functions, thus producing a more efficient practice.

32. a. At this point, it might help to watch for how well the curve is being formed and whether you can correct any problems.

33. b. A negative correlation occurs when something changes due to a lack of work. There needs to be an added sense of productivity to try and move the task forward and to make it more effective.

34. b. The Cpk has to be at least 1.5 for the best results and to show that the task in question is capable of moving forward.

35. a. The change management process is not something that a customer is likely to notice in the task. Therefore, this should not be all that relevant to the Six Sigma effort.

36. a. The mean may be adjusted to a proper total so you can better analyze what might be taking place within your work effort.

37. a. The Voice of the Customer is critical to helping you recognize what you are getting out of the Six Sigma work and to ensuring that the project is properly reviewed.

38. b. Always look at the function at the start to help you recognize what has to be completed.

39. d. The RPN number is gathered by multiplying the S, O and D numbers in the FMEA chart together.

40. d. Each of these problems may be identified through a general analysis in your FMEA report. Not all problems are going to occur within each item, although a full review may help find what commonplace problems are developing.

41. c. All performance gaps must be noted at the start to give you an idea of where the task is heading.

42. b. The 8-12-week standard is appropriate as it gives you enough time to figure out the changes you want to plan in your routine.

43. b. Your goal for the method should be to review all items only once. Anything that is defective will have to be removed and repaired and then reviewed a second time.

44. a. The SPC will help you prevent items from coming back by analyzing and improving upon what you are doing. This works with statistical process control functions to make the tasks easier to manage and utilize.

45. b. The average layout helps with identifying how well a task is being run and if certain changes might have to take place depending on where you go with your work.

46. a. The NP chart is designed to review the content based on general averages in the task.

47. b. There are no particular rules for how many items have to be in the sample size when the option is used for your analysis.

48. b. The mean is the general average of the items that can be measured within the task.

49. d. The median has to be set up with a defined value based on the items that were measured. The median can still change if more items are added, although the changes that can occur will vary based on the things that might develop in the task.

50. a. A control chart will produce a review of the task to see if it is stable.

51. d. The scatter diagram illustrates how well a task is working based on the different movements developing in the task.

52. b. The predictable design should be within the main standard deviation that you are trying to manage. The median can be far from the standard deviation that is the baseline for the task.

53. d. Anything with eight or more points on one side might suggest that the issue at hand is too large.

54. d. The mean and variation are difficult to figure out as the values on the chart keep on shifting. This includes cases where two or three consecutive points appear at the top or bottom before moving to the other side and repeating the same process all around.

55. c. The USL works as the sole limit in cases where you can go from nothing to a specific maximum. The total value in your work can vary between those two, but it cannot go above the total you have planned out.

56. c. The output is the focus for identifying how well a task runs and if you are moving forward with the task as planned.

57. c. The Kanban setup will help you to identify many things pertaining to the work you are adding as well as how you'll manage any situation you come across.

58. d. The Gantt chart requires you to work with set time frames that cannot be easily adjusted. This can cause you to rush your work.

59. b. A positive movement shows that there might be a defect or other concern that has to be resolved soon.

60. d. The benchmark can be planned out based on many factors such as the ways a task will perform, how well the operations in question work and any things that might develop within the Y variable of use.

61. d. The box plot will identify substantial outliers that occur within a review to detect when something may heavily skew the mean. You can also use this to identify what is happening with a task before and after certain changes, thus helping you identify certain problems.

62. a. The nominal data is identified to monitor how certain things might change over time. These include things that focus heavily on how progressive a task might be.

63. b. A request assists you with identifying how well a task is organized and moving forward.

64. a. The visualization involved with the task helps with producing a firm layout that is easy to follow.

65. a. The goals that a business has are more important to review than anything else in the task. This includes a review of how effective solutions are managed and what you can get out of a task.

66. c. The control stage is vital for helping you with identifying the things that might take place in the work environment and how something might work well to your general benefit or advantage.

67. a. Green and Yellow Belts alike can be trained by the Black Belt provided that the Black Belt has passed his or her certification exam.

68. d. An interaction occurs when two things that are not necessarily related to one another come in contact with each other. These might not influence how a task works or how the content moves, but they can directly impact how well the routine works and what might change in the process.

69. c. Your goal is to control your thoughts in the Six Sigma effort so you will avoid thoughts based on what you might find outside a space. The goal is to keep any problems from being more of a threat to your business than necessary.

70. a. Customer outputs may entail looking at how well a task is arranged and measured based on what might be useful. This includes cases where someone might work on different tasks of value.

71. c. Different variables can arise based on where you want to go. The X variables can be thorough, but they may be unnecessary in some cases. A review can help you with identifying which variables should be chosen above others.

72. c. The fishbone diagram is also referred to as the cause and effect diagram. The layout shows the process you are working with and illustrates everything that goes into the task.

73. d. Noise occurs when something changes the process and is not overly easy for people to distinguish. This includes cases where a task might not be easy to follow.

74. d. The Scrum is designed to help everyone in the work environment get together to review different things of value.

75. b. The customer is responsible for handling the product that will be utilized at the end of the Scrum process.

76. a. An extra bit of effort may be needed to find a way to resolve problems. This includes allocating some extra space in the routine to ensure any problems involved with the Six Sigma routine can be kept in check.

77. a. The ordinal process is named for how well different items move from one spot to another. This includes seeing the first, second, third and fourth items in an order among other points.

78. a. The discrete content you work with should be planned based on what is suitable for use right now and how the content may be measured.

79. a. By working with multiple variables, you can get an idea of the variation that is taking place in your project.

80. c. The visual data is the most important part of the Six Sigma routine to use when handling descriptive statistics. These points illustrate the ways a task may be run and what you can expect out of the work.

81. b. Population reviews help you identify many things surrounding your Six Sigma task. This includes a look at how well different types of data might be generated and what makes each data set useful.

82. b. The ANOVA work focuses on the variation in the mean.

83. c. Affinities are not listed in cause and effect diagrams in that they focus mainly on the natural events that may take place in a process. The affinity is something that regularly happens and can be implied. The cause and effect diagram should show direct events or unusual points that may influence how well a task is to be run.

84. One of the best parts of assumption busting is that the process helps you to eliminate challenges, establish rules and confirm biases.

85. a. The business decisions involved in the Six Sigma task help with identifying some of the things that are causing a business to respond a certain way.

86. b. All of these answers could work, but it is the focus on clearing out waste that is important. Going lean entails removing all unnecessary tasks and processes that might cause a routine to be harder to manage than expected.

87. Random sampling ensures that every item in a population has an equal chance of being selected.

88. a. A control chart can work in the design process to identify how a task is changing. This includes a review of the data being handled as a means of figuring out how the task should be planned out over time.

89. b. Multi-voting involves getting a third of brainstorming ideas out.

90. a. Delighters are designed to be bonus features that are not too extensive or vital. These will be added to the process after you are finished finding solutions.

91. d. There is a strong potential that the values of items will change over time. Some things that are designed at the moment may not be as popular or necessary in the future. This includes cases where you have to change things around over time to keep up with competitors.

92. a. The basics in the work environment help with identifying the positives that come with a task and what might be more important than anything else.

93. b. A one-dimensional item is named for how it does not produce much variance in its work and will concentrate more on offering the same thing all around.

94. a. The Pareto analysis shows which items are responsible for the most points in a task. The analysis should reveal details on how well a task may be run and what might have to be changed for the best possible results.

95. d. The requirements come from drivers as a means of maintaining or achieving a need.

96. d. The target value should be the goal you aim to attain. This is a goal that focuses on something of value to you and may be something that is handled carefully within the task.

97. d. The general problem that occurs in a task can be interpreted as the potential failure mode event. This can be anything that can be delved into further to figure out why a task is no longer working as well as desired.

98. a. A high CRIT number or critical number indicates that a problem is very significant in nature.

99. d. You should fix anything that occurs without warning as soon as you can. This is often a sign of a more significant problem getting in the way of your work.

100. c. The FMEA process is designed to analyze what you can do to improve upon a task and therefore should be used during the lean effort stage.

Green Belt Certification Questions

1. What are the milestones in your Six Sigma plan intended to measure?

    a. Any dates in the Six Sigma period

    b. How well the Six Sigma routine goes

    c. Particular events that take place in the work environment

    d. Changes in share prices

2. How long should a Scrum segment or sprint last for?

    a. One month

    b. Three months

    c. One year

    d. As long as needed

3. What makes the DMADV process different from the DMAIC process?

    a. Focuses on new developments

    b. Works on existing content

    c. Uses a shorter time frame

    d. Uses a smaller budget

4. What is non-value-added work?

    a. Things that don't directly influence the end project

    b. General receiving tasks

    c. Shipping work

    d. Functions that review how valuable something might be

5. What is an example of a non-value-added project that is considered necessary?

   a. Reviewing the design of a package

   b. Double-checking the shipping label

   c. Identifying improperly shipped items

   d. All of the above

6. The lead time in your value-added map is distinct for how it entails:

   a. Things you cannot control

   b. Unnecessary functions

   c. Items for confirming various details

   d. How much money is utilized in the task

7. The greatest concern about an excess amount of inventory is:

   a. Excess storage costs

   b. Too many resources used

   c. More people managing the content than necessary

   d. All of the above

8. What percentage of the task should be considered when working on the project acceptability rate for the quality of the solution?

   a. 20

   b. 50

   c. 75

   d. 80

9. Stakeholders in the Six Sigma task are:

   a. Partner businesses you are working with

   b. People who will be impacted the most by the Six Sigma process

   c. Those who invest in your task

   d. General media

10. What does the buy-in entail within your Six Sigma work?

    a. A point that your stakeholders can agree upon

    b. Entering into a partnership with another business

    c. Contacting a vendor

    d. Getting a financial reorganization going

11. What types of functions does the interested person in the ARMI review handle?

    a. Configuring the Six Sigma process

    b. Planning a Six Sigma routine

    c. Staying informed

    d. Adjusting functions on the fly

12. Subprocesses on your process map will include:

    a. Anything that branches off of your initial plan

    b. Something that leads to a new Six Sigma process

    c. Multiple processes working at one time

    d. How efficient the task might be

13. A company is unable to get the materials that it needs for handling a task. This is due to a vendor not being on time. This may be interpreted as a:

    a. Constraint

    b. Bottleneck

    c. Defect

    d. Control issue

14. Mind mapping is useful for brainstorming if you look at:

    a. Possible results of processes

    b. Figuring out the problems that need to be corrected

    c. Establishing rules for the work

    d. Relationships between items

15. Anti-solution or reverse brainstorming involves:

    a. Figuring out how a problem is created

    b. Looking at your resources

    c. Analyzing what happens when people aren't on hand

    d. Figuring out what might happen if you have time constraints

16. Figure storming is different from role storming in that a figure storming process entails:

    a. What someone might do

    b. Historic events

    c. Situational considerations

    d. Philosophical considerations

17. According to the $Y = f(x)$ equation used in Six Sigma, Y is the _____ of X:

    a. Result

    b. Impact

    c. Deduction

    d. Function

18. Simple random sampling works best if you plan on sampling this percentage of a population:

    a. 10

    b. 20

    c. 30

    d. 40

19. You are working on a systematic sampling process where you are picking from a numbered group of people. You are taking in sample numbers 4, 10, 16, 22, 28, 34, 40 and 46. What will be the next one for you to take in?

    a. 50

    b. 52

    c. 54

    d. 56

20. What is an example of environmental bias in sampling?

    a. Changes in geographic location

    b. Reviewing which people are more likely to come to a spot

    c. Reviews of the economic picture at the time

    d. How much money is involved

21. When does acceptance sampling work in your task?

    a. When you have limits over what you can handle

    b. When you can work with as many subjects as desired

    c. If your business has too many variables to work with

    d. If you have no defined considerations for your work

22. How can you identify the mixture stability plot?

    a. Based on levels of resistance at the top and bottom

    b. How often the layout moves above and beyond the median line

    c. The length of the plot

    d. How long certain measurements stay the same

23. An oscillation stability readout can include all but the following:

  a. Totals above or below the median line

  b. Items of the same value in consecutive order

  c. At least four or five straight numbers above or below the median

  d. Extreme highs or lows versus the median

24. A lognormal review of your work should entail:

  a. A drop or rise after a significant start

  b. A progressive trend that moves along over time

  c. Random shifts in value

  d. Consistent values

25. A narrow distribution means that the mean in your review is in this form versus the upper and lower ends of your data values:

  a. Higher

  b. Lower

  c. More varied

  d. In control

26. The main point of a Pareto chart is that it helps you to:

  a. Review trends over time

  b. Analyze frequency of items

  c. Identify the specific problem

  d. Review how a process changes with a variation or other variable is added

27. A sudden change in the Y value versus the time-based X may be seen as the following:

    a. Response to something

    b. Level of movement

    c. Repetitions

    d. Factor

28. What is fine for an alpha risk?

    a. 0.05

    b. 0.25

    c. 0.35

    d. 0.50

29. A hypothesis test that reveals a H0 being false but you fail to reject the HO will be a:

    a. Type I error

    b. Type II error

    c. True Negative

    d. True Positive

30. The SPC process is about:

    a. Control

    b. Measurement

    c. Correcting errors

    d. Recognizing the process

31. What happens when you reach accuracy in your work?

    a. There are no sudden shifts in the values of what is measured

    b. The same result occurs every time

    c. The same person gets the same results each time he or she uses the measurement process

    d. A diverse array of results may develop

32. This amount of work in percentage points will come within two standard deviations on a bell curve:

    a. 65

    b. 75

    c. 85

    d. 95

33. The amount of work in percentage points within one standard deviation should be:

    a. 48

    b. 58

    c. 68

    d. 78

34. By multiplying together the severity of an issue, its occurrence rate and detection totals found in a FMEA review, you will get the:

    a. Risk priority number

    b. Critical number

    c. Current process variable

    d. Number of possible causes of failure

35. What can be noticed when looking at the VOC?

    a. How many materials are to be produced

    b. How far you can go with your task

    c. How many errors people can detect

    d. A customer's specific demands

36. What feature is fixed on the Gantt chart?

    a. Time frame

    b. People who can handle a task

    c. Number of tasks

    d. Duties involved

37. The top part of a chart in the Kanban process should include:

    a. Details on what order things can be done in

    b. Optional items to consider

    c. New opportunities

    d. Must-complete tasks

38. The histogram is used to identify:

    a. How often certain things occur

    b. Proportions of actions

    c. When actions take place

    d. How the process works

39. The S in the SIPOC process entails:

    a. Suppliers

    b. Sales

    c. Subsections

    d. Segments

40. Benchmarking is mainly about:

   a. Measuring a business against others

   b. Reviewing how the improvement process works

   c. Identifying finances

   d. Planning milestones

41. What should be identified first when trying to produce benchmarks?

   a. Objectives

   b. Leadership roles

   c. Revenue totals

   d. Performance gaps

42. What part of your business can be used for figuring out the benchmarks you want to use?

   a. Size

   b. Location

   c. Demographics of workers

   d. Spending totals

43. What can you review when taking a look at the benchmarks of other competitors?

   a. Public reports

   b. Advertising materials

   c. Investigation of a competitor's retail site

   d. Analysis of statistics

44. A control limit states that a measurement will:

   a. Stay around the median

   b. Work within one of the control lines

   c. Go around the mean value

   d. All of the above

45. Which chart works well when looking at a relationship between two variables?

    a. Box plot

    b. Scatter diagram

    c. Histogram

    d. Cause and effect chart

46. What is the ideal Cpk total for Six Sigma?

    a. 1

    b. 1.5

    c. 2

    d. 2.5

47. What is the ideal Cp total for Six Sigma?

    a. 1

    b. 1.5

    c. 2

    d. 2.5

48. The goal of the fishbone diagram is to illustrate:

    a. Cause and effect

    b. Future plans

    c. Employee actions

    d. Routines

49. A higher Z-value means that a machine is not capable of:

    a. Delivering items to people

    b. Running with less cost

    c. Increasing its productivity

    d. Keeping errors down

50. What happens when the Cpk is negative?

    a. Process is too expensive

    b. Process has too many loose ends or improper functions

    c. Too many defects in the way

    d. Process is not working within the customers' desired limits

51. The middle value of the data you are trying to manage may be interpreted as the:

    a. Mode

    b. Mean

    c. Median

    d. Range

52. The yield rates for a Six Sigma task were measured at 85, 91 and 94 percent. What is the first pass yield rate?

    a. 0.855

    b. 0.815

    c. 0.727

    d. 0.701

53. How can you tell that your control chart is out of control?

    a. The points repeat the same value several times over

    b. The points keep alternating between the spots over and below the mean

    c. You get a few points above the mean, then another couple below the mean

    d. There is a progressively ascending or descending line on the chart

54. What part of a process should you pay the most attention to at the start?

    a. Anything efficient

    b. Whatever might be problematic

    c. Anything complex

    d. Important points

55. What makes customer comment cards problematic?

    a. Difficult to gauge feelings

    b. Hard to study

    c. Extreme opinions

    d. Lack of numbers

56. What type of conflict resolution action is best for cases where a business is too fragile to handle some of its functions?

    a. Competition

    b. Collaboration

    c. Accommodation

    d. Avoidance

57. What will you get when you take the completed products that you have and then divide them by the original amount of the product you are working with?

    a. Rolled throughput yield

    b. Throughput yield

    c. Yield

    d. Scrap rate

58. What type of conflict point is used in an Agile task?

    a. Collaboration

    b. Avoidance

    c. Accommodation

    d. Competition

59. An Agile task is built around the:

    a. Customer

    b. Process

    c. Employer

    d. Manager

60. Which part of the Agile task encompasses the widest layout?

    a. Story

    b. Initiative

    c. Epic

    d. Theme

61. The backlog in an Agile task entails:

    a. Things that have to be done

    b. What you have done

    c. Points for competition

    d. All of the above

62. At the most, how many tasks should be used in a Kanban routine?

    a. 4

    b. 6

    c. 8

    d. 10

63. How should the workflow in the Kanban process be visualized?

    a. With a chart

    b. With a map

    c. Through employee interviews

    d. Based on experience

64. The cumulative flow diagram displays:

    a. Which tasks have been completed so far within a time period

    b. How many things have to be done

    c. What is in progress

    d. All of the above

65. SPC is designed to monitor:

    a. Yield totals

    b. How many people are working at a time

    c. The Y process

    d. Basic routine effort

66. What makes modified brainstorming a little different from regular brainstorming efforts?

    a. Added considerations

    b. Fewer parameters

    c. Fewer people

    d. Less work involved

67. A lagging indicator appears:

    a. Before a defect

    b. After a defect

    c. At the start

    d. Near the end

68. How can you identify a leading indicator?

    a. Wavering changes along the control chart

    b. A lack of action on the chart

    c. Several points moving up or down before a change occurs

    d. Points shifting around the median

69. Can you get back into a Six Sigma task after you sign off on it?

    a. Yes

    b. No

    c. After a year

    d. After two years

70. The alternate path chart shows:

    a. Multiple processes at one time

    b. A set rule for something other than the first plan you produced

    c. Many ways how you can get to the same end result

    d. How different resources may be utilized

71. Can you interrupt the process flowchart within the task?

    a. Yes

    b. No

    c. After the halfway point

    d. Within a few steps

72. What types of costs can be considered start-up costs within your work?

    a. Capital investment

    b. Training

    c. Stakeholder investment

    d. Acquiring resources

73. At a minimum, how many Whys should you ask?

    a. 2

    b. 3

    c. 4

    d. 5

74. What is the cause and effect diagram not useful for?

    a. Identifying root causes

    b. Defining the problem

    c. Quantitative data

    d. Controlling the task

75. A check sheet works when you are trying to review:

    a. Connections between variables

    b. Reasons for a problem

    c. Where data moves

    d. How often certain things happen

76. How many lines are needed for producing the spaghetti diagram correctly?

    a. 5-10

    b. 2-3

    c. Unlimited

    d. One in most cases

77. Every item in the Kanban process that you work with will be linked to:

    a. A person

    b. A goal

    c. A request

    d. A tracking number

78. Which of these steps in a prospective Kanban routine should be planned out first?

    a. Deployment

    b. Development

    c. Planning

    d. Testing

79. It's vital to allocate some space in the Kanban process for:

    a. Emergency or urgent events

    b. Sudden changes

    c. Errors

    d. Planned expansion

80. The following information may be found in a posting on the bulletin board for the Six Sigma task:

    a. When something was originally planned

    b. The person responsible for handling the task

    c. The priority or importance of the work at hand

    d. All of the above

81. Who is responsible for allowing people to sign off on a Six Sigma task?

    a. Champion

    b. Black Belt

    c. Green Belt

    d. A and B

82. How long should a Six Sigma presentation be?
    a. 20 minutes
    b. 40 minutes
    c. 60 minutes
    d. 80 minutes
83. Competition is a part of resolving conflicts when you are trying to see what ideas work best. This may be effective for things like:
    a. Two separate processes
    b. Two unique goals
    c. Different variable plans
    d. Certain research paths
84. How long can a sprint in an Agile task last?
    a. About two weeks
    b. Around a month
    c. Up to two months
    d. No defined time frame
85. The most important part of an Agile task is to focus on:
    a. Monetary aspects surrounding the task
    b. The functionality of the product or service
    c. Any technical or detailed points
    d. Where the process may work at
86. How can the requirements in an Agile task be handled?
    a. All requirements must stay the same
    b. Anyone can use the same requirements
    c. They can be flexed as needed
    d. Only the Champion can determine which points have to be changed

87. The road map on the Agile task is vital for identifying:

    a. How a task is to be changed over time

    b. Where you will go with the effort

    c. Any set plans

    d. Ground rules

88. A PRD includes everything but:

    a. Goals

    b. Designs

    c. Predictions

    d. Definitions

89. The main part of an epic is that it can be:

    a. Used to define the entire project

    b. Organize your goals all around

    c. Broken down into smaller tasks

    d. A and B

90. What is considered more important than the design of something in an Agile task?

    a. Organization

    b. Planning

    c. Brainstorming

    d. Budgeting

91. The knowledge acquisition process of the Six Sigma work takes place during this stage in the work:

    a. Design

    b. Analysis

    c. Improve

    d. Control

92. What can a control plan include as you plan the effort in question?
    a. Description of the change you have made
    b. A look at how you will monitor the task
    c. Any metrics that must be used in the process
    d. All of the Above

93. At least how many experimental runs are needed in the pilot process?
    a. 1
    b. 3
    c. 5
    d. Unlimited

94. Is there a potential for two variables to be linear towards one another on your chart?
    a. Yes
    b. No
    c. Only if they are in the same field
    d. Only if they are identical in size

95. The cost/benefit analysis can work with all but:
    a. Employee salaries
    b. Legal costs
    c. Investor funds
    d. Resource costs

96. A business is trying to replicate its processes in many departments, but only one department in the workplace is actually taking advantage of them. This failure may be interpreted as an example of a/an:
    a. Preventative issue
    b. Internal failure
    c. External failure
    d. Appraisal issue

97. The DPU in Six Sigma is a measure of what items per unit?

    a. Defects

    b. Defectives

    c. Downtime points

    d. Decorations

98. A process has produced 360 units out in an hour. What would the cycle time be in minutes?

    a. 0.167

    b. 0.667

    c. 1.333

    d. 3

99. A company produces a case that states, "In the past year, we experienced a decrease of sales by 1.5%. This resulted in a gap of about 1% under our planned goal, thus costing up to about $25,000 per month in losses." Are there any problems with the case for the Six Sigma task?

    a. Not enough detail

    b. Too much technical work

    c. No ideas on the cause

    d. Ideal for use

100.   Agility is a measure in Six Sigma based on:

    a. How flexible a process can be

    b. What you can do within a process

    c. Your ability to switch between things while on the fly

    d. All of the above

Answers to Green Belt Certification Questions

1. b. Milestones are intended to review how well the process goes and to see when people are attaining certain goals in the Six Sigma task. These milestones do not have any specific set time frames.

2. a. Each segment in the Scrum task works for about a month. You can get the sprint finished sooner if you are efficient enough at it. The overall process that the Scrum covers can last as long as needed, but each segment should only work for a month.

3. a. The DMADV process has steps that are nearly identical to the DMAIC process. The main difference is that the DMADV work is for when you've got new tasks to take care of and you want to create new products or services. DMAIC is more about improving the things taking place in the work environment.

4. a. Non-value-added content entails many small steps or routines that might not be all that important for the task. The Six Sigma task can work to remove as much non-value-added content as possible although some will always remain.

5. d. Anything that may be interpreted as being critical to getting an item shipped out can make a difference even if it is not a value-added task.

6. a. You will not be able to manage the lead time in many cases. This will entail the time spent waiting for something to be sent to you or waiting for a party to get back in touch. The lead lets you prepare for the next step.

7. d. All of these problems can make it harder for the inventory to be managed due to the excess materials that have to be stored and handled.

8. a. About 20 percent of the task should be about the quality of the process being handled. The other 80 percent entails whether the product is acceptable. The 100 percent total should entail the process being effective enough.

9. b. Any of these answers could work in some cases, but the specific people who will be most impacted by your Six Sigma effort will vary based on the layout of the task and how you are planning the work in question.

10. a. The buy-in entail what your stakeholders agree upon and support.

11. c. The interested persons will have a full review of what is going on in the Six Sigma process. They are not necessarily going to focus on lots of detailed activities in the work process.

12. c. Your subprocesses will work at the same time, but they will both move towards the same results. You will have to plan these subprocesses together to ensure the work is managed right and remains consistent.

13. b. The problem is a bottleneck in that the issue arises from one part of the process that is not working as well as others.

14. d. A mind map will assist you with producing a visual layout of all the things you're using to your advantage.

15. a. Reverse brainstorming focuses on looking at the things that might have taken place in the past and how those events might change what you are doing or where you go. You can use the reverse brainstorming process to figure out how problems are established.

16. b. Figure storming involves a look at the content based on the things that took place.

17. d. The Y variable is a function of X in that the Y will change as the X moves along. The X can entail anything that has to be measured, so long as the work is reviewed accurately and with enough detail.

18. d. Getting a larger proportion of the people in this process is best for ensuring you get a better or more diverse layout of content ready for figuring out an answer to your questions or concerns.

19. b. The sampling is being done with you working with every sixth item starting from #4. You will then go from 4 to 10 to 16 and then every sixth point from that. You will eventually get to #52 after a while.

20. c. Anything that entails things that are happening at a given time can be interpreted as environmental bias. This includes a look at the economic climate or other considerations that might arise in the review at the time it is conducted.

21. a. You can use acceptance sampling in cases where you have limits over time, finances, access to people or anything else that might restrict whatever you are trying to handle.

22. a. You may notice some levels of resistance on the top and bottom parts in places where the readout will not go above or beyond. The value will vary and may stray off from the median point, but the measurements should be consistent around the median line without veering too far away from it.

23. c. The value of the readout has to change over time with values quickly moving above and below the median. You cannot have several items in one spot in consecutive order. It is fine to have two or three of them in order though.

24. a. A lognormal look can be identified by the shift in value of something after a start.

25. a. A narrow distribution entails the mean being listed as very high. A wide distribution shows that the mean is lower in value.

26. c. You can use the 80-20 ratio in the Pareto chart to identify the specific things that are triggering the most prominent problems.

27. a. The response to a certain action might be a factor based on different problems that may occur.

28. a. The alpha risk is supposed to be as small as possible. Aim for a total of 0.10 or lower if possible.

29. b. The Type II error is going to give you a false positive.

30. a. The control effort works as the SPC process entails a review of all the points that may develop.

31. a. The accuracy entails looking at how well the process works. This includes ensuring the effort moves forward with an idea of what range the results should be at.

32. d. The two standard deviations that move past a curve will cover the Four Sigma standard, thus reaching 95 percent of the layout.

33. c. The 68 percent standard is used for the Two Sigma and will work for the most prominent or valuable data.

34. a. The RPN will give you a closer idea of what has to be done when trying to resolve a problem.

35. d. The voice of the customer is vital for identifying the issues that may arise in the workplace.

36. a. A Gantt review will entail a specific series of points surrounding when things may be handled. This includes certain time frames for starting and stopping a task. This is not included in the Kanban process.

37. d. The most important things that have to be done are on the top.

38. a. You can use a histogram to see what the most prominent things being measured in your work might be.

39. a. The suppliers you work with will provide you with the inputs you need for handling processes to create outputs that customers will want to buy or use.

40. a. A benchmarking process focuses on seeing how a team can compare with others, especially when a competitive analysis process is in place.

41. d. Any performance gaps in your work should be explored based on the problems you have developed and what must be fixed sooner for the best results.

42. a. The size and age of your business may be reviewed to identify the problems in your work.

43. a. Many businesses will post their public details to be transparent.

44. d. Anything can qualify as being within the control limit so long as the content is in between the lower and upper limit lines.

45. b. The dots listed on the scatterplot can reveal how the X and Y variables relate to each other. This may also entail many X variables working on the same Y axis to see if certain things might change in value.

46. b. The 1.5 total is a good value showing that the process can handle things within a particular level or limit.

47. c. The 2 level suggests that the work you're putting in is able to meet the standards your clients might have.

48. a. The fishbone diagram is also called a cause and effect diagram as it focuses on many functions that can develop in the work effort.

49. c. The Z-value gives you an idea of whether or not it is safe for you to expand upon the productivity level of whatever you are using.

50. d. The Cpk is a review of how well items can work within the standards the customers have. You can use the Cpk to identify how well the tasks in question are being managed.

51. c. The median is the middle value of the work. The median may be identified with ease when there is an odd number of items being measured.

52. c. To calculate the total, multiply the three percentage points by each other. This example entails multiplying 0.85 by 0.91 by 0.94.

53. c. The process is out of control if you notice inconsistent processes over how well the value can go up or down. This might entail certain outside variables that are influencing the task.

54. b. Regardless of how important something may be, the item that will cause the most significant problems will have to be addressed at the start of your task.

55. c. People who have extremely positive or negative opinions are likely to fill out those cards, thus making them problematic for VOC purposes.

56. d. Avoidance is best for when your business is too fragile and cannot handle much competition.

57. c. The basic yield comes as you are getting items that have no defects or other issues versus the items that you produced in general. You have to get a higher yield for your work to run better.

58. a. Collaboration is important for both the customers and the employees alike.

59. a. The customer should be treated as the most important figure in the process.

60. d. The theme you will work with should be explored based on the content you will work with.

61. a. The backlog focuses mainly on the things that you are going to do so you can finish the task the right way.

62. a. While there are no specific limits to how many Kanban tasks should be handled at once, it is best to keep room for up to four at a time.

63. a. You can prepare a chart that lists information on everything you are doing with your task. The columns on that chart can include as many specific details as you need.

64. d. The task shows everything pertaining to your backlog, things that were approved, anything being reviewed, the things that are in progress and anything that you have finished. Colored lines on a duration-based chart will identify how well you are completing tasks and how easy it is to move the task along.

65. c. You can use the SPC process to analyze the content at any time.

66. b. You can work with fewer parameters in the process. This is used to keep you focused on what you want to produce within the task.

67. b. The lagging indicator illustrates that a decline is arising because of some defect that took place.

68. c. You may notice a few movements in the process, although the change in the movements may come about due to the defect.

69. a. You can always get back to your Six Sigma task after signing off provided that the task in question needs to be adapted.

70. c. The alternative path chart shows how well the task moves versus the routines you wish to plan out. You can work with as many different types of tasks as you see fit.

71. a. The process flowchart may be interrupted with you choosing to end the task if certain parameters are not met at any time.

72. b. Training generally takes place as you start the Six Sigma project.

73. d. You need to ask at least Five Whys when finding a solution to a problem or a cause. You might consider using more Whys if you are struggling with something and have no real answers for the issue.

74. c. The fishbone diagram is needed for identifying the task and how you can make the work run to its best potential. The diagram should not be seen as a measure of quantitative data.

75. d. The main goal of the check sheet is to identify how often things take place. You can make inferences with the check sheet, although this might work better if you spent some time confirming results and analyzing data.

76. c. Although you have the option to use as many lines as you want on a spaghetti diagram, you must be cautious. This includes ensuring the diagram is not too jumbled. You might need to use separate colors for some lines to make the setup easier to read.

77. c. The requests in the Kanban process list details on what you will utilize. This includes a look at how well the task is being run based on the content being produced or ready for use.

78. c. The planning stage is the first part of this example to work with. The ideal goal is to plan something and then develop it, followed by testing the idea and then deploying it in the real world when the routine is ready.

79. a. As you will only have a certain number of items to work with in the Kanban process, it is best to allocate a separate space for handling an urgent task. No other items should be added to this space or else they might cause inefficiency in the overall process.

80. d. All of these features may work, although you can also add details on how much time may be spent and whether the tasks are reliant upon other things that will work in the Six Sigma routine.

81. b. The Black Belt is responsible for determining when the Six Sigma task can end. That person may also dictate if or when the task has to be reopened.

82. b. A 40-minute time frame offers enough time for about 20 minutes of question and answer setups without the audience getting distracted.

83. a. You can test two different processes in the effort to see how well they can work and if any particular changes have to be made.

84. a. You can expect the work to go on for about two weeks at a time.

85. b. Agile work is relevant to Six Sigma routines in that Agile also focuses on identifying wastes and other problems. The Agile task requires the final output be fully functional and easy to review.

86. c. Appropriate for the name of the task, the requirements for Agile can be flexed as needed.

87. a. The road map illustrates the approximate way a task will work over time. The road map may include some slight changes in how well it operates depending on what is being produced and how the subject matter is arranged.

88. c. The product requirements document should not include any predictions as they might be inaccurate or could be subject to change.

89. c. The epic should be divided down into a series of smaller points that illustrate whatever you are planning in your task and work routine. This is to give you more control over how the routine might work in question while dividing the content.

90. b. The planning process is vital for identifying the increments within which a task may be completed.

91. a. The design process requires you to look at the things that may arise in your work.

92. d. Each of the points listed here will help you with tracking your progress in getting your Six Sigma plans up and running.

93. a. In most cases, you can use a single pilot run to get an idea of where the effort is going. It is recommended that you use multiple tests to confirm what is happening with the work.

94. a. You can get two variables to be linear or collinear to where they will respond to one another in the work process.

95. c. Any costs that can be predicted or identified can work. This includes costs that you are certain will develop in the workplace. You cannot work with costs that might be difficult to predict, such as investor funds that might not come about as desired.

96. b. The problem is occurring due to something that took place inside the business. You will have to find a solution for the internal issues that keep something from moving.

97. a. A single unit can have many defects and still operate. A defective item will not work at all.

98. a. The answer is obtained by dividing 60 minutes by the 360 units being processed.

99. d. The case is fine as it lays out the basic facts and helps the team to review the possible things that might change in the task.

100.   d. The agility gives you the power to move through many tasks in the Six Sigma routine while also reducing the costs involved.

Black Belt Certification Questions

1. What is the pull in the Six Sigma routine?

    a. Moving items around

    b. Getting a task organized

    c. Inviting more people into the task

    d. Getting the product out to the public soon

2. What is the maximum number of defects that you may find in something?

    a. 5

    b. 8

    c. 15

    d. Unlimited

3. The Pareto ratio states that a vast majority of the problems that arise will be produced by _____ percent of the material.

    a. 50

    b. 75

    c. 80

    d. 90

4. Which of these is not included in the AICP process?

    a. Associate

    b. Idea

    c. Customer

    d. Process

5. You want to talk with multiple people when reviewing the VOC, but you don't want one person to dominate the focus. You can use the following to gauge the VOC:

    a. Surveys

    b. Focus groups

    c. Observations

    d. Interviews

6. The LSL of a measure is 5.55, while the USL is 5.75. Is a readout of 5.6 acceptable?

    a. Yes

    b. No

    c. Depends on the subject matter

    d. Requires extra research

7. A feature in a product is not necessarily something that a person is looking forward to, but it is necessary for the proper functioning of that item. A Kano model will distinguish this as being:

    a. Delighter

    b. Performance tool

    c. Must-have

    d. Indifferent product

8. What makes the longitudinal scope in your project charter different from your lateral scope?

    a. How long it takes for a process to be completed

    b. Points within the process

    c. How orders are made

    d. The budgetary considerations pertaining to the task

9. The as-is point in the value stream map entails:

    a. What the current situation is

    b. Where you want your task to go

    c. What you will prepare and its current quality

    d. How efficient the task you wish to plan may be

10. What makes a trigger different from a request in your value stream map?

    a. The trigger leads to a new step

    b. The trigger starts the process

    c. A schedule is produced

    d. The flow may be reviewed

11. A useful idea for making your high-level process map work is to:

    a. Organize the process by time

    b. List the monetary values of each process involved

    c. Label things with colors

    d. None of the above

12. The greatest concern with heuristics in Six Sigma is that they are:

    a. Expensive

    b. Illogical

    c. Practical

    d. Lofty

13. Your weighted rating sheet has one item at 25 percent. What will the highest score for your review be?

    a. 1.5

    b. 2

    c. 2.5

    d. 3

14. You are planning a task and you need to look at how well machines are working. You are trying to measure whether the machines in question are on or off at certain times. What type of measurement is best to you in this situation?

    a. Binary

    b. Discrete

    c. Nominal

    d. Continuous

15. What will happen if you increase the level of uncertainty in your sample size calculation for continuous data?

    a. The sample size becomes smaller

    b. The sample size increases

    c. You include more groups

    d. You restrict the population you would collect the data from

16. The sample size for discrete data should be calculated heavily based on the:

    a. Demographics of the population

    b. Proportion defective

    c. The certainty involved

    d. Your likelihood to confirm a hypothesis

17. Biases arise in the MSA or DDA due to:

    a. A lack of understanding of the subject matter

    b. A lack of control

    c. Familiarity with routines

    d. Details in the work

18. What are base examples good for within the MSA or DDA?

    a. As a guideline for your efforts

    b. To prepare you for what you may come across

    c. For confirming that a measuring instrument works

    d. All of the above

19. A special cause in your testing process may develop because:

    a. Employees are not being made available

    b. Machines are not functioning right

    c. There's a strike at one of your vendors

    d. There's a lack of funds

20. At least how many consecutive measurements should be noticed in a same-value period of stability?

    a. 5

    b. 7

    c. 9

    d. 11

21. What type of chart is best to use when measuring defects with various sample sizes?

    a. Np

    b. P

    c. C

    d. U

22. What can be considered a value-added process?

    a. Setup

    b. Storage

    c. Inspection

    d. Processing

23. A control chart helps you to:

    a. Identify how well a process is working based on the specifics you want to use

    b. How you can recreate the process

    c. Look at how well the process is performing after a while

    d. Identify what problems are in the setup and how they can be corrected

24. What process is about making sure controllable defects can be kept in check?

    a. Poka yoke

    b. Kanban

    c. Scrum

    d. Agile

25. The following may be utilized to help you with identifying any waste or non-value-added processes:

    a. Process map

    b. Pareto review

    c. Scatterplot

    d. Histogram

26. A recall might have to be conducted to keep the problems in a Six Sigma process from becoming evident to the public. What type of analysis may work in this situation?

    a. Cost of poor quality

    b. Present value review

    c. Return on investment

    d. Profit margin analysis

27. All of these are waste except for:

    a. Inventory

    b. Motions

    c. Corrections

    d. Shipping

28. Why might goods be returned to the workplace?

    a. Products are not meeting specifications

    b. The business is rejecting things internally

    c. The customers are not satisfied

    d. The costs for producing items are too high

29. What should you multiply the DPO by to get the DPMO?

    a. 100,000

    b. 1 million

    c. 10 million

    d. 1 billion

30. A customer may be identified as someone whose relationship with a product entails:

    a. Being affected by the product

    b. Buying the product

    c. Using the product

    d. Modifying the product

31. The main intention of the problem statement is to:

    a. Create a definition of what problem has to be solved

    b. Find a solution

    c. Review how long the task should work for

    d. Agree on particular dates for completing a task

32. The main goal of brainstorming involves:

    a. Answering problems

    b. Exploring causes

    c. Developing methods

    d. Finding ideas

33. When should you avoid benchmarking?

    a. When you haven't fully listed details on your processes yet

    b. When you've got a practice that goes through many fields of work

    c. When you don't know what types of successes or efforts may be utilized

    d. When the things involved can be identified in many forms

34. An attribute that you will plan out is:

    a. Discrete

    b. Continuous

    c. Measured well

    d. Difficult to explore

35. A project listed at Four Sigma will entail how many DPMOs?

    a. 308,537

    b. 66,807

    c. 6,210

    d. 233

36. All of these are measures of central tendency except for:

    a. Mode

    b. Mean

    c. Range

    d. Median

37. A subset in a population may also be called a:

    a. Geographic segment

    b. Sample

    c. Demographic

    d. Variation

38. The asterisks on the box chart should appear _____ times away from a bar:

    a. 1.5x

    b. 2x

    c. 3x

    d. 3.5x

39. The bottom part on the box in a box chart is the:

    a. First quartile

    b. Third quartile

    c. Median

    d. Mean

40. The run chart is based off:

    a. Samples

    b. Number of entities

    c. Time

    d. Hypothetical reviews

41. The middle bar on a control chart is a measure of:

    a. A control limit

    b. The median output

    c. Average output of a task

    d. The hypothetical layout for the task

42. The following in the control chart is a measure of the proportion of items that are defective when multiplied by a sample size:

    a. p

    b. np

    c. u

    d. c

43. The center line in the scatterplot is designed to show an:

    a. Average

    b. Median

    c. Range

    d. Prediction

44. When producing a flowchart, how will you let people know when you are ending a process?

    a. Create an x on the line leading to the final step

    b. Add a separate shape explaining that the process ends at that point

    c. Produce an oval shape on the step

    d. Use a different color

45. The spaghetti diagram is recommended for cases where you are trying to:

    a. Do a review of the physical layout of the workplace

    b. Assess individual machines

    c. Perform expensive tasks in the workplace

    d. Determine how many people are working at a time

46. You analyzed 100 units in your first review and 92 of them passed. What is the first time yield on the task in percentage points?

    a. 85

    b. 92

    c. 95

    d. 96

47. What is the first thing to look at as you plan your root cause analysis?

    a. A discussion of what you expected out of the event

    b. A timeline

    c. An explanation of the event

    d. A background of the event

48. How long should the timeline in your root cause analysis be?

    a. As long as needed

    b. For one month

    c. For one year

    d. During the first two stages of the Six Sigma task

49. What type of entity might negatively influence the work in your Six Sigma task during a hand off?

    a. Middleman

    b. Recipient

    c. Sender

    d. Transition team

50. What is the best possible P-value among the ones listed here?

    a. 0.04

    b. 0.07

    c. 0.15

    d. 0.5

51. The beta risk is also considered to be the:

    a. Machine risk

    b. Risk of fault

    c. Consumer's risk

    d. Shipping risk

52. Which of the following is an appropriate significance level for the chi-square test?

    a. 0.3

    b. 0.05

    c. 1

    d. 0.5

53. You are working with 6 variable levels on the first variable and 5 variable levels on the second within your chi-square test. How many degrees of freedom will you find between the two?

    a. 11

    b. 20

    c. 30

    d. 45

54. You have made 7 observations on the first variable in your chi-square test and 10 observations on the other variable. You have a sample size of 20. How many expected frequencies are you producing in this setup?

    a. 2.5

    b. 3.5

    c. 5

    d. 10

55. The P-value of a chi-square test is well above the value of the significant level. What does this mean for the null hypothesis?

    a. Further research is needed

    b. It can be accepted

    c. It can be rejected

    d. No impact will come along

56. You are looking to test a comparison of the means of two populations. Which test will be appropriate for the process?

    a. HOV

    b. Chi-square

    c. ANOVA

    d. Mood's Median

57. A null hypothesis in your review means that:

    a. There is a sizeable different between groups

    b. You have to complete a test again

    c. There is no statistically noticeable difference between the groups

    d. You can use the results in any way you see fit

58. The S in the SCAMPER process refers to:

    a. Setup

    b. Solution

    c. Subscribe

    d. Substitute

59. You are using a Likert scale to review a particular item in your task. The item that you are reviewing is listed at 8. That means the item in question is:

    a. Not really important

    b. Neutral

    c. Very important

    d. Can go either way

60. How many ideas can be produced in the 6-3-5 brainstorming process?

    a. 14

    b. 90

    c. 108

    d. 30

61. What works first in the constrained brainstorming process?

    a. Producing starter ideas

    b. Reviewing existing ideas from the employees

    c. Trading ideas

    d. Analysis work

62. The goal of a test in the assumption-busting process is to see:

    a. If the assumption is true

    b. If the assumption can be made untrue

    c. How the assumption relates to certain variables

    d. A and B

63. Your main metric for a Six Sigma task will be to review the cost and keep that total down. What will the consequential metric be?

    a. Reduced setup needed

    b. Reduced scrap

    c. Reduced cycle time

    d. All of the above

64. The visual factory entails the creation of what materials for the support of a streamlined business?

    a. Manuals

    b. Specifications

    c. Policies

    d. Attendance rules

65. The expected value of the task may be the:

    a. Mean

    b. Regressive value

    c. Cost-added review

    d. Median

66. The focus of brainstorming is to produce:

    a. Routines

    b. Products

    c. Ideas

    d. Theories

67. What works best for informal communication within the Six Sigma process?

    a. Face-to-face meeting

    b. Email

    c. Phone call

    d. Videoconferencing

68. The best way to describe a Black Belt is as a/an:

    a. Change agent

    b. Organizer

    c. Planner

    d. Assistant

69. The central limit theorem states that the distribution of the mean will be very large if the content is:

    a. Distributed appropriately

    b. Distributed disproportionately

    c. Focused more on outliers

    d. Moving along with the standard deviation

70. A confidence interval shows that the review entails confidence in:

    a. The results

    b. The accuracy of a test

    c. Specific totals

    d. A and B

71. When can an external SMED process work?

    a. When a machine runs

    b. When a machine is down

    c. When a machine is being installed

    d. Any time

72. How long should the setup time for your work be after getting the SMED process to work right?

    a. Less than ten minutes

    b. Half an hour

    c. About an hour

    d. No defined standard

73. What is the main benefit of the SMED process outside of taking less time to prepare a setup?

    a. Reduced risk of bottlenecks

    b. Added integration

    c. Cheaper production

    d. Both A and B

74. Where will the SMED process work well?

    a. On a value stream map

    b. On a Kano analysis

    c. On a Pareto review

    d. None of the above

75. What should you ask when planning your control impact matrix the right way?

    a. How long will it take for such problems to be resolved?

    b. Is the layout organized right?

    c. Are the points related to the root cause?

    d. Can these things be changed based on relevance?

76. Which of the following is not going to influence a process capability total when the process has a continuous output?

    a. Standard deviation

    b. Technology

    c. Seasonal variations

    d. Normal distribution

77. The process capability may be seen as a proportion of the following when reviewing attributes:

    a. Functional items

    b. Excess materials

    c. Nonconforming products

    d. Variations of the items produced

78. Which of the following is not a part of the implementation process in Six Sigma?

    a. Cost/benefit analysis

    b. SMED review

    c. Risk management control

    d. Audits of the work after the task is finished

79. Is SPC needed when you are working with the poka yoke process to eliminate a defect?

    a. Yes

    b. No

    c. Depends

    d. Contact a Champion for details

80. Your Six Sigma goal is to increase product volume production while also monitoring the mean and variables. You will have to review machines in the process to see how they function. What type of chart is best for use when reviewing the Six Sigma goal you have set up?

    a. NP

    b. MR

    c. Xbar-R

    d. Type I

81. The customer will feel this way about the business when the variance is removed through a Six Sigma process:

    a. Confident

    b. Loyal

    c. Interested

    d. Ready to pay more

82. You notice a point between the top spot on a bell curve and the mean on your data set. This may be referred to as a:

    a. Standard deviation

    b. Curve spread

    c. Median review

    d. Numerical total

83. The main thing to notice in the Voice of the Business is:

    a. Revenue

    b. Safety

    c. Profitability

    d. Expenses

84. The following shape may be found on a diagram to illustrate when you are switching from one point in the process to another:

    a. Triangle

    b. Oval

    c. Rectangle

    d. Diamond

85. A business moved some frequently-accessed materials to a spot where they are easier for people to find while also being closer to job-specific machines needed for completing a task. What type of waste has been kept under control through the work process?

    a. Motion

    b. Inventory

    c. Waiting

    d. Conveyance

86. A goal of Six Sigma is to reduce the cycle for a process. When will the cycle officially start?

    a. When a machine starts up

    b. When you start developing a product

    c. When you receive an order

    d. When a new time period for work comes about

87. What does it mean to standardize functions within the Six Sigma task?

    a. You are allowing the rules to be followed by everyone in the workplace

    b. The standards will not change

    c. You are keeping the rules simplified

    d. Everything is organized

88. Based on priority, what is the last thing to take note of on a cause map?

    a. People

    b. Nature

    c. Measurements

    d. Machines

89. A worker wants to measure a complicated task that includes hundreds of threads or materials at a time. Which distribution method is best for use?

    a. Poisson

    b. Exponential

    c. Standard

    d. Extended

90. The U chart is used to identify events that:

    a. Allow a process to move faster

    b. Do not conform with certain standards

    c. May be out of the ordinary

    d. Are unplanned

91. You have the option to group your customers by more than one criteria. This process is known as:

    a. Customer analysis

    b. Customer grouping

    c. Customer segmentation

    d. Customer test

92. Two people in a Six Sigma task are talking with each other at the water cooler. What kind of communication is this?

    a. Informal

    b. Formal

    c. Unclear

    d. Depends on the values of the people involved

93. How should teams be organized in the Agile task?

    a. With help from a Champion

    b. On its own

    c. With stakeholder support

    d. Through an internal analysis

94. What can be found in a user story within the Agile task?

    a. Experiences with a product

    b. How a person will use a product

    c. Designs for a product

    d. All of the above

95. When is the best time to consider using the median as a baseline for measurement in the analysis process?

   a. When you have sizeable outliers

   b. When the content is on one end of the chart

   c. When you have a smaller number of items

   d. B and C

96. While on a story in the Agile task, you are at a story point of 30. This means that you are:

   a. About a third of the way through

   b. Halfway finished with your task

   c. About two-thirds of the way finished

   d. Almost done

97. How many process increments or sprints can be used in a Scrum process?

   a. As many as desired

   b. About 10 to 20

   c. Around 3-5

   d. Unnecessary

98. A controlled variable that will influence a response in a Six Sigma task is also called a:

   a. Level

   b. Version

   c. Factor

   d. Replicating point

99. What is the first thing you should be doing in your Six Sigma plan?

    a. Figure out where the resources you want to use will go

    b. Find a sponsor for the task

    c. Determine who will be on the team

    d. Find an objective

100. What can be done to ensure a machine continues to work based on Six Sigma standards?

    a. Train the operators right

    b. Maintain all machines properly

    c. Computerize all processes

    d. None of the above

Answers to Black Belt Certification Questions

1. d. The pull requires you to get the content you are working with out to your customers soon.

2. d. You may come across as many defects in your Six Sigma items as needed.

3. c. The Pareto principle states that 80 percent of problems are caused by 20 percent of things. This can also be attributed to other activities like sales, where 20 percent of customers will complete 80 percent of the sales going through.

4. b. The I in the AICP process is for the investor.

5. a. Surveys may help you get information from groups of people provided you offer a simple process.

6. a. The LSL and USL are lower and upper specification limits. Anything that works in between the two limits as you're gathering results for a task can work.

7. c. A must-have is something that has to be included for a product to work. It is not necessarily something that will delight; a delighter is something optional that adds to the value and functionality of a product or service.

8. a. A longitudinal approach to the scope is about the length of time needed for a task to move forward. The lateral approach is about the events that take place within the process.

9. a. As-is refers to what you are getting right now in your work.

10. a. Every process involved has to work with a trigger. The request will start the process, although the trigger will help move the initial part of the request to the next step in the value process.

11. c. Adding separate colors to the high-level process map provides you with an analysis of the individual things you are planning in your task. Each color links up to a certain thing you want to work with.

12. c. Practical concerns may be too significant for a company to handle. These issues arise when a task becomes too expensive to manage.

13. c. The 25 percent total will be a part of the overall score of 10 you will use in your chart. Therefore, the highest possible number you can get out of that 25 percent marker will be 2.5.

14. a. The binary measurement option entails data that can be reviewed based on a yes/no answer or anything else that has only two possible solutions.

15. a. The sample size may be dictated by the uncertainty. You will divide the standard deviation and 1.96 by the level of uncertainty in percentage. With a larger percentage, the uncertainty increases and you will have fewer people to work with in your group. Meanwhile, a smaller amount of uncertainty produces a larger sample as you increase your chances of getting a diverse series of answers.

16. b. The proportion defective is reviewed by taking P(1-P) and then measuring this against the continuous data total you collect. P must be a positive integer between 0 and 1 and should be based on the percentage of whatever you are calculating.

17. a. Biases in the process are produced mainly by people not recognizing what is happening in the samples or events they are measuring. People might assume that certain things are taking place in the process even if they are not actually going that route.

18. d. Each of these answers may work, although many of the base example points will help with reviewing how well measurements are handled. This includes an emphasis on how effective the process might be.

19. c. Special causes are things that might not be in your control. A vendor you get in touch with going on a strike, or anything else negative that may happen to that vendor is something to carefully consider when planning your work.

20. b. You can review any length of stability with the same numbers, although you might have an easier time with determining whether something is stable if at least seven consecutive measurements are of the same value.

21. d. The chart focuses on managing different types of sample sizes as they develop.

22. d. The processing is the part of the Six Sigma work that actually involves the materials moving around in a secure environment.

23. a. You can use the control chart to see if the process is running well. While the effort can work with a time-based setup, this may work mainly with the random samples that you choose to work with.

24. a. Poka yoke is about ensuring the problems in the workplace are addressed appropriately.

25. a. The process map reviews the general things that take place in the process you work with. You can use this to find unnecessary or excessive materials that might be utilized.

26. a. The cost of poor quality review may help with reviewing not only the costs associated with repairing things, but also how much of a hit the business might take.

27. d. Shipping processes may work with certain movements depending on what is being handled. This should be a value-added process that does not create excess waste, provided the routine works appropriately.

28. c. Any returns will be caused by the customers themselves not being satisfied with whatever they are utilizing.

29. b. The DPMO is a measure of defects found in every million opportunities.

30. a. The effects of a product should be measured based on what might work in the process of generating something.

31. a. The problem statement analyzes the issue at hand, thus allowing the team to have ownership of sorts on what should be done when trying to resolve the issue.

32. d. The brainstorming process should not be interpreted as a process for handling difficult issues. Rather, it is about finding ideas that may be used for future solutions for the task.

33. a. A benchmark works when you have an idea of where you're going with your task.

34. a. The discrete nature of the attribute shows that there is a consistent sense of knowledge involved with something. The attribute may be a factor that directly influences the variable.

35. c. The total number of defects per million opportunities will decline when you're getting into more Sigmas or standard deviations.

36. c. Range is a measure of dispersion or variation.

37. b. The sample can entail any grouping of the population, thus allowing this to be called a subset.

38. a. The 1.5x outlier on the box chart shows how a significant outliner can always arise.

39. a. The first quartile shows where 25 percent of the data in a readout will be listed. The readout shows how well the process works while ensuring it's adequate for managing different tasks.

40. c. The run chart illustrates the amount of time that has elapsed in a process. You can use the chart time to illustrate how well certain functions are handled.

41. c. The average output or mean for a task should be used as a base for the control chart. You can use this to analyze how well the process operates.

42. b. The np is a measure of the p or proportion. The np is different in that it is a look at what is defective.

43. a. The center line can be produced through an analysis of the many points on the charge.

44. c. An oval shape will illustrate when something is finished in your task. You have the option to create a different shape, but that is completely optional. The oval lets the user know that the process is starting or ending, provided that the shapes are different based on the type of step being discussed.

45. a. You can look at how well people are moving from one machine or item in the workplace to another. The review gives you an idea of what is happening in your work environment regardless of the number of people involved. You may use the spaghetti diagram to see where things are moving in a given task.

46. b. The first time yield is produced by dividing the items that passed the first yield by the total number of things that developed in the first time process. The routine may work for cases where you need to analyze your work at the start.

47. c. The explanation is needed to help understand the background of the task.

48. a. You can use a timeline for any type of long-term project.

49. a. A middleman might not be fully aware of what you are doing with your task.

50. a. The P-value needs to be less than 0.05 if possible.

51. c. The consumer's risk entails the potential for a Type II error to be committed.

52. b. The best significance level in the chi-square test should be between 0.01 and 0.1.

53. b. The (r-1) x (c-1) equation would be utilized, with those two integers represented being the details on the variables involved.

54. b. The (Nr x Nc) / n equation will work here. The n is for the sample size, while the other two points are for the observations used at the level of each of the points you are working with.

55. c. The P-value has to be higher in value for it to be rejected at this point.

56. c. The ANOVA test is designed for reviewing the means of those populations.

57. c. The null hypothesis can suggest that the results being generated may not be as significant as you might have expected them to be.

58. d. The start process entails a review of the solution parameter and how a concept is to be planned out.

59. c. The content is highly important if it gets an 8 score. The importance of the task at hand is measured based on a score of 0 to 10.

60. c. The process involves the generation of three ideas by each person in a five-minute span six times over. There will be six people involved with the process. Therefore, the 6-3-5 process will generate 108 new ideas.

61. a. Starter ideas are always included at the beginning to review what the people working on a task might already understand or believe about a task.

62. d. You have to look at what has caused the assumption to be true and then review it versus the things that might have created an issue within the work environment.

63. d. Anything that can take place as a result of the Six Sigma task can be interpreted as a consequential metric if used appropriately.

64. a. The specifications involved with the Six Sigma effort can help with illustrating concepts, and the policies help people know what to do. But for visual details, manuals and other signs will help the most with identifying what can be done to manage particular tasks.

65. a. The mean is the average and therefore should be seen as the expected value based on the general reviews you're trying to have work for you.

66. c. The ideas produced within the task can be as extensive and distinct as they have to be.

67. a. It might be easier for smaller quantities of data to be transferred between people during a face-to-face meeting.

68. a. The nature of the Black Belt as the change agent is important in that the process will help you with managing your content and organizing your data.

69. a. The equal distribution ensures that the mean is easier to determine. You will not focus much on outliers or other items that might improperly skew things.

70. b. The confidence interval focuses mainly on the accuracy of something. This includes expressing a sense of confidence that a problem will be resolved within a specific time frame.

71. a. The external review can occur when the machine is fully operational and when you know how to control the setup.

72. a. The SMED requires the setup time to be less than ten minutes, hence the name of the process.

73. d. The general arrangement of the SMED task ensures that the process works in moments without a risk of causing any problems in the manufacturing effort. This includes working to produce a cleaner setup for making products that only takes moments to manage.

74. a. The value stream map can be accentuated with an SMED chart to help identify how the startup process works with less time as needed.

75. c. The matrix may help you to identify problems with the chart and how well the Six Sigma routine is being run.

76. b. The results may be the same when the same kind of technology is used. The outside factors that may influence how the business runs will play a larger role in the process.

77. c. The design of the process should be reviewed based on how well the process can produce effective materials. This includes ensuring that the items being handled are appropriately organized.

78. a. The CBA is designed for when you're trying to analyze the contents of whatever you are trying to produce.

79. b. The SPC process should be easy to handle if managed right.

80. c. The X-bar chart focuses mainly on means and how they may vary between items in one environment. This also works for multiple materials.

81. a. Any of the answers can work, but the key part of removing variance is to instill a sense of confidence in the process.

82. a. The length of the standard deviation will vary by each process. You may use a software program to identify how well organized your work is.

83. c. The general goal of the VOB is to ensure that the profits increase. This may work through either a reduction in expenses or a control in expenses followed by an increase in revenue depending on the general task being planned out.

84. d. A diamond shape distinguishes when you're going to a new process. The square or rectangle is for a basic step. The oval is for when you're starting or stopping the process on your chart.

85. a. By moving things appropriately, you are keeping people from having to move around too much to try and accomplish a task.

86. b. The development process is the basic time when the cycle starts. The receipt of a new order is not correct as there are no guarantees such an order will be sent out. Also, the process should be in place before an order is received, thus reducing the time frame necessary for the task to be fully completed.

87. a. There is a potential for the standards to change. But the key is to standardize the process to where anyone can work with the same standards for producing something of note.

88. a. Six Sigma processes should be the same in quality regardless of the people responsible for certain tasks. You must review how the project is run by machines first while also assessing the work environment. You can then measure your standards and work with the people who are assisting you with the task.

89. a. The Poisson distribution method works with the assumption that the task will involve several materials being handled at once.

90. b. The chart looks at errors and problems that may arise.

91. c. Segments may be produced to create a clear idea of what you are looking for.

92. a. The informal nature of the communication is due to the fact that a task is not necessarily designed to be formal. Rather, it entails talking about some Six Sigma tasks without necessarily having the materials needed for the discussion immediately on hand.

93. b. The group in the Agile process can be formed on its own without any outside problems influencing the task.

94. d. The user story is designed to be as thorough as needed. This includes points on how a product or service will work and how effective the setup might be.

95. a. Outliers can heavily influence the mean's value. The median keeps the impacts of such outliers from being a threat to the measurement process.

96. a. The total value of the story point is a measure of how far you have gone in your work. You will have completed the story when you get to the 100 point. At 30, you are only about a third of the way through the task as you have planned it.

97. a. You have full control over many things to help you move forward with the task and make the most out of the content you want to use.

98. c. The factor can be measured based on any problems that might come along. The project can work with as many factors as needed.

99. d. You must plan an objective to make it easier for the task to work as desired.

100.　b. Proper maintenance functions are needed to ensure that machines work properly so all operators can get the most out of them.

Conclusion

The greatest part of working with Six Sigma is that you will find a way to eliminate all the waste in your workplace. You will find it easier to keep your business operational by getting rid of anything that might be inefficient. More importantly, the work will give you ideas of how to improve your business. You might find that your business will produce more materials and be of better use to your potential employees and other stakeholders. Your profitability may increase.

The main goal of the Six Sigma work is to ensure the task you're planning is organized right and is easy to follow. The lean process is extensive and can include many reviews pertaining to what you wish to test, your ability to measure things and how you're going to change your policies and overall organization. The good news is that there are many analytical and graphic solutions that you can use for reviewing your process. You can use these with most tasks, regardless of how big or small.

Scrum or Agile tasks are good options to consider depending on the special types of tasks you want to complete. You may use these points in your work to create a better organization for your Six Sigma efforts, especially if you are trying to work with a flexible plan or a shorter series of sprints.

It is understandable that Six Sigma might be a challenge for you to manage at times. The process is extensive and requires plenty of analytical work. But Six Sigma helps you to figure out the things that should be done so you'll have an easier time with moving forward.

Remember that you will come across plenty of competition in your field of work. You might be impressed with how well some of those competitors operate when all things are considered. These entities might have used lean processes in the past and, because of that, may now have an easier time providing quality products and services to their customers. They may also have happier workers who understand what they are doing in their work. You deserve to be on even footing with those competitors.

Be sure to review this guide regularly if you're going to begin a Six Sigma project or if you're planning on getting your certification. We wish you the best of luck with your Six Sigma project. We feel that your work should be easy to manage if you follow the guidelines in this book.